JWK

... *And Even*

ESSAYS ON MAN,

NEW YORK

f You Do . . .

MANNERS & MACHINES

BY

Joseph Wood Krutch

1967

WILLIAM MORROW & COMPANY, INC.

To my brother Charles E. Krutch

The essays in this volume have been published in *The American Scholar, Audubon Magazine, The Freeman, Harper's Magazine, House & Garden, House Beautiful, The New Leader, Playboy,* and *The Saturday Review.*

Published simultaneously in Canada by George J. McLeod Limited, Toronto.

Printed in the United States of America.

Library of Congress Catalog Card Number 67-29840

CONTENTS

I . . . Men & Machines

II . . . Manners & Morals

III . . . The Two Cultures

IV . . . *As I Like It*

. . .   . I

Men & Machines

. . .   .

Why I am not going to the moon

It was, I believe, a mountain climber who invented the phrase "because it is there" to explain why he wanted to climb a particular peak. Because ours is an age devoted to all sorts of unexamined enterprises his phrase has passed into popular speech and the very frequency with which it is invoked is a striking indication of the fact that many of the things we do, many of the ends we pursue, cannot be justified except by saying that, after all, these things can be done and these ends can be pursued.

Yet we cannot, after all, study everything that could be studied or do everything that could be done. Wisdom would seem to suggest that we ask not only what can be done, but what is most worth doing—but that is exactly what the "because it is there" philosophy refuses to recognize. As Thoreau said, it is not worthwhile to go halfway round the world to count the cats in Zanzibar. But there are, I presume, cats in Zanzibar and they could be counted. Better yet, the number could be pretty accurately estimated by a scientifically planned sampling. But before approving such an enterprise as one we ought to undertake, I would want some sounder reason than simply the fact that the cats are, presumably, there.

When President Kennedy was asked why our government was so eager to get someone to the moon, even he could think

3

of no better answer than the catchphrase "because it is there."
Now, I am willing to believe that there may be better reasons.
They may be military, and if there are sound military reasons
I somewhat reluctantly yield to them. But I dismiss as mere
foolish excuses most of the others I have heard—such as the
prestige value of beating the Russians or, most farfetched of
all, von Braun's suggestion that colonization of the bodies in
outer space is the best solution to the population problem.

   At the risk of provoking the scorn of all the proponents of
pure science, fundamental research, and so forth (as well as of
all the "because it is there" boys), I would like to say that I
have not yet heard any argument that seemed to me to justify
the enormous expenditure of time, money and brains upon this
particular enterprise. Henry Adams said that the Middle
Ages believed building cathedrals the thing most worth doing,
just as the mid-nineteenth century in the United States gave
the same sort of priority to railroad building. In our own time,
exploration of space seems to have won a similar priority. We
seem to regard it as not only worth doing but even more worth
doing than anything else and, therefore, worth anything it may
cost. But there is, it seems to me, no doubt that this inevitably
means less time, less money, and less available brainpower to
be spent on other things that, in addition to being there, seem
to have stronger claims upon our attention.

   That we should be dazzled by the sheer wonder of what man
has been able to do is not surprising. The technical problems
solved are surely the most difficult ever attacked by science.
Out of nowhere has suddenly appeared a whole new race of
experts who seem to move easily in a realm of thought and
practice that most of us cannot even enter. Within a few years
they have accomplished what the most extravagant follower of
Jules Verne would not have dared imagine except for some
distant future. Yet the very wonder of it makes it difficult for

us to maintain any sense of proportion. To question its value is likely to seem mere impudence. Yet it ought to be at least questioned.

I am not thinking exclusively in terms of the argument that the money spent might be better used to relieve the sufferings of the poor, although that is itself an argument not quite so easily disposed of as Philip Morrison, professor of physics at Cornell and formerly a group leader at Los Alamos, assumed when he wrote recently in *The New Leader:* "The claim of each act we carry out in common must rest on its merit and not on the general thesis that no rich, strange, useless thing can justly be bought while some men lack necessities. . . . Those who built the Acropolis forgot the Helots; those who sailed the Indies thought nothing of the landless peasants."

The poor we have always with us and those who cite that text do not always seem to remember the context—which might seem to make it support Professor Morrison's thesis. The comment was made as a reply to those of the disciples who had rebuked a stranger woman for pouring upon the head of Jesus a rich ointment which, they pointed out, might have been sold and the proceeds given to the poor. "The poor ye have always with you but me you have not always with you." But the question is not merely whether *any* rich, interesting, or beautiful thing can justifiably be bought while some men lack necessities. It is whether, in this particular case, the enormous expenditure is justified when it means neglecting, not only many men, but many other things with at least as much claim to being "rich, strange" and (possibly) useful as well.

Like the poor, this problem has always been with us and in one form or another probably always will be. But in times past men did have one guide in deciding *which* rich and strange thing was worth spending time and brains and money to create or do: They believed (as we do not) that one thing was intrinsically and absolutely better, wiser, or more to be admired than something else. They did not have to fall back on any "because it is there" argument because they had not, like us, been reduced by moral and cultural relativism to a sort of impotence that leaves us powerless to defend one choice as opposed to another and that therefore encourages us to do whatever can be done and to offer no reason more persuasive than the simple "because it is there to be done."

If we do indeed do some things that should have been left undone and do others less worth doing than those we neglect, none of that can be blamed on science itself. The great but limited field of its competence is knowing (pure science) and doing (technology). It cannot—as the wiser of its practitioners admit—evaluate. Though it can teach us how to get to the moon, we need something else to tell us whether or not we ought to go there.

Hence it is that if science is not to blame, some scientists are—just insofar as they encourage the now almost universal belief that science is omnicompetent and that any problems that cannot be solved by the scientific method (and that means all questions involving evaluation) are simply unsolvable or, essentially, meaningless. The tendency to fall back upon "because it is there" as the only answer to the question why a certain thing should be done is simply a demonstration of the inadequacy of science alone as a guide for either society or for the life of an individual.

Three centuries and a half ago Francis Bacon wrote in *The Advancement of Learning:* "We are much beholden to Machiavelli and others, that write what men do, and not what they ought to do." This was perhaps a useful observation at the time; but the situation in the intellectual world is now by no means what it was in Bacon's day. And of all the threats to civilization perhaps none is greater than that which leads sociology to ask only what men do do and technology only what can be done, or, to use again the popular phrase, "what is there." By banishing "ought" from the vocabulary of our sociology, and by asking of our technologists only what they can do rather than what is worth doing, we are making ourselves passengers in a vehicle over which no critical intelligence pretends to exercise any control and which may, indeed, take us not only to the moon but to destinations even less desirable.

Some will no doubt answer that many of the advances of science are due to boundless curiosity concerning things that seem to have no possible application. But such curiosity is much safer when it leads us to know whatever we can know rather than to do whatever we can do. We have a tendency to rush from knowing to doing without pausing for reflection. Technology, if not science, has sometimes entailed penalties when it has taught us how to do things better left undone. This fact was seldom noted even by a few until quite recently when a minority began to wonder whether or not it would have been better for everybody if the secret of the atom had never been penetrated. Curiosity, even scientific curiosity, can open a Pandora's box as well as a treasure chest. And one should use a certain amount of caution in lifting the lid of any box whose contents are unknown.

Primitive man suffered from both a lack of knowledge and a lack of know-how. He believed a great many absurd and often troublesome things that were not true. He had a very limited knowledge of how to do what he wanted to do. But this last limitation was also something of a safeguard, even if a rather unsatisfactory one. He could not destroy his environment as disastrously as we can destroy ours, and he could not kill as many of his neighbors as he would have been glad to kill if he had known how. Perhaps his intentions and desires were even worse than ours, but he didn't know as well as we, how to implement them. We know only too well. Know-how continues to leave know-what and know-whether further and further behind.

I do not know just how military expenditures compare with those incurred in connection with the exploration of space. But except for defense, no other single enterprise of the government is financed on so lavish a scale. This surely suggests that those responsible for giving it this unquestioned priority assume that of all the achievements possible in our generation this is the one most important. But does anyone seriously believe that this is true? That if a good fairy should grant us one wish we should say, "Let me get to the moon, and beyond"?

Consider, for example, the population explosion: not only what it has already done to make life difficult and ugly, but also what it threatens to do in the future. In the minds of many thoughtful people it is a danger to mankind that may be as great as that of atomic warfare—the one threatening us with too many people, the other with a world in which there will be none at all. One could easily fill a book full of statements by responsible persons that say just this in one way or another. One moderate comment from Dr. Walter Hoagland, president of the American Academy of Arts and Sciences, will suffice. In a recent *Bulletin of the Atomic Scientist* he described experiments that demonstrate to his satisfaction that in animal populations overcrowding produces various pathological conditions, including a fatal adrenal malfunction called the Stress Syndrome. He believes that the same thing will happen to human beings under similar circumstances, and this seems to dispose of the assurance that the feeding of a monstrously overgrown population will present no serious problems to an ever-advancing technology.

Dr. Hoagland went on to suggest that we can "do nothing and just wait for the Stress Syndrome or a new virus to do its work," or we can "leave the solution to some trigger-happy dictator with a suitable stockpile of atomic weapons." On the other hand, so he suggests, we might just possibly "decide on an optimum population for the world and by education and social pressure try to see that it is not exceeded."

Admittedly, that last suggestion, though the only sensible one, involves problems to which the solutions are not at the moment by any means obvious. But it is to President Johnson's credit that he has given, more clearly than any other high government official ever has, recognition to the fact that the population explosion should be reckoned with somehow, sometime. Not long after his inauguration the foreign aid bill contained this sentence: "Funds available to carry out this provision may be used to conduct research into the problems of population growth." True, the implication seems to be that no such problems exist in our own country. And the very fact that so timid a statement should mark an epoch is itself enough to demonstrate how casually, almost as a parenthetical afterthought, we approach what is, in actual fact, the second if not the first greatest threat to the future of mankind. Suppose that we had got no further in our plans to explore space than the provision in an omnibus bill for funds "to conduct research into the problem of space travel." Would that not suggest that we didn't think it very important—just something that might be looked into some day and at leisure?

Historians of ancient Egypt say that what we would call its "national income" was, during its days of greatness, very high. But the standard of living endured by the majority of its population was very low indeed because all of the income above what was essential to the barest existence went into the pyramids and other extravagances.

Now, no one could say that such a situation exists today in the United States. A good deal of our national income goes, not only into welfare, but into the pockets of citizens who buy with it what they like—whether that be education for their children, books and pictures and music for themselves, or (in

somewhat more numerous instances) the most expensive automobiles their income (plus available credit) will get them.
But future historians (if there are any) may wonder that we
put into our rocket motors and all that goes into the making of
them so large a slice of the national income.

Once, for several centuries, the Western world was united
in the belief that the most important task it could possibly
accomplish would be the recovery of the Holy Sepulcher. It
sacrificed thousands of lives, to say nothing of vast wealth and
a large part of its manpower, in the attempt to achieve something that few of us today can regard as having been more than
an irrational obsession. Yet to a large section of the intelligent
men of that time the enterprise must have seemed as obviously
important as landing on the moon seems to us. But is not the
moon, like the Holy Sepulcher, a mere symbol? It is not even
in the hands of the infidel—though I suppose that if the Russians get there first it will be considered to be. And I wonder
if, at some not too distant date, our crusade will not have come
to seem no less incomprehensible than that of our forefathers.

Why don't we devote to the problem of overpopulation an
effort as determined as that we are making to get to the moon
before the Russians? Why, even at long last, do we do no more
than to say that a small part of a large fund may be used to
"conduct research into the problem"—but not to take any action?

The most important of the answers to this question is not
the opposition of moralists or the indifference of those who see
in what they call a "bumper crop of babies" an everincreasing
market for the baby foods it will eat and, a little later, for the
cigarettes it will smoke. The most important reasons are, first,
the fact that this problem is far more difficult than the problem
(stupendous though it is) of how to get to the moon; and,
second, that the solution, if there is one, cannot be reached by

the methods that have yielded such astonishingly successful results when applied to all the problems that do not involve human nature and that therefore yield to mechanical solutions. That the technological problem of birth control has been solved, that our so triumphant know-how includes the know-how of contraception, is quite typical of our age's greatest strength. That we do not know how our know-how can be applied to promote a good life is equally so. If a Cousteau suggests that we build undersea cities and a von Braun gives the even more preposterous suggestion that we colonize the planets; if, moreover, these are taken seriously by some, it can only be because these are purely technological solutions and it is upon technology that most of us rest whatever hopes we may have for a decent future.

I remember having read, some fifteen or more years ago, a book by Willy Ley in which was discussed the conditions that would have to be created before a rocket could break away from the earth's gravity and proceed indefinitely toward whatever object in space it had been pointed at. To do that, if I remember correctly, the rocket would have to be capable of a speed twice what it had been possible to achieve up to that time. This critical speed was named "the escape velocity." And though the ironic implications of the term did not strike me then, they do strike me now. Perhaps one of the reasons we are so attracted by the problems of space exploration is that absorption in them helps us forget the more difficult problems lying right at our feet and that an "escape velocity" is precisely what we have achieved.

A good many science-fiction stories have been written about the survivors, sometimes the last surviving couple, on a depopulated earth. If I were to try my hand at that kind of fiction I should imagine a pair of astronauts who had escaped to the moon and who looked back at an earth where the Stress Syndrome produced by overcrowding had at last involved, not only the exchange of the Russian and American overkill stock-pile, but also the smaller but effective contributions from what are now called—but by then wouldn't be—the undeveloped countries. Our astronauts had brought along the equipment necessary for the return journey. But it did not take them long to decide not to use it.   —*Saturday Review*

NOVEMBER 20, 1965

. . . . . .

Invention is the mother of necessity

We are all aware (and we are all very frequently told) that technology has created a world that even our own parents would not have believed possible and that many of them would have contemplated with alarm. Most of this new world we take so completely for granted that we merely turn switches, dial telephones and board jet planes without asking questions and certainly without any vivid sense of their novelty or of the fact that we really know almost nothing about how they work or how they came to be.

The vast majority of us had nothing whatever to do with their creation and certainly were never given any chance to say whether or not we wanted them. We have been carried along on a tide and, although for the most part we have been willing to believe that "progress" really does represent a pro-gression toward something desirable, it can hardly be said that we *willed* any of the things that have happened to us. In a very real sense, the telephone, the radio, the television, the automobile and the airplane were thrust upon us. And as the newest developments come to involve more and more esoteric principles and problems, the proportion of our citizens who can comprehend, much less work creatively with them, must become smaller and smaller.

One need only read the popular magazines and those advertisements that reflect even more accurately the attitudes of the popular audience, to perceive that most of the members of this audience have, so far, felt no doubt concerning the desirability of our new world and have not ceased to believe that even faster transportation, more completely automatic conveniences, and still stranger machines will create a still happier world of tomorrow, of the day after tomorrow, and of that future that lies ahead "as far as thought can reach."

On the other hand, it is surely a fact of possibly enormous significance that a minority began a few decades ago to doubt the common assumption that "progress" means progressively greater happiness and to suspect that there is a danger in machines which we seem to control but which show an increasing tendency to control us. On a somewhat lower level, it is obvious to anyone who, like me, has read even a very few science-fiction stories that the Wellsian dream has turned into a nightmare.

Not long ago the statement was made, complacently rather than anxiously, that if all of the telephones now functioning in the United States were operated as they were only a few years ago, then the entire female population of working age would be insufficient to manage the switchboards. Just how accurate that statement may be I have no way of knowing. But, accurate or not, it suggests the undeniable fact that we are more and more dependent upon mechanical devices and that this makes our whole civilization very vulnerable. Hundreds of different and complicated machines must continue to function or a paralysis followed by death would soon ensue. What happened last November [1965] when one small piece of electrical equipment failed will be long remembered—but not, I am afraid, long enough. In fact, on second thought I am not sure that it would do much good to remember it.

One of H. G. Wells's early stories had to do with a giant brain encased in a glass box from which it controlled world society. Break that glass and chaos would ensue. This is very nearly the situation in which we find ourselves. If there is a next world war—and it seems hard to believe that man will suddenly abandon an activity that he has persisted in since long before history began—it may well be by far the most destructive ever known; not only because of our vastly increased power to kill, but also because even a few small bombs could break so many links in the intricate chain of technology, every part of which is dependent upon every other part, that the loss of a few links would make the whole useless. We would be reduced to a simplicity we have forgotten how to live with.

Years ago when I happened to be reading a volume of late Roman history I realized suddenly that the ancient world ended and the Dark Ages began when the army of Belisarius cut the Roman aqueducts and, overnight, turned Rome from a community with a water supply, said to have been comparable to that of a modern city, into a Dark Ages town where a few wells and cisterns had to serve a large population. A calamity even greater, but no less easy to imagine, might introduce us to a new Dark Age.

Evolutionists always point out that any animal species that comes to be dependent upon a particular feature of its environment is in danger of extinction. The ivory-billed woodpecker disappeared because he could not survive without that abundant supply of decaying trees that had been eliminated from our well-managed forests. On the other hand, the undemanding English sparrow survived even the near-disappearance of the horse whose droppings he had so successfully exploited. He was adaptable enough to do without horses or, for that matter, without almost any other usual feature of his environment.

For a few hundred years it seemed as though the machines man had invented made him more secure, less at the mercy of nature's caprices. He was ceasing to be (as the English farmer complained in describing his occupation) "too dependent on the Almighty." But conveniences and facilities, which begin as no more than convenient and useful, turn rapidly into necessities as the population increases and as our life is more and more organized in ways that take them for granted. Cities got along without electricity for thousands of years. In many remote parts of the world, large areas are still so little dependent upon it that to cut it off would not create a major catastrophe or even a serious inconvenience. But suppose that bombs or sabotage were to deprive a major part of the United States of its technological lifeblood by making electricity unavailable, not only for a few hours, but for months. Goods could not be moved in; garbage could not be moved out. Before long we would be in a situation almost as impossible as that of the ivory-billed woodpecker deprived of his decaying trees.

Because I have already lived a little longer than the average man does, I have witnessed rather more than he of the recent accelerating take-over by indispensable machines. The automobile, radio, airplane and even the telephone were either invented or permitted to become indispensable to our society within my memory. I can imagine, as the majority of today's citizens cannot, what life was like without them. But the memory would do me no good if they were to disappear.

It is significant, moreover, that the newer technological devices depend upon principles more and more esoteric. The internal combustion engine, the telephone, the moving picture, the acoustic phonograph and even the airplane could be understood by the average child. In fact, three of these marvels were invented by tinkerers rather than by scientists. But if the laws governing the application of nineteenth-century physics were relatively simple, electronics, as distinguished from electricity, belongs to experts only. You and I know how a moving picture or a telephone works. But if we read an account of the way in which our television set works, it is hard to credit. And just in so far as our elaborate technology depends upon highly trained experts, just to that extent does the dependence make us more vulnerable. Once we needed little more than arithmetic to get along with our world. Then, unless we depended entirely upon others, a smattering of calculus was necessary to know what our betters were talking about. Now, within a very few years, anyone who cannot program a computer is as dependent upon those who can as primitive man ever was upon his witch doctor. What is perhaps even more alarming is the fact that even the experts depend upon other experts and, also, upon the existence of machines which they could not make for themselves if these machines happened to be destroyed.

In grammar school I learned (but of course long ago forgot) how to extract a cube root by the arithmetical method. Recently I have asked several professional mathematicians if they could perform that operation, and was told with a smile, "Of course not. You extract a cube root with a slide rule, a logarithm table or, nowadays, with the aid of a computer." But since most engineers could not calculate a logarithm table (a very lengthy job, by the way) or improvise a slide rule, much less construct a computer, even engineers would not know how to reconstruct the machinery of our civilization if it somehow collapsed or was destroyed.

A grim joke, current just after the end of World War II, consisted of the remark that, whereas the most important weapon of the next war would be the atom bomb, the most important weapon of the war after that would be the bow and arrow. This is as good a way as any of stating the fact that a calamity could so destroy all the mutually dependent features of our technology that generations, perhaps even centuries, would be required to build them up again by beginning at the bottom of the pyramid which rests upon a hundred primary tools and materials, none of which are available to man in the state of nature or, for that matter, were available to, say, Periclean Athens. What could an electrical engineer do on a desert island if he didn't have any copper wire?

Many people must be wishing that the secret of atomic fission had never been discovered. Some may even suspect that the invention of the airplane was a misfortune. Without it we would have much less reason to fear Russia or China, and would be spared the enormous expense and effort of defense—to say nothing of the possibility that such defense may prove inadequate. But we are saddled with the airplane and the atom bomb, and it looks as though we would have to live—or die—with them.

In a book written some years ago I compared the forces we have summoned up to the bottle imp in an Oriental story. The all-powerful imp will obey all commands except one. He will not get back into the bottle no matter how sternly he is commanded—and we cannot get rid of the powers we have acquired. Not long thereafter I met (I believe in the pages of the *American Scholar*) a perhaps more telling comparison that Thomas Mann suggested, between modern man and Dr. Faustus. Having sold his soul to the Devil, Faustus has what appears to be a completely obedient servant. But the time comes suddenly when the servant will obey no longer. Instead of doing what Faustus bids, he carries his onetime master off to Hell.

Could anything short of the nearly total destruction of our civilization and, along with it, most of the inhabitants of all the "developed countries," rescue us from our own dangerous devices? Is there any possibility that we may voluntarily stop short of either complete dependence upon machines or, worse yet, a war in which both sides would suffer to an extent probably unparalleled since the days when conquerors, as a matter of course, put the conquered population to the sword?

Some sort of change of heart would certainly be necessary before we could begin to arrest, or even slow down, our increasing dependence upon increasingly complex machines. And although the man in the street still thinks of a brighter future only in terms of more, rather than less, technology, there are at least a few who are beginning to ask if we are not becoming more and more dependent and vulnerable rather than more and more independent and safe. That is, at least, fairly encouraging. But the problem of deactivating atomic weapons is even more difficult because a prerequisite seems to be an increasing consensus that appears less, rather than more, likely than it did only a few years ago.

Dr. Johnson (here, as my readers have learned to expect, he comes again) was once asked if *anyone* believed in the truths of religion in the same sense that one believes in the facts of everyday life. Johnson closed what was evidently an uncongenial topic to an uneasy Christian like himself by a firm and simple, "No, sir." Now, if most of those who say that mankind seems about to destroy itself really believed that statement "in the same sense" that they "believe the facts of ordinary life," we might manage somehow to escape the danger. But it is all but impossible for us to do so, and until the threat is seen to be more real than we can actually believe it to be, we will not take it seriously enough to help us find a way of avoiding it.

—*American Scholar*
SPRING, 1966

. . .   .

Is man a machine?

"Is man a machine?" To this question—and it is the most inclusive commonly asked today—the answer given by many scientists, and quite widely accepted by the general public, is "Yes."

No other form of atheism is quite so absolute or holds so many implications for the future of our species. It banishes from the universe not only God but humanity itself. Before we accept it, we should examine the evidence very carefully.

Mechanism is, of course, as old as Lucretius, and in the seventeenth and eighteenth centuries Descartes and Malebranche gave it a new turn. But it was not until the nineteenth that enough props were put under the theory to make it seem other than inherently preposterous. Even then, the more responsible—Darwin and Huxley, for instance—sometimes hedged slightly in parentheses; but others were, or had been, completely dogmatic. I don't believe in the existence of the soul, said one, because I can't find it in my test tube. The brain, said another, is merely a gland that secretes thought—just as the liver secretes bile. Novelists and playwrights sometimes followed suit, and our own Theodore Dreiser thought he really said something when he indulged in such pontifications as that love was merely a matter of chemistry—as though that told us anything at all.

Very few responsible scientists would today make any of these absurd statements. Though most of them may find the concept of "soul" unnecessary and unsatisfactory, they would readily admit that if it did exist the test tube would not be the place to look for it. And most of them would agree also that whatever the relationship between the brain and "soul" may be, the analogy with liver and bile is not very apt. Even during the heyday of simple mechanism the physiologist who said he could make a better optical instrument than the eye, was answered by another, "But you couldn't make it see." And even though we have, in recent years, learned more and more about the mechanical processes that accompany life, there is, among many, a greater willingness to admit that something eludes explanation and that we are less and less sure that we know what "material" and "mechanistic" mean.

Every explanation leaves something unexplained. Consider,

for example, the mystery of heredity. When Mendel's neglected laws were rediscovered we were inclined to say, "Now
we understand." But we understood only the laws governing
certain of the processes, not what lies behind them. Thomas
Hunt Morgan then discovered the role of genes, and at last we
said, "We really do understand." But how do the genes do
what they do? "Nucleic acids," says the latest theory, and we
are satisfied again. But how does nucleic acid do what it does?
Only an act of faith can convince us that there is an answer to
that question and that it is at last a real answer.

Without that act of faith we are left wondering if we are not
following a will-o'-the-wisp, so far as ultimate understanding
is concerned. We are merely learning more and more about the
describable processes without coming any closer to understanding what they mean or what legitimate conclusions may be
drawn concerning the ultimate mystery of life.

In the light of science many old metaphysical questions require restatement in new terms. But they do not vanish as some
scientists try to believe that they do. Consider, for example, the
old dispute between materialism and what was called idealism.
To the arguments of the materialists, the idealists objected that
no bridge, no contact even, can be imagined between the universe
of consciousness and that of matter. They are incommensurate
and no communication between them is possible. Because we
cannot see how matter could become thought we are forced, so
it was said, to assume that one must be some sort of shadow of
the other. Consciousness, said Thomas Henry Huxley, must be
some sort of illusion. It is more likely, replied idealists like F.
H. Bradley, that the material world is illusory. After all,
our own consciousness is the only thing of which we have direct
consciousness and therefore the only thing we know to be real.

Nowadays we may prefer to state the problem in different
terms. We may even suggest a different solution to it,
namely that just as matter and energy may be equally real

aspects of the same convertible ultimate, so may matter be a form of thought, or vice versa. But the problem arises again in connection with any attempt to present physical or chemical process as an *explanation* of consciousness. Recently *Life* magazine gave to an otherwise excellent account of the most recent discoveries in biochemistry the indefensible title "Scientists Close In on the Secret of Life."

The discoveries in question concern the role of certain chemical substances in the most intimate functionings of the living cell. They may make it possible for the biochemist of the future to change the hereditary characteristics of man himself and, as the *Life* article recognizes, the implications of such a possibility are terrifying. But to me it seems no exaggeration to say that, despite all the new knowledge concerning the processes that accompany life, life itself is still just as unique and inexplicable as it was before biochemistry was even thought of.

Doubts somewhat like these have arisen in a sufficient number of first-rate contemporary minds (including first-rate scientific minds) to provoke a suggestion. If we look back to the middle of the last century as the time when men became convinced that man, as well as the universe in which he lives, is a machine, then the twenty-first century may look back upon ours as the century when the structure of materialism as an inclusive philosophy began to crumble.

Biology had, of course, been following physics, but presently physics itself began to reinforce the doubts that were growing in the minds of some biologists. The unpredictability of the individual atom, the transformation of matter into energy, the realization that the experimenter could not be wholly separated from the thing observed—all made even the mechanism of the unliving seem less mechanistic. It would be instructive to compare the opinions on this subject held by some of the most distinguished living physicists. (Incidentally, they will also afford telling evidence against the familiar contention that scientists, unlike humanists, agree with one another because, again unlike humanists, they deal with facts and know what they are talking about.)

Hear first the mechanist George Gamow, developer of the quantum theory of radio activity and professor of theoretical physics at George Washington University. In a book called *Mr. Tompkins Learns the Facts of Life* (supposedly written down to the comprehension of such as you and me), Professor Gamow sets forth his materialistic conviction in the following words: "The mechanistic point of view is . . . that all phenomena observed in living organisms can be reduced in the end to regular physical laws governing the atoms of which that organism is constructed. . . . Basic manifestations of life like growth, motion, reproduction, and even thinking depend entirely on the complexity of the molecular structures forming living organisms and can be accounted for, at least in principle, by the same basic laws of physics that determine . . . inorganic processes."

Now turn to P. W. Bridgman, Nobel Prize-winner in physics and Higgins Professor Emeritus at Harvard. His remarkable, quite different book, *The Way Things Are* (1959), is almost a *mea culpa*, since it gives his reasons for rejecting mechanism and behaviorism—both of which he formerly inclined to—as embodying the only truth. His treatise (unlike Professor Gamow's) is too long, complicated, and subtle to be analyzed here. It admits the utility of mechanistic theories as working tools for the discovery of certain aspects of reality, but insists they neglect other tools that reveal other aspects. I think it would be fair to state one of his most fundamental conclusions like this: About a century and a half ago the great mathematician Laplace announced the thesis of scientific determinism by declaring that if we knew what physicists called the current "state" of everything in the universe we would be able to deduce from that present state everything that had happened and everything that ever would happen. "With earth's first clay they did the last man knead / And there of the last harvest sowed the seed." Professor Bridgman replies, not only that we never could know completely the "state" of the universe at any moment but also that, even if we could, there are some realities in human consciousness which could not be so determined. Physical science has no word for these realities and cannot deal with them.

Expressing great admiration for that extreme behaviorist, his onetime colleague B. F. Skinner, Bridgman feels compelled to add: "I do not think that Skinner's solution is the only possible one, or that it is a solution which takes into account all we can see or that is significant." Unless, in other words, you stubbornly deny the reality of consciousness and maintain that it can be dismissed simply because it cannot be dealt with by the methods of physical science, you must somehow take it into account. One might say (I am perhaps risking oversimplification) that Professor Bridgman opts pragmatically for the open universe of William James as opposed to the closed universe of Laplace, Skinner, and other behaviorists. At a minimum, Professor Bridgman is saying that one of the oldest philosophical questions—namely, how immaterial thought may make connection with material objects and what the nature of that connection is—has not been solved; also that it cannot be solved by simply denying the reality or the importance of either.

To this one may add something Schopenhauer pointed out and Jung has reemphasized: It is logically absurd to say that we "know" the physical world, but not that we know our consciousness, since it is only through the consciousness that we know (or rather deduce) any other reality. From the strictly logical standpoint the most radical solopsism is more easily defensible. Consciousness is the only thing we do know, and it is logically possible that nothing else—no external world and no consciousness other than our own—has any existence.

On the question whether law may properly hold an individual responsible for his acts, Professor Bridgman says: "At present the only technique we have for dealing with our fellows is to say that they are similar to the sort of creature we are ourselves. We disregard determinism when dealing with ourselves: we have to disregard it also, within reason, in our everyday contacts with our fellows." (Incidentally, the Soviet government, after toying with the theory that no one is responsible for what the forces operating upon him cause him to do, now recognizes the pragmatic necessity of treating malefactors as though they were free and responsible; in the case of the political offenders, it has an ingenious dodge when it calls prisons "mental hospitals" and thus punishes without calling it punishment.)

Cautious in its qualifications as Professor Bridgman's treatise is, I think we can call it definitely on the side of those of us who resent being called mere predictable and manipulable machines. But I will not lean too heavily on him because I remember a mildly ironic warning given me by Paul Tillich in the course of a private conversation. Never, he said, rest your philosophical argument upon a scientific opinion. The trouble with scientists is that they reverse themselves too frequently. They may have been against you yesterday and on your side today, but the next theory to come along may very well be against you again!

It is perhaps not surprising that once you say, "The brain is a mere machine," you soon find yourself saying "a mere machine can be a brain"—which is, of course, precisely what some of the more extravagant promoters of the computers and their offshoots do say. But if I may judge from the rather extensive, if somewhat scattered, reading I have done on the subject, the tide has turned here also; some, at least, of the leading experts insist that, remarkable as the machines are, they are definitely not brains. When we make them seem so it is by using a misleading vocabulary—as when, to take the simplest example, we call recorded data "memory," though it is no more memory than is the recording on a phonograph record. Norbert Weiner, inventor of the popular term "cybernetics," has recently warned that we had better not go too far in trusting "feedback" rather than the control of our own intelligence. Mortimer Taube, an expert on data-processing machines, has published a book on the subject which concludes that "man-machine identity is achieved, not by attributing human attributes to the machine, but by attributing mechanical limitations to man," and the British neurophysicist Sir Francis M. R. Walshe has approached the subject from the other end.

He wrote: "I give you a simple example in a recent monograph upon *Brain, Memory and Learning* (W. R. Russell, Clarendon Press, 1959), an excellent monograph on its clinical side, where the writer says 'the traditional reasons for separating man from brain seem to be disappearing, and in the same way the separating of psychology from brain physiology has become somewhat artificial . . . consciousness is simply the occurrence of cerebral alertness.' " To this Sir Francis Walshe replies: "Equating consciousness with 'cerebral alertness' is pure tautology, and the sentence would mean as much or as little if he put it back to front and made it read, 'Cerebral alertness is simply the occurrence of consciousness.' " One might also describe Russell's definition as Polonius-style: "For to define true madness, what is it but to be nothing else but mad?"

As in the nineteenth century, attempts to make man a pure machine come up against the stubborn fact of consciousness—a unique phenomenon as undiscoverable as the soul in any test tube. The mechanical brain exists only because a real brain creates and manipulates it.

It is true that certain enthusiasts have gone so far out on a limb as to predict that since consciousness is merely "alertness," we will someday create a machine so alert that it will become conscious. But that is a mere "someday." Until a computer begins not only to propose and answer questions, but also to debate with another computer whether or not they are both mere machines (and loses his temper in the process), sensible men are justified in doubting that anything resembling a brain has been constructed out of tubes, transistors and cables.

A few years ago I wrote a piece called "The Abacus and the Brain." More recently I had the privilege of a brief conversation on the whole subject with Simon Ramo, engineer-president of one of the great electronics firms experimenting with, among other things, a machine for translating from the Russian—which machine is, incidentally, founded upon a sort of automatic dictionary of words and a similar dictionary of phrases. I asked him, "Would you say that one of your so-called thinking machines is more like a brain or more like a complicated, mechanically operated slide rule?" "Definitely," he replied, "more like a slide rule."

Professor Ralph Wycoff is another distinguished scientist who has discussed the general subject with great subtlety. A brief quotation is worth giving, though it inadequately represents the complexity of his thought: "The unique behavior of living matter is not to be foreseen from the observed properties of its inanimate constituents, nor can man's potentiality for conscious thought and feelings be deduced from the simple forms from which he has evolved. . . . Nothing you or I will ever do will be incompatible with the nucleic acids and proteins within us but it does not follow that what we think and elect to do could be predicted if our genetic composition were fully known."

Perhaps the reader began to wonder some paragraphs back why a mere lay essayist should be wading in over his depth to take part in a controversy that is none of his business. In fact, it is or ought to be the business of everyone, layman or expert.

Much of the climate of opinion in the age we live in will depend upon current notions concerning the nature of man and the extent of his powers. As the late Richard Weaver put it, "Ideas have consequences."

If the machine can be a brain more efficient than the one we were born with, then we should turn more and more of our decisions over to it, and if our brains are machines then we are indeed no more than what the extreme Marxists say we are— helpless products of an evolving social and technological system that we only seem to direct. If this is true, then adjustment to things as they are turning out to be is the only wisdom. A good deal has been said about the fact that man is becoming the victim of his machines, but to become the victim of mechanism is a worse fate, and one from which there is no escape.

To me there is nothing more hopeful than the perhaps inconclusive signs that many scientists are beginning to perceive the fallacy in mechanism. But it is also grimly amusing to see how desperately those who do want to believe in it try to explain away whatever seems to cast doubt upon their premise.

Consider, for example, what the distinguished British geneticist C. H. Waddington has to say in an otherwise generally sound and admirable recent book called *The Nature of Life*. In a discussion of target-finding gunsights that seem to exhibit a sort of inherent purposefulness, he compares them with living organisms. He concludes: "It remains true to say that we know of no way other than random mutation by which new hereditary variations come into being, nor any process other than natural selection by which the hereditary constitution of a population changes from one generation to the next. But if one confines oneself to the remark that the basic processes of evolution are not finalistic [*i.e.* endowed with purpose], this, while true, can no longer be regarded as adequate. The nonfinalistic mechanisms interact with each other in such a way that they form a mechanism that has some quasi-finalistic properties akin to those of a target-finding gunsight."

What Professor Waddington seems to have overlooked is something that, to me, renders false the analogy he suggests. His machines that, like the target-following gunsight, exhibit "quasi-finalistic properties" do so because they were devised by men who were endowed with a complete, not merely a quasi, finalistic capacity. Until he can show us a cybernetic mechanism that designs itself, no such machine suggests how seemingly purposeful organisms could have come into being—except through the actual purposefulness of something either outside or including themselves. What Professor Waddington's analogy really suggests is the old watchmaker-and-watch analogy, and he is in danger of leading us back to the argument from design as proof that the universe was created by a mind outside of nature—which is a good deal further than I (who have my doubts about orthodox Darwinism) am ready to go.

—*Saturday Review*
JANUARY 18, 1964

· · ·   · · ·   · · ·

If God is dead does human nature exist?

Like many of my contemporaries I find the question "Is God Dead?" likely to result in nothing except semantic confusions. For one thing the term has been defined in too many ways to be surely meaningful. Even a precise definition would commit us to dealing with a question too large and remote for a rational answer in terms of our experience. There have been times when it could be asked and such times may come again. But I at least must settle for questions much less inclusive yet carrying some of the same implications.

Suppose I ask, "Is there any such thing as human nature? Are there beliefs, enterprises and ways of life consonant with that nature and others which are not and never could be made consonant with it? Or can human nature adjust to anything?" Should we ask, for instance, not merely "Which society provides for the most efficient and equitable system of production and distribution?" but also "What society is most in accord with human nature?" Similarly, should we ask not merely "What education best fits a man for living in his world?" but also "What kind of education and what kind of world would best accord with his nature?"

Such questions, I realize, have been increasingly unpopular since Hobbes expounded the theory of what Locke was to call the *tabula rasa*. Start with that theory, and all the relativisms—social, cultural, moral and aesthetic—logically follow. On a blank slate anything can be written. Man is whatever society makes him. Vice is not a creature of hideous mien unless you have been brought up to call some particular thing vice and to call it hideous. There is no use asking whether or not a custom or a society or a procedure is in accord with human nature. The sensible thing to do is to adjust the human being to whatever his society has evolved.

Do we have to accept this conclusion? The eighteenth century faced it before us and put up a fight against Hobbism. If, it said, the good is not what is in accordance with God's will, it is at least what is in accord with nature. And there is, the eighteenth century was convinced, something to be so called. Moreover, nature's law was assumed to be discoverable—in morals and in aesthetics as well as in jurisprudence. Whatever all men had agreed upon was according to nature, and thus nature (including human nature) set up its own absolutes.

But the fight against relativism which the eighteenth century put up turned out to be only a delaying action. Presently nature was criticized out of existence just as God had been. There isn't, said the critics, anything in religion or morals or art upon which all men actually have agreed. The more you learn of history and the more you study cultures other than your own, the more obvious it becomes that men can believe, do and want the most irreconcilable things. What any people calls—as all peoples do —the law of God or the law of nature is merely the custom of its community. And there, up to the present day, the matter has rested.

Of course, few of us—perhaps none—consistently follow such convictions to their logical conclusion. I have heard the most uncompromising relativists denounce the crimes of the Nazis when they ought to have said simply: "Their culture is not the same as ours." I have even heard relativists proclaim with quaint inconsistency that we oughtn't talk any longer about what people "ought" to do. Even the Russian Communists urged the workers to unite when it should have been obvious that, according to their own theory, only the dialectic of matter could determine whether the workers would or would not unite. Nevertheless, ours is a world in which, increasingly, law, public opinion, education and the social services have been based upon the assumption that men are whatever their society makes them and that we should always ask not what it is in their nature to be, but how they may be adapted and adjusted to prevailing conditions and tendencies.

Because all of this implies a definite answer to what is to me the grandest of all questions, I naturally wonder whether the common answer is justifiable and permanent, or whether we shall someday swing again in a different direction and discover evidence, now neglected, that human nature really is something in itself and that it does provide certain absolutes, valid at least in the human realm. Have the anthropologists been so preoccupied with the collection of materials to demonstrate the enormous *differences* between cultures that they have overlooked some things which are common to them all? Have the experimental psychologists been so busy conditioning both animals and men that they have paid little attention to the resistance to conditioning which both can put up?

One little straw blowing in the winds of psychological doctrine is worth noting. One school has begun to wonder whether instinct on the one hand and the conditioned reflex on the other really can account for all the behavior of living organisms. Of course, a brain which carries written upon it only a system of instincts is far from actually being a blank slate. But that is by no means all. Some members of a new school have happened to remember: (1) that birds know by instinct how to fly and do not have to be taught; (2) that though seals do not know instinctively how to swim, they are very easily taught to do so; and (3) that you would have a very hard time indeed teaching most songbirds to swim. In general then, there are not just two classes of animal behavior (inborn and learned) but also a third—that which is not inborn even though the ability to learn it easily is.

So astounded were some when their attention was called to this obvious fact that they began to wonder if the same might be true not only of skills, but throughout the whole psychic realm of beliefs, tastes and motives. The old thesis of the moral relativists was that since no one was born with the "innate idea" that dishonesty and treachery are evil, the conviction that they are is only the result of social education. The opposite could just as easily be taught; value judgments, so they said, are merely the rationalized prejudices of a given culture.

But, ask the new psychologists, isn't it possible that some moral ideas are more easily learned than others; that what the eighteenth century called natural law, natural taste and the rest is real, and that it consists of those beliefs and tastes which are most readily learned and most productive of health and happiness? Perhaps you can condition an individual or a society to think and behave "unnaturally," just as you might possibly teach a robin to swim. But men who have been conditioned to think or behave unnaturally are as unhappy and as inefficient as swimming robins. As the biologist Roger J. Williams puts it, "There are blanks and blanks. The blank brain of the child is capable as time goes on of accepting, digesting (perceiving), and acting upon a multitude of impressions that the brain of a rat is quite incapable of handling." What is true of a rat is not necessarily true of a man.

Is this belaboring the obvious? Not anything so obvious that the implications have been inescapable for those who preferred to ignore them. What difference does it make whether or not certain ideas are "innate" if the capacity to entertain those ideas and not others is? In that case the blank slate goes out of the window and every unqualified relativism along with it.

We are back, it seems to me, to the eighteenth century and one of the most discredited exponents of eighteenth-century ideas. Pope put it thus: "Nature affords at least a glimm'ring light; / The lines, tho' touch'd but faintly, are drawn right." What Pope thought of as a metaphor may turn out to be biologically accurate. On the not quite blank slate the lines are touched too faintly to constitute an automatic instinct. They are much like the latent image on a photographic plate. They are imperceptible until developed. But what development will reveal must already exist. There is, then, such a thing as human nature. What we are born with is not a blank slate but a film already bearing a latent image.

No doubt—as Pope went on to say elsewhere, as experimental psychologists prove in the laboratory, and as educators as well as dictators have too often demonstrated—the lines may be "o'er laid" and the unnatural cease to seem a creature of hideous mien. But the conditioners have to work at it—hard. Men believe in, for instance, the reality of good and evil much more readily than they can be made to accept cultural relativism.

Such an assumption is, at least, one which no valid science forbids us to make, and if we make it we are saved from the nihilism of present-day cultural and moral relativism as the eighteenth century was saved from the nihilism of Hobbes. In a sense, God—or at least a useful substitute for Him—exists. We have again some point of reference now lacking in every inquiry which sets out to determine what kind of society or education or culture would be best for us. One thing is no longer as good as another provided only it can be shown, or made, to exist. We can stop talking exclusively about what can be done to men or what we can make them into, and talk again about what, in themselves, they are.

This will involve what is certainly no easy inquiry. One of the most terrifying of Pascal's *pensées* seems to range him with the enemy: "They say that habit is second nature; perhaps nature is only first habit." To distinguish correctly between the one and the other is one of the most difficult tasks we could set ourselves. The eighteenth-century doctrine of nature collapsed largely because that century was too ready to assume that any cherished prejudice or habit was really "in accord with nature"—a tendency which reached a nadir when, for example, Boswell convinced himself that verse without rhyme was "unnatural" because when he read Milton to a rustic he got the comment that the fellow "would be rhyming" but couldn't quite make it.

If "the natural" really does exist, it is certainly something definable only in terms of the largest generalities. It won't settle disputes between Big-endians and Little-endians. Monogamy, for instance, is probably not "natural" and polygamy "unnatural." But perhaps the conviction that some code, rather than none, should govern the relations between men and women is "natural." Human nature and the societies in which it can function reasonably well are enormously variable. But perhaps they are not limitlessly so. Those anthropologists and those historians of morals who have gathered so much material to prove that the variety is limitless overlook the fact that their evidence actually suggests the contrary. They may demonstrate that a specific action that is considered just at one time and place was considered unjust at others. But how many flourishing cultures can they exhibit in which the concept of justice did not exist? How many societies other than ours ever believed that "morals" were never anything but "mores"? Does not the evidence of the anthropologists themselves seem to suggest that this is a genuinely "unnatural" idea?

Albert Einstein, so I once read, told students at the California Institute of Technology that he doubted whether most present-day Americans were any happier than the Indians who inhabited the continent before the white man came. Nine men out of ten would, I suppose, reject so extreme a statement. But a considerable majority would probably agree that we are at least *not as much happier* as the increase in wealth, security, comfort and power would suggest that we ought to be. Neither our society, our civilization, nor our technology has paid off as we believed it would. And we neither know why nor what we can do about it. We can only go on seeking more wealth, more security, more comfort and more power.

Is it possible that we can do nothing else just because we have never inquired what it is in our nature to want most and to be happiest with? Is it possible that we really want something else also; that it is not in accord with our nature to assume that a high standard of living is the *summum bonum*, and that upon it, and upon it only, our hearts should be set? Is it possible that man is not by nature a creature whose happiness is directly proportioned to the wealth he commands and the speed at which he can travel? We go on the assumption that he can at least be turned into such a creature provided we tell him often enough that this is what he is, and provided we give him wealth and speed in ever-increasing measure. But wouldn't it be worth while to ask whether or not there is something else he wants— either instead of or also—and to see if it can be provided?

There are other such questions I would like to ask. When, for instance, I see unhappy children raised according to the theory that their nature demands "uncritical love," and when I hear that juvenile delinquency is increasing under laws which insist that no young person is responsible for his acts, I wonder whether or not both the spoiled child and the juvenile delinquent are dismayed rather than reassured by the world in which they find themselves—dismayed if only because the belief that acts have consequences and that human beings should be treated "as they deserve" is part of that concept of justice which was "lightly touched" in outline upon the not quite blank slate with which they were born.

But these are very large questions. And—as an old teacher almost inevitably puts it—the bell has rung. —*American Scholar*
AUTUMN, 1957

*   *   *   *   *   *

Men, apes, and termites

"We are, in fact, anthropoid apes trying to live like termites, and, as any philosophical observer can attest, not doing too well at it."

So wrote the late distinguished anthropologist Ralph Linton, and with true scientific detachment stopped there. Whether wisdom dictates that we should solve the problem by returning to the ape or by going further in the direction of the termite he does not say. And neither does he offer a *tertium quid*.

For the moment this caution is irrelevant. I cite him only as one example of the fact that the vision of mankind's ultimate fate as possibly that of a faceless horde united in a brainlessly efficient society does continue to turn up frequently even though it is now a cliché of science fiction and other versions of anti-Utopia.

Earlier moralists thought rather well of ants, from the time of Solomon and the legendary Aesop at least down to La Fontaine. When we first turned against this supposedly admirable insect I do not know, but sometime during the nineteenth century the tide did turn. The ant's prudence, cooperativeness, and complete devotion to the greatest good of the greatest number began to seem excessive; and it was not the sluggard but the intellectual who was advised to "go to the ant"—to be warned rather than to become wise.

The only recent example I know of a survival of the former attitude was supplied by a certain famous astronomer whose hobby is the social insects and who remarked to one of my friends something like this: "Los Angeles has appealed to me for advice on the best way of fighting the Argentine ant. Now I have a good deal of admiration for that insect. It is industrious, peaceful and socially disciplined. I can't say that I have much admiration for the people of Los Angeles. And so, between you and me, I did not give them my best advice." Still, though Los Angeles now seems to be the American city least admired except by the film-struck and a certain number of its own inhabitants, I doubt that even this waggish astronomer would really prefer the Argentine ant to the Los Angeleans.

In recent years prophets have been more fertile in imagining possible dooms than possible salvation and those who specialize in the vision of men-like-ants have cited a variety of causes and symptoms supposed to be preparing or signalizing that fate.

These include the welfare state that destroys initiative; the passion for conformity; and even the simple fact that our greatest
cities would, from a moderate altitude, look much like anthills
at this very moment.

None of these tendencies or symptoms seems to me to indicate very clearly the real process by which man might become
more like termites than like men—or even like apes. What I
propose (if the reader doesn't think all this hopelessly *vieux
jeu*) is to take the whole thing with a certain degree of seriousness as a kind of allegory (even if it is not a literal description)
of something which might possibly happen and to come up with
a suggestion concerning just where a real threat lies—a threat
close enough to be worth considering as possibly operative in the
not-unimaginably-distant future.

Let us begin with a look at what Professor Linton's termites
are really like. They aren't ants, of course, and they have been
around many millions of years longer. Their characteristics
represent a development so much further advanced in a similar
direction that an ant might say (if he had any brains), "Let
us pause and take thought lest the free and abundant life of
our species disappear and we become more like termites than
we ants want to be."

Man, so the anthropologists and the paleontologists tell us,
has been a social animal for less than one million years; ants,
bees and wasps for about seventy million; the termites for something like two hundred million. That certainly suggests that all
these insects have had vastly more experience than we with
social organization and cooperation; also, that in all of them the
effect has been to move steadily in the same direction, with the
result that they have become, among other things, a conspicuous
example of "the survival of the fittest"—though to avoid semantic confusion, we had better remind ourselves that this misleading
phrase really has no content. If you ask, "Fit for what?" the
only answer is, "Why, fit to survive," and the statement then

comes down to mere tautology: "Those survive who survive."

The ant, by comparison with the termite, leads a free and spacious life. Many species are not completely blind; he has elbow room, he walks over the open spaces, he sees something of the world, and he breathes fresh air. On the other hand, the vast majority of individual termites, belonging to the most highly evolved species, never leave their crowded fortress city, could not see anything if they did, spend their entire existence in the narrow chambers and narrower tunnels of a labyrinth where they were born and where they breathe perpetually the damp, carbon dioxide-heavy atmosphere and dread more than anything else being compelled to leave it, even for an instant. The lives of certain human city dwellers who spend their days in air-conditioned offices, pass from them through tunnels of the subway to narrow chambers in some housing development, may seem remotely analogous. But the analogy is still pretty remote.

Within one of the termites' closed cities there is only one imperative, "the greatest good of the greatest number," and that is not a conviction but a built-in response, as the result of which, for instance, "a soldier"—dependably and without the least hesitation—sacrifices his life in defense of his fellows. Some of the metaphysicians of the Soviet Union have discussed the meaning of freedom in a way which seems to say that the only true and perfect freedom consists in no longer wanting to be free; termites have reached that state—or perhaps have gone a little beyond it. They do not want anything. They merely react as they have reacted for millions of years.

Termites entered the popular imagination some years ago through Maeterlinck's secondhand account, to which he added mystical overtones suggesting that the termite community was governed by some sort of communal over-soul. The more usual view of the biologist is that they are actually nearer mere machines than even the less highly developed insects or than, in all probability, they themselves were in the very long ago before they took the road that has led them to a brainless and merely unconscious efficiency.

The recent but standard account of one of the most highly developed species is entitled *Dwellers in Darkness* and is based on an original study by the entomologist F. H. Skaif. It emphasizes what is to us the horror of the termites' existence. Like those survivors of atomic catastrophe described in science fiction as confined to their "shelter," the termites are compelled to pass their entire existence in the Stygian darkness of their fortresses because to venture out would be to meet immediate death, either by desiccation or by falling victim to marauding ants. The food problem they have solved by living exclusively upon decayed vegetation and by practicing an extreme form of the injunction "Waste not, want not." In fact those now struggling with the problem of life on a long-distance spaceship might take a hint from the termites' solution of a similar problem: "If you think for a moment, you will realize that the sewage problem inside the densely crowded community must be a difficult one and the insects have solved it in a bizarre but efficient manner . . . the food passes through the alimentary canal of several individuals until all the nourishment has been extracted from it and only a dark-colored sticky paste (used as a building material) remains. . . . In this city of endless night the inhabitants shed their skins six or seven times as they grow up and the narrow corridors would soon be choked with these empty husks if they were not disposed of in some way or other. The termites get rid of them by eating them. . . . It is the same with their method of disposing of the dead. A cemetery is not needed inside the crowded fortress because the dead are eaten by the living."

If you can forget some of these and other similar practices that are somewhat repulsive to us, and consider only the abstract

characteristics of termite society, it does seem often to approximate the ideal of certain Utopians. There is no selfishness, and
only the welfare of the community counts. There is no competition, only cooperation; no struggle for individual wealth,
superiority or status. And the state (if you imagine that it ever
existed) has indeed withered away. No laws are necessary because no one would do anything a law might exist to prevent.
And though this is so far from being a classless society that
there are many classes among certain species of ants and bees,
no one is interested in social mobility because each, like the
citizens of Aldous Huxley's *Brave New World*, accepts with
perfect docility the role assigned him. In fact there is only one
respect in which this brave world is different from Huxley's. In
the latter, reproduction was controlled but sexual activity was
abundantly open to all. The termites have adopted a more
direct Draconian system. "About ninety-five per cent of the inhabitants of a termitary are workers. These are males and females
that have not developed fully and their sexual organs are ves-
tigial and useless. As their sexual organs do not function, the
workers are denied the privilege of parenthood and they know
nothing of the distractions of sex."

Nevertheless, to quote Skaif again: "Apart from microorgan-
isms, termites are far and away the most numerous of living
creatures in Africa and they teem almost everywhere in the
soil. It may be said that they own Africa in a truer sense than
do the human inhabitants, that they were here long before man
arrived and that they will probably be here long after he,
through his folly, has gone." Harvard University's Professor
B. F. Skinner has maintained that the only criterion to be applied in judging the desirability or undesirability of any institution or act is simply the question whether or not it will
make it more probable that the society which encourages it
"will be here tomorrow." By that test the termite society is
triumphantly successful.

In any case, survival alone seems to be indeed the termites' only success. Though their way of life is the most elaborate known to any creature except man himself, they know neither joy nor sorrow. In all probability they are not conscious at all. They weigh no questions, they make no choices. They live but they are not aware of living. The adventure of life has reached a dead end. They have come almost the full circle from the inanimate mechanism back again to something hardly distinguishable from the mechanical.

Most of us would not like to think that even in the remote future Professor Linton's paradox of the apes trying to live like termites would resolve itself in any fashion even remotely analogous, and if we take the possibility as in any sense serious we might ask ourselves how the termites got that way and whether or not there is any lesson to be learned from them.

Henri Fabre was convinced that the answer was simple: it is merely that God had chosen to give them nearly infallible instincts instead of blundering brains. Modern biologists have, of course, only theories. But some of these theories are at least suggestive. No creature except man, so some of them insist, ever rested his hope of survival on his ability to foresee and choose rather than upon instinct and its inherited pattern of behavior fixed by natural selection. Yet even biologists who make such an absolute distinction between man and the other animals admit that there is also a difference in the degree to which instinctive behavior in other animals is fixed and not capable of modification by any novelty in the situation to be met. We may refuse to call it intelligence, but a cat, a dog, or any other mammal does not respond to a given situation with quite the same predictable, unvarying behavior as the termite or even the ant.

Somewhere, very far back in time, one group of primitive creatures took one road and another group took a different one.

The group out of which the insects developed came to depend more and more upon fixed, instinctive habits; the other more and more upon the ability to change, to become to some degree aware of the why and the whether of a given response to a given situation. In man instinct finally came to play a relatively minor role; awareness and the possibility of choice, major ones.

By certain criteria the reliance upon instinct worked better and sooner. The termites had a real society two hundred million years before man and (as geological time goes) almost as long as that before the earliest mammals began to show signs that they, too, might be conspicuously "successful." And though even today man himself cannot be said to have solved the problem of survival as successfully as various insects have, he somehow perversely prefers his relative failure to their success. He would rather be conscious of that failure than enjoy their unconscious success. He may even agree with Aristotle that the ultimate value of life depends upon awareness and the power of contemplation rather than upon mere survival.

Just so long as he holds to that conviction he resists the tendency to move, however slowly, in the direction of the science fictionist's ultimate horror—men like termites rather than men like gods. Is there any danger that he will change his mind and prefer the termites' kind of success?

Late in the nineteenth century Thomas Henry Huxley made an extraordinary statement: "If some great power would agree to make me always think what is true and do what is right, on condition of being turned into a sort of clock and wound up every morning before I got out of bed, I should instantly close with the offer."

Few statements have ever struck me as more shocking. Huxley seemed to be saying that he would, if he could, be a termite rather than a man. And if we have started or ever will start down the road that leads in the direction of living more like termites than like men (or even than like apes) it would be because we have not only made Huxley's choice but found out ways to make that choice open to us.

We can control population if we really want to. The welfare state is not a threat if we define welfare properly. We can resist universal conformity if we really believe that individuality is a good and refuse to go along with those who insist that the mere individual should always be sacrificed to the good of the greatest number. But once we really come to believe that men should be conditioned and manipulated into "doing what is right," we will have confessed that the remote ancestor of the insects rather than the remote ancestor of the mammals made the wiser choice.

It is at least a responsible guess, made by many students of evolution, that the termites must have once been (and that some insects still are) more intelligent than ants and termites now are; that their extraordinary (and extraordinarily successful) way of life must have evolved in creatures less mechanical than they and that consciousness, as well as the power to vary conduct within some limits, faded as their way of life made them more and more perfectly "fit to survive" while thousands of other freer creatures disappeared from the earth.

If anything like that happened to them it is not wholly absurd to believe that something similar might happen to man; that as he learned more and more how to predict and to determine human conduct, the race of men would become less and less intelligent at the same time as it became more and more "fit to survive"—though less and less fit for any of the things that man has long supposed to be the basis of his claim to be the highest of the animals.

Once when James Boswell and Dr. Johnson were discussing Boswell's greatest weakness—drink—Boswell said it was strange that a man should make a beast of himself. The doctor replied that it was not strange because "He who makes a beast of him-

self gets rid of the pain of being a man." Thomas Henry
Huxley seemed to be saying that he would be willing to make
a machine of himself to get rid of that same pain. Are there
any today who would make the same choice and are there
others, more dangerous perhaps, who—without quite facing the
implication of their proposals—are moving in the same direction?

Let us first take an example of the extreme position. Here
I return to Professor Skinner, whom I take as a kind of whipping
horse because he is so eminent, so able, so clear, and so absolute.
A few years ago I took part in a panel discussion with him in
which "survival," as the ultimate value, was discussed. Here is
a short excerpt from a transcript of the discussion:

MR. KRUTCH: Supposing you should come to the conclusion, as the
result of your investigations, that the healthiest and most enduring
society was composed of creatures whose responses had become so
automatically perfect that consciousness was no longer necessary and
would disappear, would you consider this eternally surviving group
of unconsciously functioning organisms a result you would envisage
with equanimity and pleasure?

MR. SKINNER: Yes, I would envisage that result with pleasure; but
what I would not is the condition in which that would be the case.
[I include the second clause of this reply for the sake of fairness
though I do not think I understand what it means.]

In Professor Skinner's striking Utopia, which he published
under the title *Walden II,* the citizens of his ideal common-
wealth have not ceased to be conscious but they have been so
benignly conditioned to automatically right attitudes and responses, that consciousness seems to perform no function other
than, perhaps, to give them the satisfaction of feeling that they
are still in some sense living creatures rather than machines.
This situation has been created by a technician who has completely mastered the behavioral sciences and, as the *raisonneur*
of *Walden II* points out, the lesson is simply this: What is

commonly called education is too slow a process and too uncertain in its results. Instead of trying to teach men to reason and make conscious choices, we must bypass all such processes (which probably are only epiphenomena anyway) and concentrate upon direct conditioning. In his Utopia men behave in a fashion we are accustomed to call reasonable, not because they reason but because they do not; because their automatic responses are the right ones—as they also are in a termite colony.

Now, Professor Skinner is an extremist and a very logical one. I doubt that very many of those who tell us that the hope of mankind lies in the development of "the behavioral sciences" would actually face, as he does, the logical conclusion to be drawn from that premise. But just in so far as we do place our faith in the behavioral sciences rather than in education, reason, and philosophy, we are getting dangerously close to the crossroads where the insects took one road and the ancestors of the mammals took another. It might not (at least in anything less than many millions of years) conduct us to a termite colony and the kind of life led in it, but it might well lead us to a society of the sort you find described in a science-fiction nightmare.

The concept of the behavioral sciences seems at first glance an innocent, even a hopeful, thing. But what it often seems to mean comes closer and closer to the methods by which *Walden II* came into being. The line between conditioning and what we call brainwashing (when it is practiced by those of whom we disapprove) is narrow and dim. We are indignant at advertisers who invent methods of determining just what insidious notes to sound in order to awaken the wish to own and the desire to be envied; just how to create desires that didn't exist before and probably shouldn't exist now. But the advertiser is only a minor annoyance compared with those who use the same techniques to shape the individual and his society, even though it is (as they say) with the best of intentions.

How real are individuality, reason, and the power to evaluate and choose? Not real at all, say the Skinners, who are very positive that a determinism as rigid as John Calvin's rules the universe. Relatively weak and easily misled, say others not quite so absolute in their convictions that we are less free agents than merely the product of forces. Just how free and unfree we are I do not pretend to know. What I do know is that man became civilized man by believing that reason and the power to choose are to some extent real and that they can be cultivated. The more a man or a society attempted to depend upon them, the more human the human being, and the more worthy of human beings his society became.

I do not want to be a termite, to be wound up like a clock, or to live in a *Walden II*. I hope that the species to which I am proud to belong will not come to be so obsessed with survival and efficiency that it forgets what makes survival and efficiency worthwhile and, to me at least, that includes a chance to be intelligent and aware.

Do more and more men refuse to share my preferences? Do more and more of them want to be wound up like clocks and thus spared the pain as well as the rewards of being men? Or have they simply not sufficiently considered what putting one's trust in benevolent brainwashing must ultimately lead to?

—*Saturday Review*

SEPTEMBER 21, 1963

. . . . . .

Is Homer obsolete?

A few weeks ago [summer, 1966], my wife and I sat with three friends on the very spot (so Schliemann liked to believe) where Hector said his last farewell to Andromache. There we read aloud the famous passage that describes the parting and the equally famous one in which Priam comes to plead for the body of his son. Then my mind went back more than forty years to the time when Mark Van Doren and I, on our first visit to Europe, sat down by Green-head Ghyll to read Wordsworth's "Michael." Evidently I had not changed much if I could still take satisfaction in ceremonies so completely what this generation would call corny. Neither, of course, did it seem that human nature as Homer described it had changed much in some three millennia. Both man's inhumanity to man and the pity that it generates are much the same as they were in his day.

I would not intrude so commonplace a reflection if I did not still have vividly in mind the spring number of the *Scholar* in which some (but certainly not all) of the contributors argued earnestly the thesis that we are upon the threshold of a new human nature as well as of a new physical world. I do not much regret that I shall not live to see the full development of that brave new world of still greater speed, power and noise. I can accept for others what many anticipate as an agreeable inevitability, and when one writer assures me that Euclid and Archimedes have become "simply irrelevant," I can take even that. But if certain other writers are correct, not only Euclid and Archimedes but also Joseph Wood Krutch is "simply irrelevant."

Naturally, I would not like to think this a necessary conclusion but when I read, for instance,

The new world in which we live is so unlike the past, even the past which is close to us, that in proportion as we are saturated in the Western cultural tradition, we are incapacitated for looking clearly at our actual situation and thinking constructively about it. The better we are educated, the more we are fitted to live in a world that no longer exists,

I cannot doubt that the very distinguished contributor sees me as one of those trying to live in a world that no longer exists.

When another distinguished contributor quotes with approval the remark of a young man from Harvard University, "You see, my generation does not have goals. We are not goal-oriented," I cannot understand this as anything except a radical denial of what anyone saturated in (or even superficially affected by) "the Western cultural tradition" has always taken to be fundamental: namely, the assumption that one thing, one experience, or one action is better than another and that nothing is more important than the attempt to choose one or another upon the basis of a value judgment. Here we are bid to accept what is commonly called the "because-it-is-there" imperative, or what I myself define as the "I-don't-know-or-care-where-I-am-going-but-I-sure-am-getting-there-in-a-hurry" philosophy.

Obviously if either of these contributors is correct, then my reading of Homer was rendering me less capable of "seeing our situation as it really is." I would, as another contributor suggests, have been better employed listening to the Beatles who are, so he says, "trying to tell us by the anti-environment they represent just how we have changed and in what way." Then the *coup de grâce* is given in the explanation that the school dropouts "represent a rejection of nineteenth-century technology as [this is] manifested in our educational establishments." People like me then stand revealed, not as the sturdy defenders of the humanities in an age that tends to de-emphasize them, but simply as "dropouts" from the civilization of which we refuse to be a part. What used to be described as "the best that has been thought and said" should be forgotten as soon as possible. After all, Matthew Arnold lived in the dark age before computers and atomic fission. Mechanized brains had not yet been developed beyond Babbage's elementary contraptions and even dynamite was a new invention. What could he know of good and evil, of wisdom and folly? Like many of his contemporaries he was even "goal-oriented."

To my obsolete ears the language written by my more up-to-date contemporaries does not seem to be an improvement on that of the older cultural tradition, as when, for instance, an enthusiastic proponent of a thoroughly mechanized world wants to say that man can be as happy in a very big city as anywhere else but prefers to speak instead of the "hedonic potential" of Megalopolis. Neither do I think that "the young person today is a data processor on a very large scale" is a better way of saying "is exposed to much information."

From certain other contributors to this alarming issue I do find some support. Thus when Buckminster Fuller writes that "all life has been able to succeed owing to the anticipatory design of a regenerative ecological energy exchange," it takes me a little while to understand the language, but I think he means very much what Thoreau meant when he said: "In wildness is the preservation of the world," and what I meant by glossing that passage with a comment to the effect that, of all cybernetic machines, the balance of nature is the most perfect. I am also reassured when the same contributor quotes Dr. Wilder Penfield, head of the Neurological Institute at McGill University, who wrote: "It is much easier to explain all the data we have regarding the brain if we assume an additional phenomenon 'mind' than it is to explain all the data if we assume only the existence of the brain."

Richard Hoggart, professor of English at the University of Birmingham, in England, is ready to defend literature against those who regard it as no more than part of the pestilential Western cultural tradition. "Good literature re-creates the immediacy of life," he says, and to me it seems that this is possibly the most important of its functions in an age when science insists more and more strongly that neither the experiences of our senses, of our emotions, nor even the logical processes of our minds are relevant to a reality from which we inevitably feel ourselves more and more alienated. This it is that makes

literature even more important for us than it was for our predecessors—because we find in it something that "re-creates the immediacy of life." But I fear that many other contributors, and
on the whole those most deeply immersed in the new sciences
and the attitudes these sciences encourage, would dismiss Mr.
Hoggart and me as "simply irrelevant" because we are fitted
to live only in a world that no longer exists.

Since I do not want to become a man so completely new that
everything I have thought or hoped for has become irrelevant,
I take some consolation in the thought that in some very important respects man has not changed as much as the changes in
his physical environment and his way of understanding the universe might suggest. Homer's physical world was almost in-
conceivably different from ours; so were his notions about
physics, astronomy and biology. Much of his philosophy and
a few (but very few) of his standards of value are obsolete. Yet
in reading him, I still have the sense that, so far at least, the
man of the twentieth century is not a new man at all but is as
old as Hector saying good-bye and Priam begging for the body
of his son.

Homer had never seen either the simplest wind or water
mill. The machine that so dominates our lives hardly existed
at all. His universe was governed by gods whose passions,
prejudices and vices were exactly the same as (or perhaps a little
bit worse than) those of his fellows, and neither Archimedes
nor Euclid had yet begun the process of making these gods
"simply irrelevant." Still, we have no difficulty in recognizing
his heroes as creatures very much like ourselves.

Does not that suggest that what we call human nature and
what we are accustomed to recognize as the most vivid of our
experiences are actually less determined by technology, or the
kinds of knowledge it creates and is created by, than some now
hope and some now fear?

Is the scientific and technological revolution now in progress actually any more sweeping than that which took place more slowly during the three thousand years since Homer wrote? Is not the difference between the scienceless and machineless world of his time, and that which the twentieth century now possesses and cowers under, as great as any that is likely to be between our present world and that of the twenty-first century? The heroes of the *Iliad* would be as bewildered in New York or San Francisco as we would be distressed by Troy, Ithaca or Mycenae. But if we could meet together in some grove or porch where nothing need remind us of the presence or absence of those changes that time has made in our environment, and if we were to discuss not religion, technology or science, but love, hate, tragedy, pathos, and the paradox of man's persisting inhumanity despite his capacity for pity and tenderness, then I think we would understand one another quite well and realize that in many important respects—possibly in the most important of all—we are not new men but the same old paradoxical creatures, "the glory, jest, and riddle of the world."

Bernard Shaw once expounded the thesis that the length of time a literary work remains relevant depends upon the extent to which it is concerned with manners, with morals, or with passions. The first, so he said, change so rapidly that a pure comedy of manners soon loses all point. Our moral judgments, he argued, change much less fast than our manners, but have changed importantly since the time when our earliest surviving masterpieces were composed. The passions, on the other hand, have changed so slowly that we have no difficulty in recognizing the representation of them in these same older specimens of the literary art.

Taking the *Iliad* as an example, he said that it was still alive because the passions of its heroes were fully understandable but that we could not understand the moral attitudes involved.

Achilles was a noble hero, but to us his refusal to yield up the body of Hector and his barbarity in dragging it around the walls of Troy make it impossible for us to accept him as anything of the kind.

It is true that the manners represented in Homer are completely strange to us. But it seems to me (and I believe it will seem to most) that Shaw missed the meaning of the poem in his eagerness to make his point. Is it not plain enough that the poet did *not* regard Achilles' behavior as noble but as a blot on his reputation; in short, that the moral judgment passed on the actions of the characters is so very close to that which we pass upon them that our sense of an essential identity with Homer is, in that respect also, almost as complete as it would be if neither Archimedes nor Euclid (to say nothing of Watt, Edison, Einstein and Oppenheimer) had ever lived? I wonder if the recent exploits of the new physics and the new technology will really change us much more—or if, supposing that they do, the change will be for the better.

One aspect of Homer's modernity is not reassuring, even for me. He and we are equally aware of the senseless horror of war and equally incapable of imagining how it could be abolished. The proponents of the new man will no doubt insist that this is one of the many new things that their new man will know how to do. But to date, I see no evidence to support this hope. Advancing technology certainly makes wars worse, but it is so far from preventing them that they have been, during the few years just past, more nearly ubiquitous and continuous than at any time since the Dark Ages. A careful reading of selected passages from the *Iliad* might be more likely to inspire at least a desire for peace than the pursuit of technological know-how by those who are not "goal-oriented."

It might at least suggest a goal. Rereading it refreshed my belief in the sanity and helpfulness of the European cultural tradition. Reading some of the contributors to the Spring *Scholar* confirmed my fear that many of the most able masters of the new technology are very unlikely to shape for us a better or even a, to me, tolerable future.

Many readers are no doubt too young to remember that thirty years ago we went through something rather like this once before. At that time it was Marxism and the rise of Communist Russia that were making all the ideas and culture of the past obsolete and were creating a new, socially-oriented man, while those who clung to the cultural traditions of Western Europe were already anachronisms. Lincoln Steffens, who was then in his "I-have-seen-the-future-and-it-works" phase, paid me the compliment of analyzing my attitudes as typical of those that were fast disappearing, and John Strachey devoted considerable space in his *Literature and Dialectical Materialism* to an analysis of me as a representative of a dying culture. Acquaintances who failed to convert me took me aside to suggest that, since people whose attitudes were like mine would soon be liquidated, it would be prudent of me to cast my lot with the new men even if I would prefer not to do so. Homer, as well as other portions of the culture of Western Europe, have survived while most of the socially-conscious proletarian literature of the 'thirties is forgotten. —*American Scholar*

AUTUMN, 1966

. . . . II

Manners & Morals

．．．　．．．　．．．

A commencement address

When an old man has an opportunity to address a youthful group on such a traditional occasion as this, it is certain that many platitudes will fall on impatient ears. You will then not be surprised if I begin with some very familiar platitudes. My excuse for doing this is that I would like in the end to make at least one deduction from these platitudes which is not as commonly emphasized as I think it should be. Unfortunately, however, the platitudes must come first.

This, as you are well aware without being told as often as you have been told, is a great age of science; also one in which science has come to mean more and more the techniques for acquiring power. We call it the power to control the forces of nature, but we are becoming increasingly aware that it means also power over human life including, unfortunately, the power to destroy life on an unprecedented scale—on so large a scale that it may just possibly involve the destruction of ourselves as well as of our opponents.

In one way or another these platitudes will be the theme of a large proportion of the commencement addresses delivered this week in hundreds of schools and colleges. Thousands of young men and women will be urged to devote themselves to science as the great need of our time and urged to do their part in making our nation strong. At the same time a lesser but still immense number of young people will be warned of the dangers as well as the promises of technology and not a few will be urged to avoid an exclusive stress upon it. They will be told that philosophy, ethics, religion and the arts are an essential part of the human being and that we neglect them at our peril.

Those who stress the dangers as well as the promises of technology are not always either querulous old men or professors of the humanities, though the latter are sometimes suspected of merely defending their shrinking classes. Among those who sound a warning are some who have been themselves very deeply involved in expanding science and technology. Here, for instance, is a singularly brief, trenchant statement from a great atomic physicist, J. Robert Oppenheimer:

"Nuclear weapons and all the machinery of war surrounding us now haunt our imaginations with an apocalyptic vision that could well become a terrible reality: namely, the disappearance of man as a species from the surface of the earth. It is quite possible. But what is more probable, more immediate, and in my opinion equally terrifying, is the prospect that man will survive while losing his precious heritage, his civilization and his very humanity."

Now what is this "humanity" which Mr. Oppenheimer is afraid we may lose? Is it simply poetry and music and art? Can we keep from losing it by insisting that all students, even in scientific institutions, take courses in the romantic poets and music appreciation? Well, it is partly that and the proposed remedy is good as far as it goes, but that isn't very far.

The issue is much larger. It has, of course, something to do with our increasingly greater, our almost exclusive stress upon wealth and power as the only things worth having; upon, for instance, our willingness to accept what we call "a high standard of living" as necessarily the equivalent of what philosophers used to call "the good life." It is, to use a platitudinous word, "materialism." To be human certainly means to be capable of valuing some nonmaterial things. As we lose interest in things other than the material, we are at least becoming that much less like human beings of the past and, in that sense, are indeed losing our humanity.

What I want to talk about this evening is something which seems to me even more characteristically and exclusively human than art or letters. You may call it "morality." I prefer to call it a strong clear sense that the difference between good and evil is, for the human being, the most important and fundamental of all distinctions.

As I say this, I hear from you an almost audible protest. "You don't mean to imply," I can almost hear you exclaim, "that we are not today deeply concerned with morality! Surely ethical questions are among those of which our society is most deeply aware. Has any other age ever talked so much about social justice, ever professed so much concern for the submerged common man? Has any other ever appeared to take more seriously human rights, political and economic rights, the rights of racial minorities, the rights of colonial peoples? Do we not acknowledge, as no age before this ever did, our responsibility for what we are for the first time calling 'one world'? Isn't ours the great age of social consciousness as obviously as it is the great age of science?"

All this I readily grant, but I am also aware of a strange paradox. It is often said, and my observation leads me to believe it true, that this seemingly great growth in social morality has, oddly enough, taken place in a world where private morality—a sense of the supreme importance of purely personal honor, honesty, and integrity—seems to be declining. Beneficent and benevolent social institutions are administered by men who all too frequently turn out to be accepting "gifts." The world of popular entertainment is rocked by scandals. College students, put on their honor, cheat on examinations. Candidates for the

Ph.D. in social, as well as in other studies, hire ghost writers to prepare their theses.

The provost of one of our largest and most honored institutions told me just the other day that a questionnaire was distributed to his undergraduates and that forty per cent of them refused to say that cheating on examinations is reprehensible. Again I seem to hear an objection. "Even if this is true, haven't these things always been true? Is there really any evidence that personal dishonesty is more prevalent than it always was?"

I have no way of making a statistical measurement. Perhaps these things are not actually more prevalent. What I do know is that there is an increasing tendency to accept and take for granted personal dishonesty. The bureaucrat and the disc jockey say, "Well, yes, I took presents, but I assure you that I made just decisions anyway." The college student caught cheating does not even blush. He shrugs his shoulders and comments: "Everybody does it, and besides, I can't see that it really hurts anybody."

Recently a reporter for a New York newspaper stopped six people on the street and asked them if they would consent to take part in a rigged television quiz for money. He reported that five of the six said "Yes." Yet most of these five, like most of the college cheaters, would probably profess a strong social consciousness. They may cheat, but they vote for foreign aid and for enlightened social measures.

Jonathan Swift once said: "I have never been surprised to find men wicked, but I have often been surprised to find them not ashamed." It is my conviction that though men may be no more wicked than they always have been, they seem less likely to be ashamed—which they call being realistic. Why are they less ashamed? I think the answer is to be found in the student's reply: "Everybody does it, and besides, I can't see that it really hurts anybody."

Precisely the same thing was said in many newspapers about the TV scandals. If you look at this common pronouncement, you will see what lies behind the breakdown of private morality as opposed to public, of personal honor as opposed to social consciousness. If everybody does it, it must be right. "Honest," "moral," "decent" mean only what is usual. This is not really a wicked world, because morality means mores or manners and usual conduct is the only standard.

The second part of the defense, "It really doesn't hurt anybody," is equally revealing. "It doesn't hurt anybody" means it doesn't do that abstraction called society any harm. The harm it did the bribe-taker and the cheater isn't important; it is purely personal. And personal as opposed to social decency doesn't count for much.

Sometimes I am inclined to blame sociology for part of this paradox. Sociology has tended to lay exclusive stress upon social morality, and tended too often to define good and evil as merely the "socially useful" or its reverse.

I open, for instance, a widely-used college textbook of psychology to a chapter headed "Morality." It is a very brief chapter and in it I read: "We call a man moral when his actions are in accord with the laws and customs of his society." No qualification follows, no suggestion that a thing may be evil even though sanctioned by law and custom. Certainly no hint that under certain conditions a man should be called moral only when he refuses to do what a bad law permits or an evil custom encourages.

If you accept this psychological concept of morality as no more than mores, then you are logically compelled to assume, for instance, that in Nazi Germany a man who persecuted Jews was a moral man, that one who refused to do so was immoral since persecution was certainly both the law and the custom in the country of which he was a part. I doubt that the author of this textbook would have followed his logic to that extreme, but he gives no reason why one should not do so. He certainly implies that a student may cheat on examinations and a public official take bribes without ceasing to be moral if cheating and bribe-taking are the common practice of his group or his colleagues.

What social morality and social consciousness sometimes leave out is the narrower but very significant concept of honor as opposed to what is sometimes called "socially desirable conduct." The man of honor is not content to ask merely if this or that action will hurt society, or if it is what most people would permit themselves to do. He asks first of all if it would hurt him and his self-respect. Would it dishonor him personally? He is not moved, as the cheater often is, by the argument that cheating would not do society any harm and even, perhaps, might enable him to "do good" because it would help him to get a job in which he would be "socially useful."

Two generations ago the world was genuinely shocked when the Imperial German Government dismissed a solemn treaty as a "mere scrap of paper." Today we only shrug when a government breaks a treaty. Statesmen are not expected to be men of honor, only to do whatever seems advantageous to their government.

The cheating student has come to believe, perhaps even been taught, that immoral means simply "socially undesirable," and that what everybody does is permissible since, after all, "moral" means no more than "according to custom."

When some scandal breaks in government, or journalism, or business, or broadcasting, the usual reaction of even that part of the public which is still shocked by it is to say that it couldn't have happened if there had been an adequate law supervising this or that activity. College examinations, government bureaus and television stations should be better policed. But is it not usually equally true that it could not have happened if a whole group of men, often including supposed guardians of public morality, had not been devoid of any sense of the meaning and importance of individual integrity? May one not go further and ask whether any amount of "social consciousness" plus any amount of government control can make a decent society composed of people who have no conception of personal dignity and honor, of people who, like students, don't think there is anything wrong in cheating?

It was a favorite and no doubt sound argument among early twentieth-century reformers that "playing the game" as the gentleman was supposed to play it, was not enough to make a decent society. They were right; it is not enough. But the time has come to add that it is nevertheless indispensable. The so-called social conscience, unsupported by the concept of personal honor, will create a corrupt society. Moreover, I insist that for the individual himself, nothing is more important than this personal, interior, sense of right and wrong and his determination to follow it rather than to be guided by "what everybody does" or by the criterion of mere "social usefulness." It is impossible for me to imagine a good society composed of men without honor.

I shall not labor the point further. But I will assume the privilege of a commencement speaker to give advice; and what the advice comes down to is this: Do not be so exclusively concerned with society and social conditions as to forget your own condition. You are your own self and you cannot shift the responsibility for that self to world conditions, or social conditions, or the mores of your civilization. That you cannot shift this responsibility is your burden. It is also your ultimate resource.

The time may come when you lose hope for the world, but it need never come when you lose hope for yourself. Do not say "I will do what everybody else does." Be, if necessary, a lonely candle which can throw its beams far in a naughty world. And I say this not only because I think that in the end that is best for society. I say it first of all because I'm sure it is the best and happiest course for yourself. If you must be pessimistic about the world, if you must believe that society is corrupt, then do not see in that any reason why *you* should be corrupt. Be scornful of the world if you must, but base your scorn on the difference between yourself and that world which you think deserves your scorn. Some will say that if you do this you run the risk of spiritual pride. I think the world could do with a little more spiritual pride because there seems to be so little of it about.

You will be told that you risk thinking yourself wiser and better than the common run of men. I hold that this, too, is preferable to being content not even to try to be better and wiser and more honest than they are. You may think that personal integrity and self-respect are not what you want more than anything else. You may say to yourself that putting them first would make it too difficult to get along in the world and that you want to get along in the world; that you would rather have money, power and fame than personal self-satisfaction. You may even say that you want money, power and fame so that you can "do good in the world." But if you do say any of these things, you will be making an unwise choice. You will be surrendering something which cannot be taken away from you to gain something which can be taken away from you and which, as a matter of fact, very often is.

We hear it said frequently that what present-day men most desire is security. If that is so, then they have a wrong notion of what the real, the ultimate, security is. No one who is dependent on anything outside himself—upon money, power, fame or whatnot—is, or ever can be, secure. Only he who possesses himself and is content with himself is actually secure. Too much is being said about the importance of "adjustment" and "participation in the group." Even cooperation—to give this thing its most favorable designation—is no more important than the ability to stand alone when the choice must be made between the sacrifice of one's own integrity and adjustment to, or participation in, group activity.

No matter how bad the world may become, no matter how much the mass man of the future may lose such of the virtues as he still has, one fact remains. If you alone refuse to go along with him, if you alone assert your individual and inner right to believe in and be loyal to what your fellow men seem to have given up, then at least you will still retain what is perhaps the most important part of that humanity which Mr. Oppenheimer fears we may lose.

—Delivered at the University of Arizona

JUNE 1, 1960

. . .   .

The sloburbs

At Los Angeles we were told that the San Francisco Airport was fogged in, and we were given a choice. We could go to a hotel for the night and hope that the weather would clear or we could resign ourselves to a nine-hour bus ride. I chose the bus while reflecting sourly on the paradoxes of today's travel. A few months before I had come to San Francisco from Tokyo in exactly the same time it would take me to get there from Los Angeles. But one compensation—if you can call it that—did develop. I got the most extensive view I have ever had of what is now commonly called the sloburbs. Also, the fullest realization of their horror.

Nowhere are they worse than in the Los Angeles area and nowhere are they more extensive. For several hours the same dismal scenes changed so little that it was hard to believe one was moving at all. Gas station, motel, car lot, bar, hamburger stand; then gas station, motel, car lot, bar and hamburger stand again—all bathed in the hellish glow of neon. Daylight would have made everything look shabbier but not more attractive.

Los Angeles can, of course, be accused of no more than a bad eminence. Nearly all American towns, even quite small ones, present a more or less extensive version of the same picture. The newer and the faster growing the community the more it intends to be a sloburb and nothing else, and sloburbs are so much alike that if you were carried into one blindfolded you would often find it impossible to say not only where you were, but even whether you were north or south or east or west.

Tucson, where I now live, is no exception. In fact, it is rather worse than many because so much of its explosive growth is recent and takes the form of rapidly spreading sloburbs. They have not yet reached the area where I live but they are creeping towards it, and as I drove home the other day through spreading ugliness I was again amazed that this sort of anti-city could be so characterless. Everything looks improvised, random, unrelated to everything else, as though it had no memory of yesterday and no expectation of tomorrow.

Nor is this true only of the motel, bar, hamburger-stand complex. It is almost equally so of a new kind of "business district," which is less a district than a ribbon of commercial establishments growing longer and longer as "downtown" shrinks or stagnates. Here the repetitive succession is not unlike that of the only slightly frowzier parade of eateries, drinkeries and sleeperies. The supermarkets (one every few hundred yards) are the most imposing of the commercial establishments. Between them come drugstores (which sell more toys, sporting equipment and sandwiches than they do drugs), dime stores, TV repair shops and auto supply emporia in a sort of procession which is repeated as soon as the repertory has completed itself.

Yet this is far from being a depressed area. It is actually a very prosperous one and real-estate prices skyrocket in what is only a little better than a sort of shantytown. Poverty, I reminded myself, creates slums and slums can be even uglier. But

I wondered if ever before in history a prosperous people had consented to live in communities so devoid of every grace and dignity, so slum-like in everything except the money they represent. They are something new and almost uniquely unattractive—neither country nor village nor town nor city—just an agglomeration without plan, without any sense of unity or direction, as though even offices and shops were thought of as disposable, like nearly everything else in our civilization, and therefore not worth considering from any standpoint except the make-do of the moment.

A real metropolis has a quasi-organic unity. There is a nerve center more or less elaborate which includes whatever public buildings, theaters, auditoriums and major commercial emporia the community can support. From the impressiveness of this nerve center one can judge pretty accurately just to what degree it is a metropolis rather than a town or a village. Its suburbs and even its slums are related to the whole. But a large sloburb like that which surrounds and all but engulfs Los Angeles differs from that of the village on the highway in nothing except area. You could cut a piece of it and set the piece down anywhere and you could not tell that it had grown up around Los Angeles, rather than where you found it. A suburb implies a city to which it is attached but what we are increasingly developing are huge agglomerations which cannot be called suburbs because there is no urbs to own them.

Why, then, have the sloburbs become the most characteristic aspect of modern America? Why are they the only real urban development new to our time, as much our special contribution to the look and feel of our environment as the skyscraper was that of the first half of the century?

If you accept the now usual assumption that whatever we do or are is the necessary result of "evolving technology," then the answer is easy. Technological progress has made the population explosion supportable and necessitated rapid growth. The automobile has made us mobile, and prosperity has not only created the demand for the superfluities to which two-thirds of the enterprises in the sloburbs cater but also encouraged the tendency to regard everything, including architecture, as disposable. Stores, office buildings and even churches will be "turned in" for new ones in a year or two. That is progress.

If on the other hand you believe that evolving technology is only half the story, that human beings are capable of resisting as well as of yielding to pressures, then the question why we have consented to the sloburbs remains; why we are to all appearances so contented with them. Remember that sloburbs are the product of wealth and abundance. The motel-café regions cater to those who have much leisure; the merchandising sloburbs depend at least as much upon what might be called luxury goods as they do upon necessities. Why is there so little luxurious, or even decently dignified, about the buildings which house them, the merchandising methods they employ? Why should an abundant society be content to accept communities so obviously the antithesis of that "graceful living" which the service magazines talk about and declare to be nowadays open to all?

Some of the frequent answers to that question also are easy: Americans have no taste, no sense of dignity, no ability to discriminate between the informality to which they are committed and the slovenliness of the sloburbs. Their civic pride does not extend beyond pride in increasing size and that prosperity which means that most of its citizens are making money building sloburbs or operating them. Given the primary fact of profit, nothing else is very important. Certainly aesthetic considerations are not. Arizona, for instance, tempts the tourist with the pretense that its proudest boast is its natural beauty. But it really prefers billboards, as is evidenced by the fact that it recently again rejected the offer of the national government to grant a bonus if it would keep the main highways clear of them.

These also are, of course, familiar charges and not without an element of truth. But they are not quite the whole story, not quite fair. The typical American is not indifferent to everything except profit. He is merely indifferent to some of the things which others consider important. He has, for example, an enormous faith in schooling—which he assumes to be the same thing as education. In Tucson, for example, by far the most imposing buildings are the absurdly elaborate schools, which the same citizens who prefer billboards to scenic grandeur, seem willing to support through very high taxes. The consensus seems to be essentially this: It is just that citizens should be taxed heavily and also expected to contribute generously. But they should never, under any circumstances, be prevented from making a profit. Hospitals also seem to be among the non-profit institutions to which citizens point with pride. But they are unwilling to do anything to slow the spread of sloburbs. The zoning regulations are a farce. If an area is zoned for residents only, that usually means that no business can be established there until somebody wants to establish one—at which time the zoning is promptly changed. Order, dignity, grace and beauty are things that are simply not worth paying even a small price for. Schooling, recreation and health should be supported. But the other parts of, and provisions for, the good life are not the community's business. Perhaps this tolerance is part of the kindly slovenliness in manners and morals to which we seem more and more inclined. But it is enough to permit the development of communities which it is impossible to imagine an earlier generation submitting to without protest.

Some years ago I decided that for me the city was paying diminishing returns and I moved away from it. This was a choice I have never regretted but it was related to my time of life as well as to certain aspects of my temperament. It did not mean that I had no regard for cities and what they have contributed to civilization. But the sloburbs have none of the advantages of country, village or genuine city life. They do not, like real cities, provide a sufficiently large minority of citizens of intellectual and artistic taste to support cultural institutions proportionate to the size of their populations. Neither do they provide that "life of the streets" which is another of the chief attractions offered by a real city. Anywhere in a sloburb one may buy gasoline, cocktails, beer and hamburgers. But one cannot go window-shopping or indulge in any of the other activities which in New York or San Francisco draw strollers down the streets of the urban core. Neither, of course, can one breathe fresh air or enjoy the beauties of nature. One can only breathe gas fumes and revel in the glow of neon. Of all the places into which one's lot may be cast, few—not even those minimum-security prisons called garden apartments of the sort I pass on my way once or twice a year from Manhattan to Kennedy—strike me as more dismal.

Thinking of a real city as something analagous to a living creature where highly differentiated organs are all related to, and coordinated by, a central nervous system, I found myself wondering to just what sort of creature an individual sloburb might be compared. Most of even the so-called primitive organisms are wholes in the sense that the parts are related to one another and cannot exist except in connection with some center. You can't, in most cases, just break off a section and expect it to survive. Neither can most of such simple organisms grow indefinitely without any natural boundaries or shape. Hence, if a sloburb is analagous to any living thing it must be, I think, to one of the myxomycetes or slime molds. These remarkable blobs found especially in damp, rotting logs have no shape, no characteristic size and no community center. They consist of an agglomeration of one-celled individuals without a trace of the differentiation characteristic of even the more primitive multi-cellular organisms. You may break one blob into a hundred pieces and each will prosper as satisfactorily as it did when it was part of a larger blob. Put the pieces into contact again and they will merge much as the sloburbs spreading out from two communities merge when they meet. And given favorable conditions, the size of the blob grows and grows without there being any theoretical reason why it should not ultimately cover the earth. Such an eventuality might make a good horror movie. But no better than one that showed the whole face of America covered ultimately by one vast sloburb.

—*American Scholar*
SPRING, 1965

. . .   .

They order these things worse in France

Last year [1965] my wife and I spent five months in France, much of the time holed up in one of the least disturbed of the tiny medieval villages that dot the Maritime Alps. Three years before, we had gone around the world in the company of a generous friend and in considerably fewer than eighty days. Such displacements are too commonplace to provide an excuse for many travelers' tales, but one does usually return with a few hundred feet of home movies to be inflicted upon barely polite friends. What follows is something of much the same sort.

We might begin with a shot of almost any European highway or city street, but I choose Cannes because it happens to be only thirty miles or so from my tranquil village. Those of us who are accustomed to think of American traffic as crowded and dangerous can hardly believe our eyes. A few years ago it was said that one out of every seven French drivers had killed someone, and it is surprising that the rate is not higher—as perhaps by now it is. One would have guessed that the automotive psychosis would be more violent in our own country than anywhere else, but that is far from being the case. No attempt is made here to limit the tendency that is everywhere visible, for motorcars to take over both the city and the country and to assume that their needs come before any others. In the long stretch of Cannes' seafront, Croisette, there is not a single traffic light, and if there are any traffic patrols I have never seen one—although I have seen a racing car weaving at sixty-miles-an-hour in and out of the other crowded and speeding cars.

As for the numerous pedestrians who must cross this speedway to get from the beachwalk to the town, they are merely tolerated and must look out for themselves. It is true that there are yellow-striped passages here and there that are supposed to give them the right of way, but woe to him who assumes that it will be granted. For one thing, unless the nearest car is some distance away it would be impossible for it to stop, and in practice the pedestrians must congregate at these points and wait (often for a long time) until some short gap in the triple line of speeding cars makes it possible for them to dash frantically across. Watching them I have been reminded of chickens in a Mexican village scattering before an onrushing bus. The pedestrian is now a third-class citizen disfranchised and deprived of his rights. If there will probably be no peasant revolt, that is because most of these pedestrians are, on other days or at other hours, transformed into motorists and will exercise the motorist's prerogative as arrogantly as though they had never been pedestrians. They will do as they have been done by.

As for the drivers, they kill one another as exuberantly as they kill the outlawed pedestrian. When they collide without killing all the occupants in one or both of the cars, the survivors show an increasing tendency (as the newspapers are persistently noting) to come to blows, sometimes only with fists, sometimes with knives or that equally dangerous weapon, the easily detachable spike-heeled shoe by which use the driver's female companion attempts to give the *coup de grâce* to his opponent. That this motor madness is a psychosis is recognized. But since by some curious twist all modern societies assume that the motorist (perhaps it is rather the motorcar itself) may not be in any way restricted, nothing is done about it.

I have driven an automobile for fifty years and owned one for forty-five. Like most of my fellow citizens, I would hardly know how to do without this means of transportation although, unlike the majority of my fellows, I have never thought of it as anything more than simply that. But that we are paying a tremendous price for it becomes everyday more evident. The highways, overpasses and cloverleaves use up more and more of the countryside; parking lots and garages occupy more and more of the scarce city areas; and junkyards piled high with the debris left after the increasing number of wrecks disfigure the outskirts. And, of course, the air we breathe is poisoned. Obviously, the automobile is riding mankind, not vice versa. But we are told that our economy would collapse if people did not buy more and more, larger and larger, faster and faster, and more and more expensive cars. If one's own car is a convenience, everybody else's is a nuisance.

Now let us move out to my village only a few miles away. It is officially in the Department of the Var, but geographically it is on a hilltop in the Maritime Alps. It first comes into history in 49 B.C. when the Romans conducted water from the nearby stream to an already existing village. During the late classical, the dark, the medieval and the renaissance days, it was repeatedly colonized and repeatedly depopulated by wars, by pestilence, and probably by the attacks of the Mediterranean pirates from whom the hillside site gave some protection. The new church which now serves the community was built in the thirteenth century, but there are standing ruins of the vault of an older one that goes back to the tenth. There are also some still-standing walls of the house occupied by the medieval lord of the manor. But the oldest now-inhabited houses are said to go back to the twelfth century, although there are others probably not older than the fifteenth or sixteenth. On a clear day you can see from the large public square the Mediterranean and in it the two islands on the nearer of which the Man in the Iron Mask was once confined. Swallows build under the tiles of the red roofs, and in the fields beyond the cuckoos call incessantly. The hillsides round about are strewn with limestone fragments and are cut up into small fields separated by literally miles of dry walls, representing a labor that the New England builders of similar works might have hesitated to face. The mayor, who is also the local historian, tells me that they represent the work of several centuries; the most recent were built in the sixteenth.

During the eighteenth century there were as many as a thousand inhabitants but there are now only about a hundred and fifty, and the village rests in a tranquillity that is no doubt near to, but nevertheless not quite, stagnation. The cash income of many of the inhabitants is probably below that of an American sharecropper, but they do not consider themselves poor folk—probably less because of what we would call their standard of living than because, after the French fashion, many of them own little patches of land in addition to the houses they live in. Some of the latter have no "conveniences" whatever. Water is drawn at public taps or fountains, clothes washed at long outdoor troughs. But many of the citizens keep a few chickens, cultivate garden patches sometimes several miles from their homes, collect linden leaves to sell for the infusions that old-fashioned people in the cities still drink, or in a few cases grow lavender for the perfumeries of Grasse not many miles away. There is a one-class school for the few remarkably clean and well-behaved children. Electricity is available for those who want or can afford it and the community has installed a TV set in one of the many unoccupied buildings. A sign on the door says that those who take advantage of it in wintertime are requested to bring one stick of wood to contribute to the fireplace.

I know how easy it is to idealize the simple life and to assume that the cheerful poor are more content with their lot than they actually are. In certain respects the simple life is more complicated than that which is highly organized. But there is no doubt that there is a tension, a frenzy, even, in Cannes, as in most large cities, which the inhabitants take for granted unless they happen to live for a while in a village like this where it does not exist. Here most of the inhabitants have little and must spend an enormous amount of time in tasks that the city man has somehow done for him. And yet, if they do not have more leisure, they at least move at a more leisurely pace, and they seem less driven by the desire to get ahead, perhaps just because they do not see how they could possibly do so. And perhaps it is because there are so few people here that they are almost invariably cheerful and polite to strangers whom they seem to welcome—not, like most city dwellers, to resent. I suppose that the young people have a tendency to drift away. The older—and some of the young—would not on the other hand, I think, want to change their way of life.

I would certainly not want to live permanently in Mons, not even with the special comforts and privileges I enjoyed there. I am not saying that this is the good life—I am merely wondering if there is not some feasible happy medium between it and the stresses that go along with our developed technology and our overpopulation—if there is no choice between stagnation and frenzy.

Why do the Cannoise drive at such insane speeds from one

place to another while most of the Monsoins stay so tranquilly put? Are the former victims of a death wish or is the explanation, as I am inclined to think, less melodramatic but equally sinister? Can it be that they rush madly from one place to another because there is nowhere they really want to be, and because they can conceal this dreadful fact from themselves only by seeming to be terribly eager to get to whatever temporary destination they have invented for themselves? And can it be that the inhabitants of Mons remain quietly in their village because that is precisely where they do, genuinely, want to be?

To proceed from, say, Paris to Hong Kong by slow stages is to grow gradually accustomed to the change. To leave the Georges V, and within a very short time to find oneself face-to-face with the incredible boat slum in Hong Kong, is to be jolted into a very keen realization of the differences possible to the human condition. Travelers who pride themselves on their sophistication often look down upon those who employ guides. But a really good one, like our Chow-Chow in Hong Kong, does a great deal more than merely point out the sights. He bridges the gap between the spectator and the spectacle. Nothing that I saw in Hong Kong seemed to me more significant than Chow-Chow's reply when we expressed some sympathy with the long hours of labor that both he and his wife submitted to. "I want to work; I do not care to be entertained." Or than a proverb that I heard from him (attributed, of course, to Confucius) which was alone worth going around the world to hear: "The local ginger is never hot."

Now comes a shot of a movie theater in Tokyo. The huge, lurid poster advertises *The Sands of Iwo Jima*. But how, I asked the highly intelligent woman guide, do the Japanese feel about that? Why, she replied, they have no partisan feeling at all. The war belongs to a past that has been wiped away.

"What did you do during the war?"

"I had just finished college when it began. I spent the years working in an ammunition factory and practicing how to stab Americans with a bamboo spear."

"How do you feel about the bomb?"

"Strange as it may seem, it was a kind of blessing. We had been told that if we were invaded we must all be prepared to die to the last man and the last woman fighting in the streets. We were prepared to do just that. Only something inconceivable and overwhelming could have changed such a resolution. We could hardly believe our ears when the Emperor advised us to surrender. Now we are very glad that we did."

Obviously, not all Japanese feel that way. Was our guide merely telling us what we would like to hear? I do not think so. She did not seem given to that kind of diplomacy.

I have saved for the last, three shots which I consider the best. Two made on the plane journey, one during the recent visit to Cannes.

The first is a brief glimpse of nighttime Beirut, where it is disturbing to see that the neon tube has learned to write the sinuous Arabic script. Scene two is a street in the modern section of Damascus. A few feet ahead of me are a man and his wife with two small children, each of the children holding the hand of one parent. All are dressed in modern European clothes and might be mistaken for any upper-middle-class American and his family, practicing togetherness on a Sunday morning. But as I pass the group and risk a backward glance I see that the wife is, despite her otherwise quite Western outfit, wearing the long, opaque veil from her eyes to below the chin.

Now comes a bit of montage of which I am particularly proud. We cut to a few feet taken this past summer on the Croisette at Cannes, down which parades a good-looking young woman in what is now called a monokini—which coinage, although likely to offend the purist, is convenient and will probably delight the descriptive etymologist with its seeming assumption that the "bi" of bikini means "two."

I have, on various occasions, indicated my resistance to many of the relativisms now current. But I must admit that the modest and the immodest seem to be almost entirely a matter of the mores, and just how much of what part of the female anatomy may decently be exposed is purely a matter of habit, sometimes easily modified and sometimes stubbornly persisted in. By strollers in Damascus, however much they may be in other respects Europeanized, it must obviously seem that for a woman to appear without a veil is simply to walk naked in the streets. In Europe, on the other hand, custom has changed so rapidly that within my memory the Sennett bathing girls in knee-length skirts and black cotton stockings were pleasantly shocking and purely theatrical, since no woman bathed in such a costume. Today the scantiest of bikinis is not only acceptable to the wearer but is not usually disapproved of by parents who had found the Sennett girls quite risqué.

Yet each innovation is, for a short time, often vigorously denounced or even forbidden. The young lady of the Croisette was presently spotted by two gendarmes who seized her by the arms and legs and carried her kicking into a building to whose back door a Black Maria presently drew up. From the newspaper I learned that she was fined three hundred francs—a pretty stiff penalty in a country even less inclined than ours to inflict punishments; and where, for instance, a few weeks later a drunkard who had killed his father was given a suspended sentence.

It seemed a ridiculous fuss to make over the exposure of a few inches (although I admit they are rather eventful inches) of the female torso, almost all the rest of which is by now perfectly familiar to even the most puritanical bachelor. If a modest woman, as Hamlet maintained, will not bare her beauties to either the sun or the moon, then why should the face—surely the most individual and most easily recognizable as well as the

most intimate part of the body—not be the most carefully veiled against the gaze of the casual stranger? Is it not as likely as any other feature to provoke a man to that lust of the eye which, so Scripture says, is already an adultery? And if one unveils the face, just where does reason stop and licentiousness begin? Although I have a certain hankering after absolutes, I do not know where to find one in this area, of either morals or aesthetics.   —*American Scholar*
                                                                  SUMMER, 1966

.   .   .   .

Where's the fire?

Suppose you are driving an automobile at seventy-five miles an hour. No matter how cunningly made, how expensive and how efficient the machine may be, no matter how expert a driver you are, you still can't for the time being do anything except keep it on the road. You can't even think about anything else. Your hands are full, your mind is occupied. You may (as many do) find the occupation more exhilarating than any other you have ever experienced. But you will not enjoy the scenery, ponder philosophical questions, or conceive works of art.

What our so astounding and (in its own way) so successful technological society demands of those deeply involved in it, either as planners or as executants, is something very much like driving a high-speed automobile, and it threatens to become even more like manipulating a space capsule in orbit. This society is tremendously powerful and most ingeniously contrived. It operates at great efficiency and at very high speeds—economically and politically as well as technologically. But to keep it on the road requires the full attention of all who are concerned with its operation. It threatens at every moment to get out of hand and we are terribly (if often only half-consciously) aware that a moment's inattention or an unforeseen circumstance will reduce us and our wonderful machine to a flaming wreck, from which it is unlikely that either the driver or most of the passengers will escape with their lives.

Those of us who are inclined to moral, intellectual or aesthetic criticism—who are, as it were, standing by the roadside as one racing car after another plunges past—rebuke the occupants for what seems to us too little concern with the occupations and values we hold to be the most important and the most characteristically human. But busy as they are, they can hardly be expected to indulge in contemplation or do anything except keep the vehicle on the road—if they can. Under the circumstances it is perhaps futile as well as unfair to expect anything else. Granted the condition of the modern world, those who accept and participate in it can hardly be other than what they are. We cannot change them and they cannot change themselves, so long as they hardly dare take their eyes off the road.

"Why drive so fast?" we ask. "Why build machines that can be driven at such speeds and quite possibly demand more of the human brain and nerves than they are capable of giving?"

To these questions there are several common answers. The most pessimistic is simply that this is where we find ourselves— at the wheel of the racing car. It is, as our forefathers said concerning the predicament in which certain other individuals found themselves, "the position in which God in His wisdom has thought fit to place us," or, as we now translate the phrase, "the situation inevitably created by our evolving technology." We couldn't change even if we wanted to. And to the suggestion that we might at least slow down, the reply—not without considerable justification—is that there is a whole line of other cars (other peoples, other nations, other classes) just behind, and that if one car were to stop it would inevitably be destroyed by a rear-end collision.

A more cheerful answer is this: "But we like driving a fine car at high speed and we don't really care whether or not (as you doubt) it is getting us anywhere. It's the going we enjoy; the sense of power and speed. For the sake of that intoxicating sensation we gladly surrender those pale satisfactions that you say are to be found in the good life of art, intellect and contemplation. We don't miss them. In fact, we never tasted them. The future belongs to people like us who know how to enjoy what merely frightens you. As for the danger of a smashup— well, we all have to die sometime. If the automobile has created threats to life, medicine has reduced others. We do live dangerously but you can't get away from the fact that, even so, the average life-span is now longer than it was in quieter ages."

Those who reason thus are, I suppose, the true children of our age—much more our representative men than the alienated or the beatniks. Possibly, they are also the children of the future.

Some of them, if they have a touch of philosophy, may suggest that what we call "living dangerously" will become in time less dangerous than it is now, because the human being will adapt, by conditioning and perhaps even biologically, to the new situation. He will develop quicker muscular reactions to cope with the greater speed of his vehicles, and nerves rugged enough to remain relaxed under what now seem hardly bearable strains, such as those to which the executive and the statesman, as well as the racing driver, are subjected.

Perhaps natural selection will see to it that exactly this will happen and the process may be already under way—as a certain scientist whom I am not at liberty to identify, undertook to demonstrate in a privately printed essay which he called his contribution to the Darwinian Centenary.

With tongue in cheek he offered this demonstration: Despite the fact that automobiles grow continuously faster and more dangerous to operate, the number of traffic deaths in proportion to the number of cars on the road has actually decreased. This surprising fact, he suggested, can mean only that natural selection has been busily removing both from the road and from the breeding stock those who ought not to be driving our dangerous contraptions. Only the fittest survive, and if the automobile manufacturers will only cooperate by continuing to make their products more and more dangerous, they will hasten the time when all except those with the nerves and muscles of racing drivers will have been eliminated from a world to which they are no longer fitted.

All such spoofing aside, I do not know how to make a counter-statement likely to carry any conviction, so far as the true children of our age are concerned. I do not see how the civilization we have created (or which, as some would prefer to put it, has created itself) could provide very favorable conditions for the development of the good life as I define it. Neither do I see how this civilization could be simplified or even slowed down, without catastrophe, unless the simplification and the slowing down were brought about very gradually by a dominant minority that believed (as only an insignificant minority does believe) it would be desirable to do so. For the individual there seems only a pair of alternatives. He may join with the spirit of the age or he may ride the juggernaut as infrequently as is possible, taking good care at other times to remember that juggernauts are notoriously dangerous to pedestrians also.

Technology itself cannot make us more competent to evaluate its creations; and although it will no doubt perform many wonders still no more than dreamed of, I do not think that its blessings and benefits will be of a kind different from those it has already conferred, perhaps too abundantly, upon us—namely, even greater speed, power, wealth and possibly health.

And unless these are the only things we need, I think it unfortunate that most people should assume that it is to science and technology alone that we must look for any improvement in the human condition.

With that large majority that does assume, consciously or unconsciously, that speed, power and wealth are in themselves quite enough to make a good life, we dissenters cannot argue. But we do have to register a protest against those who maintain, not that we don't need any other culture, but that there has already emerged a new scientific culture that performs, or at least will presently perform, all the functions that the other culture, now obsolete, formerly performed for us; that such a purely scientific culture can supply ethical guidance, aesthetic satisfaction, standards of value, and a view of the universe that the human being will find congenial rather than alien.

This defense of orthodox science as the basis of a culture as well as of a technology goes back at least as far as Darwin himself who insisted in the last paragraph of *The Origin of Species* that "there is a kind of grandeur" in his vision where "from the war of nature, from famine and death . . . the production of the higher animals [he did not yet quite dare say man] directly follows," although I think the qualifying word "kind" is here very important. C. P. Snow happens to be at the moment the best known proponent of science as the better of the two so-called cultures, but he is by no means the only one. Rather surprisingly, Aldous Huxley in the little book published just before his death sketched very unconvincingly his outline of what such a complete culture would ultimately be like. Even more recently the *Nation* (January 4, 1964) devoted most of one issue to a long dialogue called "The Abacus and the Rose" by J. Bronowski, whose *Science and Human Values* was a best seller a few years ago. In this new dialogue Bronowski sets up a couple of straw men—one a member of the Establishment, the other a professor of literature who seems to have taken all his ideas from Professor Leavis. After these two have been demolished by a scientist, the latter takes the floor to proclaim that the scientific culture has already been formulated and accepted by those sufficiently advanced to understand it:

> We are making a unity . . . a complete culture, a unity out of variety. I will tell you what a molecular biologist is. He is a man who unravels the secrets of life by using the tools of physics. He shows—we have shown—that the structures of biology become intelligible when we treat them, not as a string of mysteries, but as strings of molecules. Those are the changes in the picture of the world that we strive for. That is the universal unity in which we believe. I wrote a poem once about art and science and the unity of all things.

The poem that follows is cast in heroic couplets (which seem a curiously old-fashioned literary form for so convinced a proponent of the new culture) and its clincher is reached when the author declares that if he regards living creatures not as mysteries but as strings of molecules, "an icy sweetness fills my mind." This phrase reminds one immediately of Darwin's "a kind of grandeur," although Mr. Bronowski does not seem to share a certain dubiety that led Darwin to say not "grandeur" but "a kind of grandeur."

I am well aware that not all biologists, not even (or perhaps especially not) those who are, like Bronowski's Professor Potts, specialists in macromolecular biology, believe that the living processes become completely intelligible "when we treat them, not as strings of mysteries, but as strings of molecules." Professor Adolf Portmann, for example, in his recent *New Paths in Biology*, a good deal of which is concerned with macromolecular studies, sounds almost as though he were replying to Professor Potts: "Many biologists take the view that the study of the fine structure of living matter is *the* essential task of biology. This view ignores one very important aspect of life—subjective experience. No amount of research along physical or chemical grounds can ever give us a full picture of psychological, spiritual or intellectual processes."

If a "scientific culture" should ever succeed in recognizing both the reality and the importance of these aspects of life and in somehow integrating them with its "strings of molecules" instead of continuing to dismiss them as some sort of delusive epiphenomenon, then it will have absorbed rather than replaced the older culture and it may indeed prove to be all we know on earth and all we need to know. But until it does recognize and have something adequate to say about what are to the human consciousness the realest and most important parts of the experience of being human, it will be no substitute for even the completely prescientific parts of literature, philosophy and metaphysics.

Even a race of men that had come to find Professor Potts's "icy sweetness" enough, would still have nowhere to look when faced, as all men sometimes are, with the necessity of deciding what is right or wrong, good or evil. And even so dedicated a scientist as Vannevar Bush not merely confessed but passionately insisted, in a lecture on scientific motivation, that neither the Potts brand of philosophy nor the Potts kind of poetry provides any such guidance:

From the preservation of the mechanistic universe some recent writers have gone on to formulate a code of ethics as though it followed in logical consequence. This code, in summary, is very simple. Man controls his destiny; let him so control it as to build for himself a better life. That is good which leads in this direction. The code is laudable enough as far as it goes; but it is incomplete and without a logical base in the facts from which it purports to be derived. For it is based on a tacit assumption that the mechanistic account of the universe that has been constructed within the accepted limitations of science is in fact a complete account, and a proper basis on which to build a complete ethical code. This is to assert that there is no reality beyond those things which we can measure with a rule or time with a clock and that value can be deduced from a statement of fact. But man's motivations emerge from his entire experience. The seat of ethics is in our hearts, not in our minds. Our ignorance is vast. At every turn, as we reach boundaries beyond which strict definition and logic, measurement and manipulation, cannot be applied we are confronted with a mystery. Our little minds have carved out a region within which science has proved a guide through the murk, leaving blanks and emptiness, but building a consistent conception. . . . But to imply that we now grasp the sorry world entire, that we can now draw final conclusions, is to mistake a first step for a journey. We have a useful formulation, within its realm, but have thus far proved little on which to judge our duty or our mission.

In this paragraph, so it seems to me, a very distinguished scientist made, by anticipation, an unanswerable reply to C. P. Snow and to all proponents of the so-called scientific culture. The simple statement that value cannot be deduced from a statement of fact sums up in a very few words what some refuse to recognize. If one agrees with Vannevar Bush that science cannot establish standards of good and evil, and that for this very reason a purely scientific culture is impossible, then it follows that a civilization based upon science alone can only be one in which know-how has replaced the pursuit of wisdom. And there are at least a few of us to whom it seems that too much undiscriminating know-how is what makes it possible that our physical world as well as our civilization is about to perish.

—*American Scholar*
SUMMER, 1964

. . . .

The fun explosion

Stern censors usually denounce their contemporaries as "pleasure-mad." Our age being one when sociology gets more attention than the fulminations of the moralist, the preferred term is "fun-oriented." For although this term is also sometimes pejorative, it is not always so. A few years ago, for example, Daniel Lerner published in the *American Scholar*, an article not explicitly taking sides, but giving a very tolerant description of the "fun-oriented" society.

"The theory that every man has a right to comfortable conditions of life is," he said, "the economic counterpart of the theory that every man has the right to be continuously entertained. . . . The old Puritan ethic (or perhaps, more exactly, simply Protestant), with its emphasis on effort, achievement, struggle, and success, has yielded to a whole new array of words expressing the new concept of right conduct and a good life."

About the same time, Miss Katherine Hoskins, writing in the *Hudson Review*, took a more positive stand: "I sometimes think that our volatility, our lack of memory, our wastefulness, and other qualities that seem weaknesses could be the virtues of two hundred years from now. I can imagine a new ethos, a different hierarchy of values into which our characteristics would fit. . . . A world more fluid, more abstract—where all things are easily picked up, easily put down. A world without monuments and where one didn't save string, an era of present rationality and charm, wherein the ego has learned grace and poetry and uses them."

Now it is true that there are distinctions between what being "pleasure-mad" on the one hand, and "fun-oriented" on the other, implies. "Pleasure-mad" suggests dissipation accompanied by the search for madder music and stronger wine. "Fun-oriented" sometimes suggests only golf, picnics, cookouts, and all sorts of innocent happenings. Still, one does shade into the other.

It has always seemed to me strange that the left-wingers who despise the "privileged class" and find no virtue except in "the worker" should suppose that if everybody had the equivalent of inherited wealth everybody would be fine. The rich playboy has always been an irritating phenomenon, but in the past he was never numerous enough to constitute a serious problem. Many members of the middle and lower classes now enjoy the "privileges" that were once abused by the rich only, and maybe that is why the youth problem grows. At least this seems as reasonable a theory as the more popular opposite, which is that society deprives too large a proportion of its members of the goods they have the right to expect. As a Tory might say, "They seemed to behave better when they had even less."

A few days ago I stood on a busy street corner in Tucson watching the young people go by and asking myself if I saw in them the emergence of the new and healthily fun-oriented type. I concluded that the first step (if it really is in that direction) had obviously been taken. Physically, they were a healthier-looking, more confident lot than one is likely to see in any other country. Among the young women (in whom of course I was most interested) there may have been few who could be singled out as great beauties, but the level of physical attractiveness was certainly high—and obviously high on the list of their ambitions. Since their models were those of the movies, the television screen, and the fan magazines, the almost universal effect aimed at was that of the siren—the dangerous woman—or what Hollywood calls, somewhat inelegantly, the "sexpot." But this was despite the fact that few of them had the temperament to go with this outward show, or were capable of fulfilling the promises their appearance seemed to hold out. Instead of going on to a career of devastation, most of them are destined to end up in a few years pushing a cart in the supermarket—the cart being used as transportation for one or more kids until such time as the space they are occupying is needed for prepared baby food. Though their heads will be crowned by large curlers they will be definitely "fun-oriented" rather than "pleasure-mad."

In one other respect I think I can see, even in the faces of the youngest, that they are also already living in that new world "where all things are easily picked up and put down," and where there are no "monuments." Translated, this means that they have gladly accepted our "civilization of the disposable," in which everything from Kleenex to automobiles is to be casually discarded and in which, instead of looking for a usable past, they are so completely unaware that any past exists that they have no need to reject it. They really were "born yesterday" and the last thing that would ever occur to them would be to familiarize themselves with the best that has been thought and said. Their beauty (if you can call it by so exalted a term) is the exact opposite of what Pater thought he saw in the Mona Lisa. None of the sorrows of the world have come to rest on their faces and if the eyelids are a little weary that is only because their owners were up late last night having fun.

If you assume (as they unconsciously do) that there is no such thing as the wisdom of the ages and that there is nothing to be learned from even the mistakes of the past, then perhaps they are right in being happily ignorant of it. But I find it hard to believe that the slate should be wiped quite so clean.

Presently I found myself thinking, in my old-fashioned way, about Matthew Arnold's classification of his contemporaries, and I think that it requires some modification if it is to be applied this hundred years later. What he called "the Cultured" are perhaps as numerous (which is also as few) as they were in his time. But if I understand aright another of his distinctions, there are fewer Philistines and more Barbarians, *i.e.*, fewer who have rejected culture and chosen vulgarity, more who are simply unaware that culture exists. The values of the Philistine—comfort, money and power—are consciously held and therefore not wholly unexamined. His thinking may be vulgar and directed toward the achievement of vulgar ends, but it is at least thinking of a sort, and the choices are deliberately made. The Barbarian does not really think or choose at all with his conscious mind. He merely finds himself living in a world of physical sensations, quite unaware that any other existence is possible. I know that we spend millions on schools, that no other nation is so supplied with libraries, that paperbacks proliferate, and that even TV devotes hours to "education." But I have the feeling that a very large number of youths of both sexes are as untouched by all this as though it did not exist.

In addition to Arnold's categories one must of course establish a new one, either nonexistent or unnamed in Arnold's day: the category of the Alienated. This category includes two subdivisions, into one or the other of which the existentialist and the beatnik are placed. Both have one thing in common with the Philistine because both have rejected "culture" in Arnold's sense, though they often know more about it than his Philistines did. They differ from one another in that the highly intellectual existentialist is depressed, while the beatnik has taken only one step away from the fun-oriented society and finds the *summum bonum* to be not fun, but "kicks."

Lytton Strachey once remarked that when Victorians "lost their faith" they reacted to the loss in different ways. To some it was merely a burden laid down; to others it was more as though they had lost a portmanteau that they continued to look nervously about for. The beatnik and the existentialist react in a somewhat analagous manner to their own loss of faith in the whole system of beliefs and values of the Western world. And to me the discouraging fact is that, if, as seems to be the case, the existentialists will be the teachers of any Barbarians who decide to live "an examined life" instead of an unexamined one, there isn't too much to choose between the two. In fact, I am inclined to think that I would rather live among the modern Barbarians than in a society really dominated by the completely alienated—whether existentialist or beatnik.

For those of us who live in the United States, our world is almost completely without monuments in the literal as well as in the figurative sense, and I wonder if this absence of physical monuments does not encourage our unawareness of the monuments of thought and feeling in which the Barbarians refuse to interest themselves. When (as seems to be increasingly the case) the schools make a halfhearted effort to call some attention to them, we, so the pupils reply, are "modern" and can't be bothered with what ought to have been disposed of long ago. In many schools, it seems, the attempt to present culture has been given up in despair, "assigned reading" now being any book the pupil cares to choose—with the result that, so I am told, one class in a Tucson high school is "studying" *Peyton Place*.

Even in New York there are few physical objects outside museums to remind anyone of the fact that the city has a past; and to the Barbarian a museum (which he does not often visit) is the only proper place for anything that was made more than twenty years ago. Buildings are not disposed of quite as quickly as automobiles (just as automobiles are not disposed of as quickly as Kleenex), but there is little desire to keep any of them long. What a fanatical antiquarian called "vandalism" we call "modernization." As a result, even the most ambitious public structures are almost in the class of consumer goods, with the stress on "consumer" and, by consequence, on consumption.

I am told that even the Parisian is losing interest in his

"monuments" and is quite reconciled to seeing them replaced by modern structures of either the glass-box or the Corbusier variety. Yet of all great cities, his is the one in which monuments of both the remote and the recent past are most conspicuously integrated into the whole city—to which they contribute so much of its character. These monuments are lived in and with, not merely preserved. Hence the citizen does not have to seek them out but passes Notre Dame, the Louvre, and the Arc de Triomphe—each a characteristic monument of some part of his past —as he goes about his business or pleasure. In New York the most you are likely to find is the plaque that says, "On This Spot Once Stood . . ."

I do not think it is mere prejudice that has led me to believe that the man and woman on the Paris street look somehow aware of more things than do their opposite numbers in Tucson or New York; and if this is not an illusion, then it may be that their physical city has something to do with the fact. Of course, they also look less healthy, physically less imposing, and I am certain that the American would not want to give up his advantage there in exchange for what the Parisian seems to have. But is a choice really necessary?

A few years ago Robert Graves gave a speech before the American Academy of Arts and Letters, the subject of which was announced mysteriously as, "On the Word *Baraka*." It turned out that this word is Arabic and refers to that particular charm (in both the literal and figurative sense of the word) which adheres to anything from a cooking pot to a mosque that has been long used by either an individual or his clan. Mr. Graves's point was that we rarely keep anything—cooking pot or building—long enough for it to acquire even a trace of this charm, and that the central fact of our civilization is that we prefer newness to *baraka*. My objection to the new Utopia certainly includes the fact that the very concept of *baraka* will have been forgotten.

Is it—or isn't it—a cause for surprise that the age of fun should be also both an age of violence and (among a conspicuous group of intellectuals) an age of philosophical despair? Fun, violence and despair seem at first sight to make an unexpected trio, but perhaps there is a natural relation. Since you can't possibly have fun all the time, since seeking it too persistently and too exclusively is a sure way of finding boredom and frustration instead, perhaps pessimism is the inevitable reaction of the thoughtful, and violence the inevitable reaction of those who do not analyze their frustrations.

If it is true that the American family spends an average of five hours a day watching television, then what it is so doggedly exposing itself to, must indicate something about the inner life of its members. The seeming incongruity of the fun-oriented commercial that usually interrupts the most sadistic spectacle again calls attention to the kinship between the two. Suddenly, at some climax of violence, comes the "word from our sponsor." What one logically expects is an offer of heroin, of brass knuckles sent COD "in a plain wrapper," or, possibly, some direction for obtaining police protection. But the advertiser assumes that what the audience wants most is something that will keep its hair in place or get the clothes really white. Are these two things—the sadistic melodrama on the one hand, and the commercial on the other—the two competing versions of the American dream? And is it the triviality of the one that creates an appetite for thrills and excitement at any cost?

What cannot be doubted is the all-too-obvious fact that this is indeed an age of violence, both public and private. Publically, it is an age of revolutions, small wars, and riots; privately, an age of vandalism and brutal assaults that suggest the "unmotivated act" of the existentialist novel, though the perpetrator usually can give no such rationalized explanation. When, a few months ago, a Tucson youth drove an ice pick into the back of a school maintenance worker, and then said he had no idea why he assaulted a man against whom he had no grudge, the shocking thing was that, in a sense, the incident was too typical of what one reads about almost daily to cause shock. And one wonders again if the reaction against the boredom of a fun-oriented society does not have something to do with the situation.

The New York World's Fair adopted as its theme "Man's Achievements in an Expanding Universe," but its theme song (to the music of Richard Rogers) is: "Walk away from every care / This is your fun time / You are entitled to it." Walking away from every care in an expanding universe may seem to require some doing, but isn't that last clause, "You are entitled to it," the real theme song of our society? Did the natural right to *pursue* happiness become somehow the right to *get* happiness, and did that right inevitably degenerate into a right to have fun—for the simple reason that the impossibility of guaranteeing fun is less obvious than the impossibility of guaranteeing happiness? Do children destroy schools and students plunge ice picks into custodians simply because they are not getting the fun they have been told they have a right to, and are taking their revenge?

Sociologists used to blame all youthful delinquency and most adult criminality on a society that had deprived the child or the adult of decent conditions of life. But the explanation will no longer hold water. Youthful delinquents and vandals come from every strata of society—from the poor who have too little, from the rich who have too much, and from the middle classes, which seem to have just the right proportion of the things the sociologists talk about. We can't all belong to the Jet Set but few of us are too poor to join its lower-income analogue, the motorcycle set. If many at both levels have been deprived, it is not of comfort and material luxuries. Perhaps what they suffer from is being deprived of a set of values not to be found in a fun-oriented society. There we are all taught to believe that fun is what everyone has a right to; that if you do not have as much of it as you think you should, you are "deprived"; and that to be deprived is to make any protest, up to and including murder, "understandable" because society, not you, is to blame.

Still another paradox is the fact that this fun-oriented and violence-oriented society is also, on the other hand, playing a leading role in a world movement aimed at extending freedom and equality to all persons within our own country, and ultimately to all nations. Perhaps the most tragic consequence of a taste for violence is the extent to which it confuses the motives of every social or political movement, from the demand for civil rights to anti-colonial revolution, by making them sometimes genuinely what they profess to be and sometimes merely excuses for violence. Students strike and riot for absurd, as well as for legitimate, reasons. One is not quite sure whether the inhabitants of Cyprus wanted independence for reasons credible to human dignity, or merely in order that Turks and Greeks might indulge in the fun of killing one another; whether a Southeastern confederation wants to be a self-governing nation out of legitimate "national aspirations," or whether the greatest national aspiration is to be strong enough to attack and subdue its neighbors. Surely the unholiest of united fronts is that formed by the union of those who have a passion for justice with those moved only by a pathological lust to destroy. And it is all the more dangerous because even individuals are sometimes self-deceived.

The apologies for a fun-oriented society seem to assume that security and abundance are automatic as well as permanent, and that somehow or other they will continue to bless those who have put "having fun" before everything else. Theirs would be, it seems to me, a rather ignoble Utopia and it is certainly an impossible one. At this moment one cannot be sure whether we are headed toward a world more just and happier than it has ever been, or whether (as the news of yesterday and today seems often to suggest) toward a dark age where violence, both private and public, is normal and almost continuous. The fun-oriented are not likely to be of much help in settling the question.

—*Saturday Review*
JANUARY 16, 1965

. . .   .

The age of violence

"I very much like to torture animals," so writes Salvador Dali in his modest *Diary of a Genius*. One of his deepest regrets is, as he goes on to say, that he has never had the pleasure of watching a lion die of starvation.

Now lions are expensive luxuries, but rats and other small animals come cheap, and a modest equivalent of the experience denied Dali is enjoyed by many adolescents in high schools that buy from one of the largest biological supply houses complete starvation kits that include various deficient diets and thus provide for a refinement which only modern science has made possible. The victims eat, but they die even more slowly than if they were entirely deprived of food. Thus the pleasure of watching them is prolonged, and it may be justified on the ground that it is "educational."

A century ago Charles Darwin told a Royal Commission that experiments involving cruelty to animals were "damnable" unless they contribute important knowledge unobtainable in any other way. And when Thomas Henry Huxley heard of a vivisectionist who said that he might give his victims an anesthetic to keep them quiet but not to spare them pain, Huxley wrote, "I would willingly agree to any law which would send him to the treadmill." Certainly high school students have no need to prove for themselves that dietary deficiencies can be fatal, and they learn nothing but hardness of heart from either these experiments or from some of the others now popular— such as, for instance, the inoculation of rodents or chicks with cancer. In their literature class they probably read "The Ancient Mariner" and are asked to comment upon:

> He prayeth best who loveth best
> All things both great and small.

But a bright student might be inclined to reply that praying in schools is forbidden anyhow, and at least one teacher is reported to have brushed criticism aside by explaining that students were sternly forbidden to regard their victims as pets or to take any interest in them as individuals. Another teacher, when asked why it was necessary to perform actual experiments when published accounts and photographs were available, replied that "using live animals fascinates the youngsters." He added that it wouldn't do to stop the experiment before death ensued because death made it "more dramatic" and "the children are not convinced unless the critters die."

There are, of course, laws against cruelty to animals, but I have never heard of a case where they were invoked to prevent any torture that claimed to have a scientific purpose. In fact, many, though not all, laboratory physiologists have bitterly opposed all the various bills introduced (chiefly, so far, without success) that would set up standards governing the treatment of laboratory animals—Senate Bill S1071, for instance. But does anyone dare say that no laboratory worker could possibly have a touch of sadism in him or even that routine familiarity with torture might make him callous? The very fact that laboratory experiments are conducted behind closed doors makes it all the more desirable that some sort of control or inspection be provided for. In England, where all possibly painful experiments must be licensed by the Home Office, eighty-eight biological Fellows of the Royal Society answered a questionnaire in which they were asked whether or not they opposed these existing controls, whether they believed they prevented the highest level of medical research, and whether they found in their own experience that control seriously frustrated legitimate results. Of the eighty-eight, only one replied "Yes" to any of the three questions; the rest gave a "No" to all three. Among comments from eminent persons were:

Sir Francis Walshe, F.R.S.: "A wide familiarity with the literature of experimental neuro-physiology leads me to think that in other countries where no such rational mode of control is used, quite a few futile and unnecessarily painful animal experiments are carried out by persons not always qualified to do them."

Professor A. T. Phillipson, deputy director of the Rowett Research Institute: "I am glad to hear the Americans are trying to introduce a bill similar to our Office Act."

Professor A. Habbow, F.R.S., director of the Chester Betty Cancer Research Institute: "I have, of course, been most interested to learn of the American bill and sorry to hear of opposition to it."

Nobel Prize-winner Professor H. A. Krebs: "I am very glad indeed to support a movement to introduce in the United States legislation similar to that operating in Great Britain. My answer to all three questions which you formulated at the end of your letter is a simple 'No.' "

One similar bill was recently introduced in one of the American state legislatures, whereupon an amendment was offered specifically exempting high school laboratories from any supervision or restriction. In the Middle Ages any cruelty was justified if it could be said to be in the defense of true religion; much the same is true today, if science is substituted. But one does not have to oppose all vivisection to ask that the experimenter should be required to show not merely that he could learn something from some horrible cruelty, but that what he could learn is important enough to be alleged as an excuse. I wonder, for instance, about the experiment recently reported to determine how much fire dogs could breathe without dying. The experimenter said that the Army "wanted to know." Why it wanted to know was not explained, but perhaps it was in order to make sure that its flame throwers were sufficiently lethal.

We like to tell ourselves that civilization has made us more humane. Our newspapers no longer carry advertisements like the following, from a British periodical in 1730: "A mad bull, dressed up with fireworks, is to be turned loose . . . likewise a dog dressed up with fireworks; also a bear to be turned loose. N.B.—A cat is to be tied to the bull's tail." Bear-baiting was officially prohibited in England in 1835, and a few years earlier, the first law making cruelty to animals an offense *per se* was passed—over, incidentally, vigorous opposition in Parliament by those who called themselves anti-sentimentalists. Nevertheless, it sometimes seems that Emerson's Law of Compensation really does work—both ways. Perhaps there is less suffering inflicted upon animals that is frankly for pleasure, but there is probably much more of it—quantitatively, at least—in the interest of scientific knowledge.

Killing for fun and death as a spectacle are not, however, unknown today. In Tucson, Arizona, the head of a certain printing organization that opposes most of the present game laws, abandoned the usually mealymouthed, gun manufacturers' explanation of the wholesome effects of killing animals for fun (*i.e.*, outdoor exercise, contact with nature, making fathers pals with their sons, and so forth) for the statement that children ought to make early contact "with life and death." And frank though that was, it wasn't quite completely so. What he meant was not "familiarity with death" but "familiarity with killing," which is a rather different thing. And there is surely some doubt that there are not enough opportunities today to become familiar with that. We who have had the privilege of living in the Century of Progress have, as a matter of fact, had more opportunities to take killings of one sort or another for granted than had either our fathers or our grandfathers.

Perhaps it is because there has been so much killing in our time that there seems to have been a reversal of the once-evident trend away from ritual violence. Perhaps the fun-killings, staged by some of the veterans' organizations that invite young folks to club rabbits to death, is only a survival of a concept of sport widely prevalent down to the nineteenth century. But there is no doubt that bullfighting (once regarded as decidedly un-American) has become a smart diversion. Nor is its popularity confined to the Southwest, where the *corridas* (a little Spanish adds a touch of chic) staged just across the border are not only regularly advertised in our newspapers but often given critical reviews. Hemingway's bloodlust no doubt had something to do with the rise of the fashion, and his celebration of the bullfight as the most refined expression of the sadistic impulse met with widespread response.

A few years ago, during a Congressional hearing, a witness introduced a memo from an advertising manager to the producer of a TV serial his company was sponsoring: "More violence and more bosoms." A great deal has been written in quite proper protest against the violence that runs so consistently not only through TV melodramas and through the animated cartoons, but also through even the Disney nature films, where ritual fights (often carefully staged) play a large part. How much all these things are creating a taste, how much merely responding to it, would be hard to know, but less has been written about the increasing element of violence, danger and death in the so-called spectator sports. American football (which a recent English critic called "not violent enough for a war, but too violent for a game") is relatively mild by comparison with air shows and auto races, though even in football there are some spectators whose excitement is increased by the fact that fatal injuries are at least a very real possibility. And as far as the air shows and races are concerned, their danger is frankly stressed in the advertisements.

The most penetrating discussion I have ever seen of the part played by the ever-present threat of death at an auto race occurs, oddly enough, in a Bantam paperback called *When Engines Roar*. These "nineteen action-packed true stories capture all the daring and drama of the greatest moments in auto-racing history" and are obviously directed at *aficionados*. But the volume does nevertheless include an article, "The Psychology of Auto Racing," by one Raymond de Beker, which is reprinted from *The Annual Automobile Review*.

Mr. de Beker cites a variety of appeals that the spectacle of auto racing can and does make: Speed is one of the more spectacular achievements of technology and all aspects of technology fascinate modern man; crowds, noise, and mass hysteria offer an escape from the troubled self, and so forth, and so forth. But the principal conclusion that emerges from the analysis is foreshadowed by the opening sentence: "Motor races are just as essential a part of modern life as gladiatorial combats were in ancient Rome."

After disposing rather briefly of the less obvious appeals, the author develops fully an analysis of the most powerful ones. "In no other sport . . . is the danger of death so imminent. At Le Mans death reaped eighteen victims in a matter of seconds . . . and though the spectators have every intention of running risks only by proxy, it happens that fate panders over-zealously to a taste that conscience scarcely dares to admit." Hence (as he might have added but didn't), it is all rather as though the spectator at the bullfight was occasionally tossed into the arena or the Roman fan at the Colosseum found himself, though no Christian, suddenly in the middle of the lions (which would have served him right enough).

Mr. de Beker then concludes: "Mankind has reached a dangerous corner. . . . [He] seeks to perceive what fate this machine holds in store for him and to experience vicariously the pains of death and rebirth it involves. He wants to know if he can become the superman who defies the laws of space, the mechanized centaur he visualizes in the champion, and avoid the catastrophe which alarms yet attracts him as flame does a moth."

When I began to write this piece, the moral I would have drawn from the bullring and the racecourse would have been implied in the question how far the spectator at either is from the Emperor Commodus, whom Suetonius describes as leaning over the box to stare intently into the face of the gladiator dying a few feet away. Now, however, I wonder if the auto race isn't, unlike the bullfight, something new rather than merely a recrudescence. Perhaps its chief significance is what Mr. de Beker makes it—as a ritual presentation of man face-to-face with the machine that he half hopes and half fears may put an end to him at last. —*Saturday Review*

MARCH 27, 1965

. . .   . III

The Two Cultures

. . .   .

Are the humanities worth saving?

In his sentimental moments even the tycoon sometimes puts in a word for the good old days, and he may, like Henry Ford, support a museum to preserve their relics. In somewhat similar fashion nearly everybody professes to regret "the neglect of The Humanities." Any discussion of education or of contemporary civilization is likely to include a formal bow in the direction of Culture, much like the equally formal bow in the general direction of Religion. "Oh yes, I almost forgot. There is also God and the humanities—very important things of course, though I haven't time to discuss them now."

Nevertheless, the tycoon is not anxious to bring the good old days back, and relatively few people are actively interested in the humanities, no matter how seriously they profess to take them. Compare the contents of any "class magazine" with that of a corresponding publication of the nineteenth century. Compare, for example, the modern *Harper's* or *Atlantic* with the same magazine two generations ago. Politics, sociology, and— to a lesser extent—science have now almost a monopoly. Any sort of writing whose appeal is primarily to what are still somewhat vaguely called "cultural interests" is almost nonexistent. Yet it was the staple of these same magazines not so very long ago. About such things their public has obviously ceased to care very much.

If, despite the parlousness of the times, there really is a case for The Humanities, why does the public continue indifferent? Can it be because that public, though willing to support liberal arts colleges much as it is willing to support churches, is not very clear in its own mind what the humanities are about or what they are for? Would it be wise for a time to talk less about their sad neglect and more about what, if anything, they are?

The word itself is exceedingly vague. Interpret it broadly as "whatever concerns the human being" and there isn't much it cannot be made to include. Interpret it as narrowly as it is sometimes interpreted and it ceases to mean much more than "polite accomplishments," analogous to the needlework and flower-painting which ladies were once supposed to dabble in, principally in order to demonstrate that they really were ladies rather than something economically and socially inferior. Those —and there are many—who unconsciously define the word thus, quite properly relegate all the activities it implies to idle upper-class ladies and to those timid, ineffectual males who are tolerated in a realistic society because of the entertainment they provide for these same refined ladies.

A subtler approach is the attempt to give real meaning to the concept "humane" by a process of elimination. In contradistinction to *what* are certain pursuits so described? To that question the Renaissance scholars who gave us the word would probably have replied something like this: "Why, humane learning is so called to distinguish it from divine learning or theology; also, of course, in contradistinction to those 'illiberal' studies merely mechanical or immediately utilitarian in their aims. More specifically, 'human' means what you find in the writers of Greece and Rome."

Unfortunately, time has tended to destroy the usefulness of these definitions without supplying us with a good one that is currently workable. "The humanities" does not mean merely the Greek and Roman classics because, however valuable or even indispensable they may be, they do not now contain all humane knowledge. "Humane" does not mean merely "profane" as opposed to "sacred," because nearly everything with which the modern world concerns itself is "profane" in that sense. And, though the term still does mean "without immediately useful application," the development of the sciences has raised a new confusion. They are no longer necessarily "illiberal" and they are not always merely immediately practical in their aims.

Deny the adjective "humane" to all scientific knowledge and you impoverish the concept of the humanities to a point where it is even more likely to suggest little more than "elegant accomplishments" plus "a pious concern with the notions and achievements of the past." You encourage the idea that the humane is not merely nonscientific but actually anti-scientific; that it implies a flight from modern knowledge, and that therefore "the humanist" is necessarily some sort of old fogey, a quaint and curious adherent of a lost cause, worth tolerating only because he embodies some charm to which we make a faint nostalgic response.

At the other extreme is the position taken up in the late nineteenth century by those who followed the lead of Huxley. To them modern science is simply the form that humane learning has assumed in our time. Chemistry and physics and biology *are* Culture. To study them is not only to master specific facts but to reap at the same time all the benefits supposed in the past to accompany the study of the classic curriculum.

When we lament today the neglect of the humanities, or discuss solemnly what should be done about it, we get nowhere, partly because we do not define what we mean by the term and frequently vacillate between several possible meanings.

Even when we try to face the crucial question of the relation between, and the rival claims of, "the sciences" and "the humanities," we seldom get beyond two vague notions: First, that the sciences are "humane" when they are taught as "cultural" rather than "professional" subjects; and second, that "the humanities" include also certain considerations and concerns which science cannot, or at least does not yet, take into consideration. But neither of these notions is very precise or very helpful. What are "the cultural aspects" of science and what, if anything, are the realities with which science cannot or does not deal?

Of these two questions the second seems to me the more important as well as the more difficult. Unlike certain nineteenth-century educators, we are aware that the physical sciences are not merely utilitarian. We no longer dismiss college courses in chemistry as "stinks" or assume that physics is merely something which the future engineer must learn. Science has influenced philosophical, ethical and religious thinking so profoundly that even those who regard the so-called scientific philosophies, religions and systems of ethics as erroneous, must recognize that any "cultured" man needs to know something about them as surely as a cultured atheist needs to know something about Christian doctrine and history.

But there is much less agreement on the other question. If the modern humanities are still to be something more than "science taught in such a way as to emphasize its cultural values" along with, perhaps, a certain amount of historical and antiquarian lore, then what is this something? What is its hard core? Is it anything except some knowledge of those irresponsible fancies with which the prescientific age permitted itself to dally and which we try to regard with condescending tolerance? Are there any important "humane truths" which are non-scientific?

Most of us who call ourselves humanists do believe that we deal with such truths. But we have not succeeded very well in making them seem real to others. Discuss the humanities with any scientifically-minded person. Even though he is one of those who will grant, at least for the sake of peace, that "the humanities ought not be neglected," the chances are that he will find it very difficult to say why, or to imagine what these same humanities may be, unless they are, essentially, not much more than a game some find it nostalgically agreeable to play with the naïve, disorderly, and usually erroneous notions which amused the childhood of our civilization. That there are any realities that can only be investigated by nonscientific methods, he can hardly believe. Yet unless there really are some such, then we take the humanities too seriously rather than not seriously enough.

Sometimes—though not often enough—official science admits that its field, though large, is limited; that its methods are not applicable to every subject of investigation; that it is not, in a word, omnicompetent. Yet it has extended its range so widely and produced results so impressive that neither the scientist himself, nor the public which he has so properly impressed, pays much attention to disclaimers. Both are prone to believe that the limitations of science leave little reality unexplored. And since we can hardly expect the scientist, even at his most modest, to define for us what he does not claim as part of his province, we must define it for ourselves, and what I propose is simply this: Let us examine the positive claims rather than the negative admissions of science, and see what that leaves over as a possible subject with which the humanities alone may deal, in their admittedly less positive manner.

By science's more modest practitioners we are sometimes told that its subject matter is *all objectively verifiable truth,* and that its method is *experimental verification.* It deals with what can be proved and, especially, *with what can be measured.* Could we then define the humanities by stating a simple opposite? "Humane learning and humane studies are those which concern themselves with what cannot be experimentally verified and is not susceptible of measurement." That, I think, would clear the air.

Science has often misled the age when scientists have claimed scientific authority for statements which were not based upon any experiments and did not involve any accurate measurements. The humanities have often done themselves a disservice when, as often, they have rejected genuine scientific truths or when, as is nowadays more common, especially in connection with fiction and drama, they have claimed a kind of scientific authority for their own productions. But unless we are willing to affirm boldly that there is a large area of elusive truth which it would be fatal to neglect, but which nevertheless cannot be dealt with by any scientific method; unless we are willing to admit also that in this area doubt and dispute must rage, perhaps forever, because what is included within it cannot be measured or subjected to controlled experiment, then there is little use in "defending the humanities," because there is little left to defend.

Most of what are called "the cultural aspects of science" lie within the area of the humanities as here defined. So also do so many other vastly important matters that it is the field of science rather than the field of the humanities which seems, by comparison, restricted—so restricted indeed that science itself comes to seem only an astonishingly effective method of dealing with very limited subject matters. If we permit ourselves to contemplate the truths which cannot be verified and the values which cannot be measured, we may well wonder that any age dared to neglect them. Yet neglect them we did, and it may be for that very reason that a civilization which has made so many careful measurements and performed so many triumphant experiments is, nevertheless, a civilization which has come justly to fear that the human race itself may have no future.

Since the days of Francis Bacon there have always been individuals who maintained that only "facts"—positive and verifiable knowledge—are worth bothering with. But never before our own, has there been an age when most people made this assumption so uncritically, that they ask in all innocence for so much as a single example of something important and knowable which cannot be measured or made the subject of an experiment.

Suppose we consider, for example, that reality which is called "happiness." Pope described it as "our being's end and aim," and though there have always been some—Bernard Shaw is a modern instance—who dismissed happiness as unimportant, even scientists usually admit that most of us continue to pursue it whether we ought to or not. Yet "happiness" is something which falls almost completely outside the purview of science. Its various degrees cannot be measured. The conditions which produce it cannot be controlled. We cannot demonstrate that an individual man either is, or is not, happy. In fact, his emotional state cannot even be safely inferred. We know perfectly well that many a man who "ought to be happy" and many a man who "acts as though he were happy," isn't.

To banish these undoubted facts the positivist is forced into an absurd and disastrous subterfuge. Knowing that science cannot deal with subjective states and being committed to the contention that only scientific knowledge is useful, he cannot escape the conclusion that such subjects as happiness are not worth thinking about at all. We should, he says, devote ourselves instead to those objectively measurable and controllable factors which, so he blandly assumes, determine subjective states. Since we can make some sort of approximate measurements of "the standard of living" we will adopt the convenient assumption that happiness varies directly with the standard of living. Hence, though we cannot profitably talk about happiness, we can talk (and how!) about welfare. The two ought to be, approximately, the same thing.

No assumption could, of course, be falser. Literature may be unscientific but it has never made the mistake of assuming that prosperity is the same thing as happiness, or that people are happy when "they ought to be." Yet this simple fact is in itself enough to suggest both what the subject matter of the humanities is, and one of the functions humane works of literature, or art or philosophy *do* perform.

These works concern themselves with, for instance, happiness, contentment and joy—as well as with their opposites. Their first and simplest function is to keep us human by acknowledging, as the scientists do not, that "the merely subjective" is vastly important in human life, that we are not merely "economic men" or "members of a social group" or "psychological types" but Men to whom such unmeasurable, unverifiable, uncontrollable realities as happiness are at least as important as any which can be measured, verified, or controlled; that in a word, the subjective is the very core of our being. Because the Founding Fathers were essentially humanists they asserted man's right to Life, Liberty, and the Pursuit of Happiness. If they had not been humanists, it would have been to the Pursuit of Welfare, or even of a High Standard of Living!

Totalitarian governments boast that their aim is the establishment of a scientific society. Some would-be perfectors of what we call Western democracy seem to cherish a similar ideal. But no society that based itself exclusively upon what can be learned by the scientific study of man could consistently recognize the existence of happiness as distinct from prosperity, welfare or a "high standard of living." Nor could it, for that matter, recognize as real any aspect of any man's inner life. Yet, insofar as a democracy tends to ignore that inner life, just to that extent does it obscure one of the most important distinctions between the facts and the theories of totalitarianism and the Western tradition.

Without humane learning no man can remain what we now call Man. Either he will slowly become so extraverted and adjusted that he is actually no more than one of those figments of the imagination with which scientific politics and sociology deal, or his individual awareness of his truest and vividest inner life will alienate him from his fellow beings because he will have no communication with them in terms of that inner life; because he will meet no public acknowledgment of the fact that any other human beings live any such lives, or are, indeed, human at all. Politics unites the outward actions of men; "the humanities" unites their thoughts and feelings. It draws them together in spirit.

But this is by no means all. Indispensable as is the function which consists merely in revealing that an inner life is something not unique but shared, different as mankind would be had "the humanities" never publicly acknowledged its humanity, the great creators of the humane tradition did not stop with the performance of this function.

Though they were deprived of both measurement as a tool and of experiment as a method, they went on to investigate as well as to describe the phenomena with which they dealt. They drew conclusions from observations which cannot be rigidly controlled and projected upon human beings as a whole, experiences which they knew only from their own. Even the assumption that men other than themselves have any consciousness or desire can be made only by such a gratuitous projection. And though by such methods they have not "proved" anything, they have carried conviction; and it is by the power to convince rather than by experimental verification that we test the validity of any work which claims a place among "the humanities."

As a result of such unscientific procedures as it can employ, the humanistic enterprise has built up that store of ethical convictions, moral principles and standards of value by which men live, as surely as it has created an awareness of their intimate selves and the correspondence between one intimate self and another. The body of humanistic knowledge is neither wholly consistent with itself, much less is it demonstrably true in any objective sense. But it is, nevertheless, a body of imperfect knowledge indispensable to civilization.

In a profound posthumous essay published in *The Virginia Quarterly,* under the somewhat misleading title "Americanism," Santayana recently provided an original approach to the great underlying problem of today. The modern world, he says, began in the sixteenth century when Western Europe came first to realize fully that knowledge—at least a certain kind of knowledge—is power. The determination to acquire that kind of knowledge launched the most dazzlingly successful enterprise any group of human beings ever embarked upon. And if the most recent consequence is the growing fear that power, getting out of hand, will destroy the race that released it, there was another unnoticed consequence that preceded all such fears.

The very success, so patent and incontrovertible, of the determination to pursue relentlessly the newly-opened source of power, favored the unconscious conviction that the knowledge which does confer power is the only kind of knowledge there is. True knowledge, as opposed to mere fancy on the one hand and mere pedantry on the other, comes thus to be defined as simply "that which confers power." Moral philosophy, poetry and art are as contemptuously disregarded as the theology which the new age more specifically repudiated: They do not confer power—at least no power over the physical universe so evident as the power which scientific knowledge confers. And because they do not they are, therefore, not knowledge.

What can sensibility and "understanding" enable a sensitive and understanding man to do? In what way can it be demonstrated that such a man has any power at his command which the insensitive and un-understanding has not? Attempt to reply that, in the long run, sensibility and understanding make for a better and safer world, and you are told that you cannot prove it. If you fall back upon the conviction that what you *are* may be as important as what you do, you will be told that "behavior" and "action" are now generally recognized to be not only the measure of man, but the only tangible, substantial realities in any society. And so they are, once you have assumed not only that "knowledge is power," but that power is the only valid test of the importance of knowledge.

Words are tricky things. At first sight it may seem that De Quincey's famous distinction between the literature of *knowledge* and the literature of *power* is a direct contradiction of everything which has here been said. "Books, we are told, propose to *instruct* or to *amuse*. Indeed! . . . The true antithesis to knowledge, in this case, is not *pleasure* but *power*. All that is literature seeks to communicate power; all that is not literature, to communicate knowledge."

From another point of view the exact opposite may be said: "All literature seeks to communicate one kind of knowledge; all writing which is not literature seeks to communicate power." But the contradiction is apparent rather than real. Because De Quincey had never submitted to the tyranny of science he was able to mean by "power" not the ability to control directly the physical environment, but the ability to carry conviction and to arouse passion. He realized, in other words, precisely what kind of power humanistic knowledge confers upon mankind. It does confer upon us a kind of knowledge or, if you insist, half-knowledge, upon which the richness of human experience and the stability of society largely depend.

Deprive the individual and the world of all the convictions which science cannot prove to be legitimate, and neither man nor his world could stand. The question whether the humanists have revealed morality or invented it, whether they have discovered "value" or created it, is less important than the fact that but for them, mankind would never have conceived of, and quite certainly never have cherished, either. And if poets have sometimes fixed erroneous and pernicious ideas upon whole sections of the human race, at least only other and better poets have ever been able to remedy the evil.

Such at least is the affirmation which any effective defender of the humanities must be willing to make. Unless there is a kind of knowledge which is not power in the sense that scientific knowledge is power, and unless that kind of knowledge can, however imperfectly, be discovered and communicated by literature and the other arts, then the humanities are a fraud at worst, a trivial amusement at best. They certainly cannot save us and they are not worth saving. We should not be disturbed by their neglect. It would be more sensible to say, "Good riddance." —*Saturday Review*

JUNE 4 AND JUNE 11, 1953

. . .   .

The uses of literature in an age of science *

Let me immediately call your attention to the fact that my title refers to the function of literature rather than merely to the function of the writer in an Age of Science. That the writer

* Speech delivered at the Rockefeller Institute.

has such a function is seldom doubted. He can act as an independent middleman between the scientist and the uninstructed layman. Sometimes he is little more than a ghost writer, who on the one hand, shares enough of the scientist's knowledge to have some idea of what he is doing, and at the same time, enough of the ignorance and other limitations of the uninstructed layman to know how to tell this layman as much as the layman will be able to understand. Such a writer is useful; in fact, he is desperately needed by both the scientist (who needs the financial and political support as well as the confidence of the layman if science is to play its full part in society) and by the layman if the layman is not to regard science as a form of black magic which must remain totally incomprehensible.

This importance of the writer is, then, great and beyond dispute. But is there such a thing as literature which is not anti-scientific on the one hand, nor mere popular science on the other; something which concerns itself often with the same subject matter as science but in some different way? And when I say literature, I am thinking not only of fiction and drama and poetry but also, perhaps especially, of expository writing, which deals with the same facts and themes as pure science but with an approach and emphasis which is different.

Now I am not, I hasten to assure you, about to launch upon a defense of the humanities of that familiar sort which consists of vague reference to literature as a graceful ornament and relaxation, as a home of lost causes to which we pay sentimental deference, or as a land of "dreams" to which we retire when reality is too much for us. What I am trying to define for myself is a function, or rather a group of functions, which literature performs when it is neither an escape from scientific truth nor a mere popularization of such truths but a way of looking at science which is not, and need not be, the scientist's way, but which makes it easier for many of us to live comfortably in that world of science which is so different from the world our imagination gave us back in the days when imagination was free to imagine pretty much what it pleased about nature, about human nature and about a God made in man's own image.

Because literature, unlike science, is at least as much subjective as it is objective, because it is so distinctly man-centered rather than centered outside man around some concept of absolute truth to fact, literature constitutes a continuous reminder of something the man of letters believes to be true and believes that the scientist sometimes denies or forgets, namely, that science exists to serve man, not man to serve science. The man of letters is not so ready, as many scientists are, to say that we must never ask whether this discovery or that machine is likely to be a blessing or a curse to mankind and that we must be prepared, if necessary, to perish for the Glory of Science, much as Jonathan Edwards said he would be willing to be damned for the Glory of God.

The inventor of an airplane in Samuel Johnson's romance *Rasselas* refused to make his invention public, because he believed that man should not be able to fly until he had first become virtuous. We are not likely to, and perhaps should not, take quite that position. But we may appropriately accept the reminder that the power which science so abundantly supplies us with is good only so far as it is used for good ends; that if we are not willing to refuse to fly until we have become virtuous, we ought at least to realize that being able to fly will not make us either virtuous or happy—which is what the more extreme proponents of technological progress seem to assume. If mankind really does presently enter upon a scientific and technological Utopia—instead of either perishing in a catastrophe or being reduced to a mere slave of his own machines—it will be because he has remembered what many scientists who have a touch of literature in them and literature itself have in many different ways reiterated, namely, that unless man sees science as his servant rather than his all-demanding god, he may end by immolating himself on that god's altar, as the victims of religious superstition have immolated themselves upon the altars of their own, not stranger gods.

Hardly less obvious, or less often recognized, is that thorny question of values. Can science establish them and, if not, are they then necessarily either merely arbitrary or merely fictitious? To the first question, "Can science establish values?", scientists themselves give sometimes a "Yes" and sometimes a "No" answer. And if the answer is "No," those who give it sometimes answer the second question, "Are values then merely arbitrary or fictitious?" with a "Yes." And if they do answer "Yes," then they fall into the completest possible moral relativism, where the monster is as admirable as the saint.

Because this question has been so often discussed, I am not going to discuss it at length but make only two comments. So far as I myself can see, science as such, cannot by its very definition establish values. I rest my case on a very simple statement made some years ago, not by a man of letters but by an official scientist of great repute, Dr. Vannevar Bush. "A value," he said, "cannot be deduced from a statement of fact." That seems to me to be conclusive: Science is concerned only with facts, and a statement of fact cannot define a value.

If the methods of science cannot define a value, then it may be asked, "Can anything else?" Certainly neither literature nor philosophy has ever succeeded in establishing values as statements of fact, accepted as such with that degree of unanimity with which scientific statements of fact have been accepted, for a time at least. But though a given science may reach a very high state of development without concerning itself with values either directly or indirectly, literature might almost be defined as an attempt to give some account of human life on the assumption that values are of supreme importance. Literature, which deals with the scientific subject matter, may sometimes legitimately raise again and again the question whether or not the universe outside of man is actually morally neutral. I certainly would hesitate to say that neutrality has been conclusively demonstrated and I see no reason why the question should not be asked again and again as searchingly as possible. But even if you dismiss such attempts to find a human meaning in the external universe, one fact seems to me to remain. All civilizations have rested upon the explicit or tacit assumption of some system of hierarchy of values, however arrived at and however different from that accepted in other and perhaps equally successful civilizations. And it is literature in one form or another—literature oral or written—which transmits the civilization's value system, however arrived at. If science cannot establish a system of values and if civilization can't survive without one, then civilization cannot survive without literature. In an Age of Science, it is important that this literature should not be anti-scientific or ignorant of science. To be either, is to make certain that the literature will be discarded—as the fundamentalist theology was discarded in the old war between science and religion. But literature should have its own way of treating the facts and themes of science.

Let me now try to say something concerning a theme neither so easy to state, nor quite so frequently explored, as either of the two I have just been touching upon.

It used to be said that science was merely systematized common sense. Such it obviously was in the days of Galileo and such it still was, to a considerable extent, well into the nineteenth century. But no one would maintain that it is that today. Over the portal that marks the entry to modern physics and modern biology (which is coming more and more to unite with physics and chemistry) is written a sort of parody of Dante's *Inferno:* "All common sense abandon, ye who enter here."

If science began in the Renaissance, when men began to put

more trust in the evidence of their senses than in logical and metaphysical arguments, modern science demands that we reverse the process. In the first place, our senses are of little use because the facts that we are pursuing lead us into the realms of the small, smaller, and yet smaller where first our unaided eye cannot follow, then where our optical microscopes cannot take us, and at last into the realm which even the electron microscope cannot wholly penetrate. At best we have only to deduce or infer what we can never expect to see or hear or feel. What is even worse, we are now used to being told that the real but invisible world, which we cannot reach with our senses, is also not capable of being reconstructed in our minds—even that ultimate reality is not only not understood but quite possibly not understandable. The paradoxes of the metaphysicians, like that involving fate and free will, are no less unsolvable than is, say, that of the wave and the corpuscle. Yet it was to that dilemma that the enterprise of common sense ultimately conducted us.

As far back as the nineteenth century we began to realize that things were not what they seemed: that, for instance, when our five senses told us that the chair we sat on was a solid object, all five of them were lying. By now all the ordinary phenomena of the world we seem to inhabit are mere fantasies, created by senses and intellectual concepts which, one and all, are united in a conspiracy to deceive us.

And yet most of our lives is necessarily lived in the realm of appearance. Call it animal faith, if you like. But whatever you call it, our active, our emotional, and a large part of our intellectual life continues (and probably will continue as long as we are recognizable as the kind of creatures we now are) to have its being in the world of seeming rather than in the world of scientific facts. Even if you are inclined to dismiss literature as no more than an account of the universe as it really isn't, such is the universe of appearances which is in many ways more real to us than any other. If we did not have animal faith, we could not survive; and, at a minimum, literature helps us to retain an animal faith by which we can live in our human world.

The last claim I have to make is the most inclusive of all, perhaps indeed includes all the others. It is based upon the simple fact that man is, or at least always has been so far, a creature of emotions as well as of intellect. But pure science has to do with the intellect only. It is concerned exclusively with knowing and through knowing, with doing. The phrase "coldly scientific" has become a cliché. And science thus performs its special function when it is cold, in the sense that it refuses to allow its conclusions to be influenced by its emotions. But the man who is nothing but "coldly scientific" (if indeed such a creature has ever so far actually existed) is hardly a man at all.

All literature is, on the other hand, emotional. To a greater or lesser extent it also may be concerned with what we believe to be the facts of life, but it inevitably involves (as science does not) an emotional reaction to those actual or supposed facts. And this is very significantly the case with that special sort of literature with which I am concerned this evening; with that sort, I mean, which deals with the facts and the themes of science in some literary way. You may call it impure science, if you like. I am aware that some scientists despise it more passionately than they despise even the literature which is admittedly an escape from fact into the realm of fantasy and dreams. To them it seems not only childish but dangerous, something capable of disturbing and corrupting the vision of science itself. But surely it is no threat to that vision so long as it acknowledges what it is and does not pretend to be pure science.

Perhaps I can put the same thing in another way by saying that man needs not only to know but also to wonder and to love, and that science, as such, has nothing to do with either wonder or love though those two are perhaps the essential concern of the kind of literature I have been trying to defend.

I am aware that certain extremists would reject everything I have said and maintain that what I have called the function of literature has turned out to be purely the attempt to preserve certain of the all-too-human weaknesses which the true scientists have by now got rid of for themselves and which they believe are destined in time to cease to cripple, as to date they have always crippled, all attempts to create a thoroughly rational and scientific civilization.

A few months ago I came across a very clear statement of this position in an imaginary conversation written by J. Bronowski in which he celebrates the macromolecular biologist as the man who has at last enabled pure science to answer all the needs of the human being. "He is," and I quote, "the man who unravels the secret of life by using the tools of physics. He shows—we have shown—that the structures of biology become intelligible when we treat them, not as a string of mysteries but as strings of molecules. That is the universal unity in which we believe."

Bronowski then goes on to compose a scientific poem which is quite as bad as Erasmus Darwin's famous "Botanical Garden" and proclaims that when he regards biology not as a string of mysteries but as a string of molecules, "an icy sweetness fills my mind."

If this is indeed not only all we know on earth and all we need to know, then I have this evening talked nothing but foolishness. But so far as I am concerned, I still do not see how treating biology as a string of molecules removes all the mystery and wonder and if it did then I would fall back upon the contention that an "icy sweetness" is not enough for me and that I do not believe mankind as a whole would be satisfied with it.

Neither do I see how an understanding of the macromolecular structure of the living cell can throw any light on any question involving either ethics or aesthetics. If such knowledge is indeed all we know on earth and all we need to know, then the only conclusion which can be drawn is one which some positivist philosophers have drawn already—namely, that all questions involving ethics or aesthetics are, as they are fond of saying, "meaningless questions."

If they are not meaningless but fraught with meanings and consequences of tremendous import, then we must attend to even those often contradictory hints which literature in various forms has attempted to communicate.

We may *say* that good and evil, like ugliness and beauty, are merely the prejudices of a given society but few people have ever consistently acted upon that assumption and no society which as a whole acted upon it, could last for long.

Of all scientists the physician is perhaps the one who is most aware of ethical problems and he sometimes says that medicine has an ethic, but I do not see how it can be deduced from the science of medicine itself.

Consider the case of those Nazi physicians who thought it ethical to perform upon human beings experiments which shocked those physicians who adhered to other political (not other scientific) creeds. Their scientific training was the same. They knew the same facts of anatomy, physiology and pathology. They would have agreed upon the diagnosis and treatment of any suffering patient—assuming that they wanted to relieve him. Whatever made the difference between them was the result of beliefs and attitudes derived ultimately from non-scientific literature.

The ultimate concern of all science is an answer to some question *how* this or that happens or *how* this or that can be done. The question whether or not something *should* be done is one to which science as such can give no ultimate answer.

Science is concerned with know-how not with know-what or know-whether.

Shortly after the end of the Second World War Dr. Robert Oppenheimer entered upon the current discussion of that threat to the human race which the discovery of atomic fission had raised. He concluded by saying that what he most feared was not the physical destruction of mankind, not that the race of human beings would lose its life, but that it might (and the phrase is his) "lose its humanity."

Ever since I first read that statement I have wondered just what he meant by it and the only answer to that question that I can arrive at is simply this: "Man will have lost his humanity when and if he has become concerned exclusively with questions concerning *how*, not at all with questions concerning *what* and *whether*."

During the Middle Ages, when science was popularly confused with magic, it was assumed that it came from the devil and that those learned in it had lost their souls or, to return to Mr. Oppenheimer's phrase, their humanity. At the very least, science was a black art and therefore a very dangerous one.

Today, so it seems to me, the scientist is necessarily *exposed* to a similar danger. While acting in his professional or specialized capacity he must ask no question to which there is not, potentially at least, a scientific answer. He must be unemotional, objective, and neutral. He must not instinctively prefer one answer or another, must not allow himself to be swayed by prejudice, not even by prejudice in favor of what, as mere human being, he feels to be the good and the beautiful. If he abandons this kind of objectivity he risks perverting his science.

But there is nevertheless in this necessary attitude something which I am tempted to compare to the risk of trafficking with the devil.

It is opposed to certain aspects of human nature. And the

scientist can save his soul only if he leaves complete scientific coldness, objectivity and neutrality in the laboratory where it belongs and, when he leaves it, resumes interest in what I would call other aspects of truth and other methods of searching for it even though he may, if he likes, call them merely human prejudices. And it is, of course, literature which tries to persuade him to do just this.

—An abbreviated form of this speech appeared in the *Saturday Review*, DECEMBER 5, 1964

. . .   .

Should we bring literature to children?

Fifteen years ago I accepted an invitation to address an association of teachers of English. No such organization has invited me since, and there may be some connection between the two events. The announced "theme" of the meeting was something like "How to Bring Literature to Children," and I told the audience that the question was all wrong. Trying to answer that wrong question had already led to "projects" for the study of Shakespeare, which consisted not of discussing the plays, but of pasting up notebooks with publicity pictures for the movie version of *A Midsummer Night's Dream*. What they should ask, I said, was "How to Bring Children to Literature." Literature should stay right where it was. What they proposed was not education at all, but a refusal to educate.

Since that time great strides have been made in the art of bringing literature to children of all ages, from four to four-score. The great novels and plays, reduced to half an hour on radio or television, we take for granted; and somewhat more alarmingly we also take it for granted that soldiers should learn both the art of war and the ideology of democracy out of comic books, prepared for their instruction.

With my thesis I imagine that a good many people will disagree, but most of even those who do, will not want to deny the existence of the tendency which they approve of and I do not. More and more it is taken for granted not that all men, being created equal, have a right to the best, but that "the best" is whatever the largest number of people find immediately accessible and pleasing. Therefore, of course, men are best served when we attempt to find out what they like and to give it to them.

Educators used to assume it was their duty to select the great books of the world and to teach students why they really are great. Even today the Chicago group advocates a somewhat fanatically narrow version of this assumption, and has created something of a stir because of a fundamental premise which would once have been thought self-evident. But the tendency of the time is much better illustrated by a group of professors of education who have just recently proposed that the list of required reading in schools should be based upon a study (which they have just sponsored) of the tastes of schoolchildren.

That the list so compiled contained very few of the supposed classics and was very heavily loaded with books that would seem very trivial indeed to any one whose taste was more cultivated than that of the children themselves, seemed to the educators a fact quite irrelevant. The question of whether or not this was the proper way to select books for educational purposes was not even raised. But it is certainly, and with a vengeance, "bringing literature to children" rather than bringing children to literature. Indeed, it is difficult to see just what we are supposed to be getting in return for all the money spent on schools if school children simply spend their time reading what they would read anyway. It might be argued that the teachers were learning something from the pupils—namely, what the taste of uneducated children is. But the pupils were certainly not learning anything from the teachers and it would seem that the children are the ones who ought to be paid salaries—if any one should.

Would any pediatrician base the diet prescribed for the young submitted to his care, simply on an effort to determine what eatables they remembered with greatest pleasure? If he knew that the vote would run heavily in favor of chocolate sodas, orange pop, hot dogs and bubble gum, would he conclude that these should obviously constitute the fundamental elements in a "modern" child's menu?

Items drawn from the newspapers over a period of only a few weeks show clearly which way the wind is blowing. One college professor proposes that colleges should cease trying to teach college students what he contemptuously calls "literary English" and teach instead only that kind of expression which has been found "acceptable" in the student's own group. Another writes to protest the use of the word "ubiquity" in a newspaper, on the ground that many people do not know what it means. A third, going the whole way at once, urges that colleges drop from their courses of study everything which does not contribute to the student's "adjustment to society." The fact is, however, that language "acceptable to the group" is precisely what one gets in communities where there is no formal education whatsoever. The fact is also that if no one ever used any words which everybody did not know, then no one would ever learn any new ones, and the common vocabulary would gradually drop lower and lower until it contained only the three or four hundred words which are said to serve the needs of the most primitive people. As for "adjustment to society," that is something which necessarily goes on. But the purpose of education is, or at least was once assumed to be, the production of knowledge, attitudes, skills and tastes, to which, on the other hand, society would adjust itself.

Mr. Alexander Pope, whose works were not on the list of the schoolchild's favorite books, once described the progress of the learner as one in which he is, as he climbs, continuously inspired by the sight of new peaks beyond: "Hills peep o'er hills and Alps on Alps arise." In contemporary theory, whether in reference to the education of children or adults, nothing is supposed to be more carefully avoided than anything that suggests a glimpse just beyond the local horizon. Books are carefully graded according to the "age level" to which they are supposed to be appropriate. Vocabulary studies are consulted to make sure there are no words which the child at that "age level" is not supposed to know. But surely the best book for any intelligent child is often the one somewhat beyond his comprehension, and if there are some words he does not know, he may just possibly be inspired to find out what they mean.

I am well aware that the tendency that I have been deploring seems to some people to be what is meant by the "democratic movement." To me it is exactly the reverse because "democracy" seems to me to be based upon the belief—or at least the hope—that the "common man" does not have to remain common and that, given the opportunity, neither intellectuality nor artistic appreciation is beyond him. To believe the contrary and to conclude from that belief that whatever is the product of practice, cultivation, training and aspiration should be discredited and discarded, is not democratic but nonsensical. Yet a colleague of mine who attended an influential national conference of so-called educators reported that "intellectual" and "intellectualist" were the favorite terms of disparagement and that they seemed, as a matter of fact, to correspond pretty closely with the current Soviet favorites, "formalist" and "formalism." He was told that "doing" and "loving," not "intellectualizing," were the activities to be cultivated in a democracy, and my friend was angrily howled down when he protested that he himself was so boundlessly democratic that he believed even intellectual people had a right to an education.

I cannot think of anything better calculated to produce a rigid two-class society, composed of the rulers and the ruled, than this assumption that both the education of children and the instruction of the adult population are aims best achieved when a small professional group of educators, publicists, commentators and whatnot, spends its time deciding what is appropriate for the average citizen to know or think and what devices of "mass communication" will work best if these bits of information and opinion are to be transmitted without requiring of him the intellectual activities to which he is supposed to be so little given. I am by no means sure that any information which can be communicated via, say, the comic-book technique, could possibly be as important to the progress of democracy as the accomplishment of the confessedly more difficult educational feat that consists in teaching people how to read and how to find in the printed word, with all its subtlety and flexibility, a congenial method for receiving communications.

A good deal has been said about the importance of the distinction between "education" on the one hand and "indoctrination" or "propaganda" on the other. Confessedly, the line is sometimes hard to draw, but confessedly also, the difference between an educated population and an indoctrinated one is precisely the difference between a democratic society and a totalitarian society. The line, then, needs to be drawn, however difficult it may seem to be to draw it, and perhaps there is no better way to make the distinction than this: Whenever an attempt is made to convey knowledge or influence opinion in such a way that the person addressed becomes, as a result, less merely passive, more capable of criticism, and better prepared to make an effort to learn and think for himself, then what has been done to him comes under the head of education. Whenever, on the other hand, the attempt to convey knowledge or influence opinion is such as to encourage his indolence and his passivity; whenever it aims to require the least possible effort on his part and confirms him in, rather than frees him from, the existing limitations of his powers of attention and analysis, then it is propaganda or indoctrination. And it is my contention that both current educational theory as it applies to school or college students, and current methods of mass communication as they are applied to adult education in most of its forms, are tending in the direction of propaganda rather than of genuine education.

Those who are now attempting to use radio and television, however good their intentions, need to be on guard against the fact that whatever the possibilities may be, those media of communication lend themselves most easily to processes which are dubiously educational. Even the most conscientious brief version of a novel or play, even the most conscientious dramatization of a historical event, is something less than the original work of art or than genuine history. And, while we are busy congratulating ourselves that at least it is reaching people who otherwise would not meet either literature or history at all, we forget to ask how many there are who might otherwise have taken to reading if they had not had thrust upon them this lazier substitute. Mr. Fred Allen, whose remarks on television have, to be sure, sometimes been interpreted as the result of an irritation at a disturbing novelty, predicted that the man of the future would have eyes the size of cantaloupes and no brain at all. It may at least be said cautiously that we know what he means.

It has also been said that there is no country in the world where it is so easy to go to school and so difficult to get an education as in the United States. I do not think that that is really true, but I am not sure it does not threaten to become so, or that we are not in danger of destroying the educational system by our very eagerness to make it easy and efficient.

Carlyle maintained that the true university was merely a collection of books. That is certainly a very extreme statement of one point of view. But I am not certain that it is any further from the truth than the popular American assumption that the best school of any kind is the one most dominated by the largest number of professors of education, most responsive to the results of questionnaires, surveys, opinion polls and statistical compilations, most elaborately equipped with slide projectors, phonographs and radio sets. Some day we are going to have to realize that you cannot "give" anybody an education. The best you can do is to make it possible for him to get one.

—*New York Herald Tribune Book Review*
J U L Y 22, 1951

. . .   .

The prosperity of a jest

Everybody seems to be interested nowadays in what is called "communication." The lowest of the lowbrows dropped radio for television because they recognized TV as "a new medium of communication"—even if they did not call it that. The highest of the highbrows go in for semantics because that is the most esoteric aspect of the same grand subject. Meanwhile, all the in-betweens who busy themselves with World Problems talk about nothing more earnestly than mass communication.

There are—they will tell you—good reasons for all this. Never before were there so many things which the world needed to know. Never before was it so important that everybody should understand what was once the business of the ruling class alone. Intellectuals must study semantics so they can communicate with one another. Educators and publicists must study mass communication so they can reach the Common Man. And if you object that the quality of the thing communicated seems to vary inversely with the ingenuity of the means used to communicate it, they reply that it need not be so.

Perhaps television drama is not so good as legitimate drama or, for that matter, so good as the movies. In fact, perhaps it has nothing to recommend it except (a) its accessibility and (b) the charm of novelty plus the wondering admiration that the invention arouses. But, they say, it *could* be first class. There is no reason why Sophocles instead of Milton Berle, and Plato instead of Arthur Godfrey should not be piped into every home.

"Propaganda" and "advertising" are sometimes recognized as dangerous influences. They employ the techniques of communication to serve the selfish interests of individuals and groups. But that, we are told, is merely because the propagandist and the advertiser have got way ahead of everybody else when it comes to understanding how to communicate. The educator must wake up and catch up. He must take the instruments away from his opponents. They sell toothpaste and soap. They boast of creating "psychological wants" which nobody had until he was taught to have them. It is up to us to sell tolerance, good will, the scientific attitude and even perhaps wisdom itself, by similarly proved methods.

That there is a catch in all this, nobody seems to be very much aware. But there is a catch and the catch is this: The methods of the advertiser and the propagandist are not really usable for any purposes other than their own. They want their audiences to be as passive and uncritical as possible. Their methods are calculated not merely to make that audience believe what it is told, but also to believe just because it has been told. Their aim is to hypnotize and condition. The last thing they want is any thinking-for-yourself. Like the Bellman who went hunting for the snark, they have almost convinced even themselves that "what I tell you three times is true." Hence, what they are engaged in is not a kind of education but the direct opposite of education. The end result of their skill in one kind of communication is a group of listeners and "viewers" who are less than ignorant; it is a group which knows things that are not true and has become increasingly incapable of learning anything.

Nothing more clearly distinguishes a method of education from a technique of indoctrination than the fact that education demands from the subject some effort, especially some effort of attention, while propaganda does not. The advertiser will go to any length to make everything easy. The educator will see to it that something is expected of his pupil. He knows that no one can learn anything worth knowing unless he is willing to learn, as well as willing to be taught. He knows that learning how to learn is more important than any specific thing he can "communicate." And the grand question has now become whether or not the new techniques of mass communication inevitably and by their very nature weaken the power to learn at the same time that they make being taught so easy.

What so many enthusiasts of communication will not realize is that there is a point beyond which everything should not be made varied, vivid, picturesque, dramatic and "interesting." A time is sure to come when something which needs very much to be learned cannot possibly be made as vivid, picturesque, dramatic and interesting as certain other things. And when that time comes, only the individual who can turn his attention to what is most important, rather than allow it to be captured by what is most interesting, is capable of being educated.

Some years ago Mr. Clifton Fadiman used—and for all I know may have invented—the phrase, "the decline of attention." Nearly everyone seemed to recognize its aptness. It covered everything from the school teachers' complaint that children would no longer take the trouble to learn arithmetic, to the publishers' discovery that "condensations" sold better than original masterpieces and that pictures which could be glanced at were increasingly preferred to articles which had to be read. The college student plays the radio while he studies because he cannot keep his mind on his books; vacationers at the beach take along a phonograph, a deck of cards and various other pieces of paraphernalia because neither the sea itself nor any one of their other diversions can hold them for long. Even the magazines that professedly address the more intellectual audiences find it continually necessary to become more "striking." The newspapers' discovery that bigger headlines paid off was followed by the magazines' discovery that only an arresting makeup would enable them to survive. No one can be expected any longer to open a monthly simply because he has learned from experience that it will contain something interesting. His attention has to be caught by a snappy title, a striking picture, a teasing promise held out. Even among more intelligent and better-educated people it can no longer be assumed that they will *give* their attention. It has to be *caught*.

Some who are mildly disturbed by these phenomena explain them by saying rather sourly that we all "have too much," and that we are like a spoiled child who can never be entertained because he has too many toys. Others, refusing to be disturbed at all, explain rather complacently that ours is merely a world which is richer, livelier and more vivid than it used to be. But is it? Does a child who comes home from a school where he has had his "natural interests" nervously catered to, who then goes out to the movies and comes home again to a television set (this is precisely the usual routine of my friends' children) really lead a richer life than the nineteenth-century child who had nothing to do after school except read *Robinson Crusoe?* Does the adult who glances through a picture magazine, skims a news-weekly, watches ten minutes of a Senate investigation on TV, and then hears the *scherzo* movement of a symphony on the "Ford Hour" really live a richer life than his grandfather who actually read the *Atlantic Monthly?* It is not what you have available but what you take in that counts. And there are a great many adults as well as a great many children who don't seem to have time to take anything in.

Recent advertisements of a well-known encyclopedia make their pitch on the number of illustrations that this still valuable work contains and on the fact that it is "as interesting as a picture magazine." Perhaps it is. Perhaps it ought to be. But that isn't, and ought not to be, the most important thing about it. What kind of public buys an encyclopedia not because it is full, authoritative and accurate, but because it is "as interesting as a picture magazine"? It is more expensive than a picture magazine, and to buy it for the pictures is a waste of money. Is an encyclopedia wise to enter into such competition on such terms? Should a college compete with TV on approximately the same level? Or should colleges and encyclopedias alike assume that there still exists some audience for what only colleges and encyclopedias can give? Just how much should either know or care about certain techniques of communication?

Many of those who are advocating fuller use in education of "the mass communication media" seem ready to accept not only the limitations of those media but the very techniques which most outrageously pander to those who cannot or will not really attend to anything.

Suppose we listen for a moment to a spot commercial. Our advertiser knows that his hearers cannot be expected to listen for even thirty seconds while being told about the wonderful new toothpaste which, for the tenth time during the past decade, has "revolutionized tooth care," and which is now urged upon him "for your toothbrushing pleasure." Since thirty seconds is too long for the audience's span of attention, the message must be broken up thus: three seconds of instrumental music followed by some odd sound, preferably one never heard before; ten seconds of a jingle set to nervous music; then a male speaker who makes one of the large claims which Dr. Johnson already knew as the essence of advertising. He is interrupted by a female voice that gurgles, "Yes siree, that's true! That new element Abradabracan really did make my teeth sparkle!" Then the male announcer takes over again, and there is a reprise of the jingle.

Now take a step up to one of the semi-serious commercial interview programs. Stripped of the various announcements and commercials, it may last ten or possibly even twenty minutes. Yet the chances are that there will be at least two visiting celebrities as well as the interviewer. Move another step up to one of the longer, more ambitious entertainment programs. It may be studded with "names," but no one stays on much longer than is necessary to prove to the listener that he was actually there. Turn finally to a serious, noncommercial discussion program. The chances are three to one that it will present a "panel." But why? Is it primarily to promote an exchange of opinions, develop the sharpness of debate, et cetera? Perhaps. But isn't it also because no one speaker could hold the attention for that long? It takes at least two to tell about a toothpaste in thirty seconds; it takes quite a group of contrasting personalities to hold a "serious" audience for thirty minutes.

It seems to me (if you don't mind my saying so) that we have reached a point where "failure to communicate" is more often the result of a failure of attention—which no one seems to think we can do anything about—than of those imperfections in our techniques of communication which everybody seems determined to remedy, even if it means teaching patriotism through comic books, mathematics by moving pictures, and the principles of ethics as they can be expounded in a jingle set to music. Though most educated people seem to have agreed some years ago that the "commercial" is one of the ugliest and most humiliating phenomena of our civilization, some of these same people do not seem to realize how close they come to wanting to make what they call "popular education" one long commercial designed to sell science, culture and right-political thinking to people less and less willing to make any effort of attention.

Are what our school principals grandly call "audio-visual aids" usually anything more than concessions to the pupils' unwillingness to make that effort of attention necessary to read a text or listen to a teacher's exposition? Can anything be said in favor of most of them except that they are, at best, a surrender to the delusion shared by children and adults alike that the mechanical techniques of communication are interesting in themselves, no matter what (even if it happens to be genuine information) is being communicated? Are they not, at worst, merely devices for "catching" an attention which can never be given freely or held for long? How often can it be said that any movie, film strip, or recording teaches the so-called student—who has dwindled into a mere listener or viewer—more than could be learned in the same time with a little effort, or that the mechanical method has any virtue other than the fact that such effort is not required? Is there anything a picture can teach the pupil which is worth as much as that ability to read, which he stands in very great danger of losing?

What those who so earnestly discuss the problems of communication seem to forget is that its success depends upon the sensitivity of the listener as well as upon the efficiency of the transmitter. Or, as Shakespeare knew, the prosperity of a jest lies in the ear of him that hears it. What is the use of trying to make the jests simpler and simpler if the ears for which they are destined are to grow duller and duller? It is not a little learning, but a little capacity for learning, which is a dangerous thing.

At the moment, various educational institutions are making a new effort to use radio and, more especially, television for their own purposes. Perhaps, if it is not too late, they may succeed. But if they do succeed, it will be because they are more interested in what they have to communicate than in what it seems easily possible to communicate within the limitations the medium imposes. To those interested in the method itself there is nothing less suitable than a mere lecture. For purposes of true education it may very well be that there is nothing better. Fewer people will listen, but those who do will actually be getting what they might get at the college itself. On the other hand, try to use either radio or TV not as a mere mechanical means of diffusion, but as an institution which has developed its own methods, standards and techniques, and you will get a substitute for instruction as obviously inferior to what it has replaced, as most TV drama is inferior to the stage play and most radio concerts inferior to what could be heard in a concert hall.

Colleges are among the few surviving institutions that some- times put quality above quantity, that are not yet quite con- vinced that when you spread something wide that is all to the good, no matter how thinly you spread it. They may make use of the media of mass communication, but it is at least as likely that these media will make use of them. I am not at all sure that we ought to take the instruments of mass communication away from the advertisers. Perhaps we should let advertisers keep them. Perhaps we should have a little more faith in the media which are our own and which we know how to use.

—*American Scholar*
SUMMER, 1955

. . .   .

Making education more alluring

In the smallish but rapidly growing community on the out- skirts of which I live, there are an astonishing number of quite imposing public schools, and new ones are under construction almost continuously. The assumption that the cost of a building and the size of its playground are a trustworthy measure of an educational system's adequacy seems widely prevalent, but below the surface, disputes rage with violence in some communities. Should the pupil's self-confidence be protected by the rule that advancement from one grade to the next is obligatory, or should no one be graduated from grammar school unless he can write grammatically? Does "preparation for life" include some mastery of scholastic subjects, or is such mastery a mere incidental accomplishment to be acquired only by those who happen to desire it? Should every high-school student be automatically eligible for the state university, or has the university the right to enforce its own standards of minimum preparation?

All these are questions which have been debated at such length in so many places that it is not worthwhile to discuss them here. But there is a broader related question which gets less attention than it should: Do both compulsory schooling and free public education of all sorts have the unfortunate side effect of diminishing their apparent value and the eagerness to enjoy them? Would all sorts of cultural opportunities be more enthusiastically utilized if they were not so easy to get and if people were not so persistently urged and cajoled into accepting them?

Even children unusually fond of reading tend to assume that if they spend an afternoon over a book they are doing their parents a favor. Going to the movies or watching TV, however, is a valued privilege—perhaps just because they are not so warmly approved of. The majority of adults, being children of a larger growth, carry a good deal of the same attitude with them. They will pay substantially for anything which is plainly labeled "entertainment." But they expect libraries, most museums and schools to be free, concerts and lectures to be either free or priced far below what would seem normal for a play or prizefight.

The reasons for this strange state of mind are the same as those which give the child his attitude. "Society" seems very anxious that everybody should read books, go to lectures and even look at paintings. To a certain extent, therefore, we are doing society a favor when we do. It is hardly fair that we should pay for it out of our own pockets too. Such money as we have to spare should be reserved for entertainment which no one has been urging us to indulge ourselves in.

No, I am not advocating that public schools be abolished, that free libraries be closed, and that it cost as much to get into the Metropolitan Museum as it does to get into Madison Square Garden. I do suspect, though, that a substantial number of children would do better in school if attending it were a privilege, not a legal necessity; that quite a few adults and children would seek books more eagerly if they were not readily available in free libraries, many of which use posters, slogans, radio programs and other devices to persuade people to come and carry away books. I am ready to admit that the positive advantages of publicly sponsored cultural activities outweigh the side effects. But I would like to have a little attention devoted to the question of whether these side effects could be mitigated.

Educational psychologists have discussed at length a great many aspects of technique, some of them pretty farfetched. The possible bad effects of almost every educational policy or procedure have been anxiously examined. But I have never heard of one who ever took any account of a psychological fact of which even the most naïve layman is perfectly well aware—at least in connection with everything not cultural or educational: that we don't like to do what we are compelled to do, that we tend to resist at least a little bit what we are urged to do, and that things too easy to get are not very much valued.

Some say that God put the best fruit on a forbidden tree because He wanted to make sure that Adam and Eve would not fail to acquire the knowledge of good and evil. If He did, then

He was a better psychologist than we are. I would like to see a conference of educators devote a session to some such question as this: How can we get just a faint suggestion of the forbidden fruit to cling to learning of all kinds? How, also, without endangering the psychological health of the child, might we even let him suspect that his scholastic success will be determined by his ability and his industry? I have never heard of an athletic coach in a school or college who insisted upon advancing every player from the scrub team to the first. He doesn't seem to fear that the inferior players will suffer from a serious psychological trauma.   —*The New Leader*

JANUARY 17, 1955

.   .   .   .

Psychoanalyzing Alice

Most readers of *The Nation* must have seen in their daily paper some account of the adventures of Alice in the new wonderland of psychoanalysis. Many years ago, the late André Tridon undertook to explore the subconscious mind of the same little lady, but Tridon was something of a playboy, while Dr. Paul Schilder, research professor of psychiatry at New York University, was presumably in dead earnest when he warned his hearers at a recent meeting of the American Psychoanalytic Society against exposing children to the dangerous corruptions of Lewis Carroll. All of Carroll's ten brothers and sisters stammered; "this fact might have made the author unhappy"; and in any event his superficially pleasant fairy stories are the expression of "enormous anxiety."

According to the account of Dr. Schilder's speech printed in *The New York Times*, most of Alice's adventures are "calculated to fill her with anxieties" of a pernicious nature. "She feels separated from her feet, she is stuffed in and out of small holes, and she never knows from minute to minute whether she will be small or large. . . . There are severe deprivations in the sphere of food and drink. . . . The poem of the Walrus and the Carpenter is of an astonishing cruelty. The Lobster is cooked. Alice herself frightens the birds with tales of devourings. . . . The fear of being cut to pieces comes again and again into the foreground. The head of the Jabberwock is cut off. There is a continuous threat to the integrity of the body in general." Even worse, apparently, is the fact that Carroll plays fast and loose with language and the conception of time. The innocent child may never recover from the shock of "mimsey" or "wabe." "This is a world of cruelty, destruction, and annihilation. . . . One may be afraid that without the help of the adult the child may remain bewildered in it and may not find his way back to the world in which he can appreciate love relations, space, time, and words." Personally, I have never heard of a child who confessed to being dangerously terrified by *Alice,* or of an adult who attributed his downfall to a trauma received from the book in infancy. But no doubt that proves nothing. The fears inspired are subconscious also.

Now there is not, so it seems to me, any reason for doubting the large general assertion that Lewis Carroll had "complexes," or that his fantasy was to some extent at least an expression of them. Even if we leave such esoteric matters as "threats to the integrity of the body" in the hands of specialists like Dr. Schilder, it ought to be evident that his nonsense, like so much nonsense and so much wit, was a device by means of which his intelligence protested against various kinds of cant which his priggish and conventional temperament would not permit him to flout openly. I see nothing farfetched in the assumption that queens are absurd puppets in *Alice* because Carroll outwardly accepted the absurd legend of Victoria, or that the farce of the trial is largely unconscious satire of the pompous procedure of courts. Nor do I see how anyone can ponder the dilemma in which Alice is placed when she tries to choose between the Walrus and the Carpenter without perceiving a submerged La Rochefoucauld in the mild-mannered don who found his chief delight in photographing little girls. Alice, it will be remembered, thought she liked the weeping Carpenter best because he seemed a little sorry for having betrayed the oysters. But when she was told that it was he who had eaten the most and tried to shift her sympathy to the Walrus, she got a crushing retort— the Walrus had eaten as many as he could get. Only a man who had hidden somewhere in his soul a very cynical conception of human behavior could, I submit, have conceived that incident.

If we go that far we may also, I suppose, take it as a matter of course that Alice's fantastic adventures are none of them quite sane. But that is not the point. Why, of all people, should a psychoanalyst be shocked to find complexes in an artist, or afraid to have children ("polymorphically perverse" by Freudian premise) introduced at an early age to a literature the very secret of which is its successfully playful catharsis of certain all but universal obsessions? As for the satire and the cynicism which Dr. Schilder does not mention, I should say that any child is ready for it as soon as he is capable of recognizing its existence and that he is never too young to begin to laugh at those morbid fears which, the psychoanalyst himself is ready to assure us, he is never too young to feel.

In America the Philistine used to be above all else a moral man. The arts had nothing to fear from his fury except when he could discover that they were "impure." Nowadays he is more likely to discover in the most unexpected places some defiling trace of either "bourgeois prejudice" or "psychological abnormality," and to look askance upon anything that does not combine the obsession of a social worker with the "normality" of a boy scout. Some years ago when I first met a certain distinguished psychoanalyst I told him that I had observed in his many books what appeared to me to be a rather serious *non sequitur:* The first eight chapters were usually devoted to showing how abnormal most of the distinguished people of the world had been, while the last always concluded with a "Therefore, let us endeavor to be as normal as possible." I asked him if he did not suppose that a too thorough psychic housecleaning might be undesirable for those who aspired to be something more than merely "normal," and I received a remarkable if somewhat pompous reply. "I would not," he said, "like to give a categorical answer to that question, but I will say one thing. Dr. Freud and I are the only two prominent psychoanalysts who have never themselves been analyzed—and I think we have made the greatest contributions to the science."   —*The Nation*

JANUARY 30, 1937

. . .   .

Genius and neuroticism

Psychoanalysis is now one of the taken-for-granted tools of the biographer and critic, whether serious, middlebrow, or even low. It seems to me, nevertheless, that one fundamental question has never been satisfactorily answered. Exactly what is the relation between a writer's complexes, obsessions or neuroses, and his genius? An ancient gag used to run, "Photographers don't have to be crazy, but it helps." Are we compelled to say the same thing about artists?

Back in the late 'teens and early twenties when Freudianism first became a fad, an affirmative answer to this question was often implied or even given. The argument ran something like this: Closely examined, most great men turn out to have been at least a little bit queer; therefore, genius is necessarily queer. In fact, queerness and genius are the same thing. The artist's gift is the neurosis he exploits.

With shame I must confess that I was guilty of seeming to accept this absurdity in the first book I published (not counting a doctoral thesis). It was a biographical-critical study of Edgar Allan Poe, who was, among other things, a perfect sitting duck for the amateur psychoanalyst. And I chose him for that very reason. I laid great stress on his sadistic fantasies, his obsessive concern with death and dissolution, and with what seemed to be in his own life a desperate determination not to become sexually involved with any of the women whom he professed to love; also on his "Philosophy of Composition," which maintained, despite conclusive evidence to the contrary, that he deliberately chose macabre effects, which were in fact the only ones he could produce.

I am still ready to argue that the theory I evolved concerning Poe's personality is consistent. I still believe also that the "*frisson nouveau*" which Baudelaire discovered and celebrated in Poe is a neurotic shiver. But in my enthusiasm I went far beyond this. I said, or at least strongly implied, that Poe's neuroses *were* his genius and that, if we could get all the facts, such was usually the case with great imaginative writers. They are always neurotic. Unfortunately I neglected to ask why, if all geniuses are neurotic, all neurotics are not geniuses.

What I am asking now is simply this: Granted the extravagance of any mere equating of genius with mental disorder, what actually is the relation between them, especially in extreme cases like that of Poe where at least much of the unique character of the work obviously is profoundly influenced by these disorders? That great art is essentially sane, I am convinced. But it often is the product of minds which seem to be more, rather than less, disturbed than those of ordinary men.

Perhaps the reason why the contemporary critic seems rather disinclined to face this question is simply that he (and all of us) have come to believe that what used to be called "abnormalities" are part of the psychic makeup of nearly everybody, and that the genius sometimes seems more abnormal than most men simply because he gives us a better opportunity to see his mind at work. But even so, I think my question is not completely answered. To take again the extreme case of Poe, it seems certain enough that if he had been less neurotic his work would have been quite different from what it is. Would it have been better—or would it have been less original, less interesting? What would be the answer to the same question if it were asked about some other writer much less obviously "unhealthy"?

Shortly after my own indiscretion was published, I received a letter from Dr. Beatrice Hinckle, translator of Jung and then (next at least to the Freudian, A. A. Brill) the best-known practicing psychoanalyst. She approved my diagnosis and said she had met a number of cases where the pattern was the same as Poe's. But she added a vehement protest. The neurotic genius was a genius in spite of his neuroses, not because of them. Mental illness was never anything but a handicap. This seemed to me then, and still does, as much an overstatement as my own opposite thesis. Poe would certainly not have written what he did if he had been "normal." It's there that the problem arises.

The whole question comes to my mind again because I have just been reading several reviews of the new fourteen-hundred-page edition of Beethoven's letters, many of which had never before been accessible and which, so the reviewers all seem to agree, are painful reading for those who admire Beethoven the man, no less than the music he wrote.

Here is a case far more complicated than that of Poe; the relation between the man and his abnormalities is far less simple. "Liegeia" and "The Fall of the House of Usher" (to say nothing of such astonishing productions as "Berenice" and "The Pit and the Pendulum") obviously bear so close a relation to their author's own neurotic fancies that the one seems a direct expression of the other. Though Poe has given artistic form to his obsessions, they and the stories they inspired are qualitatively almost identical. But whatever the "Ninth Symphony" may express, no one would be likely to call it obviously "sick" in the sense that Poe's writing usually is. On the basis of the works alone, the understandable image of Beethoven has been of a heroic figure struggling manfully against a cruel fate and transmuting his agony sometimes into tragedy, sometimes into a joy that transcends the suffering over which an abounding vitality triumphs.

This is the way in which he has usually been pictured by admirers who assumed (and wanted to assume) that the man and the music were identical. That element of stormy protest which is so different from anything to be read into the cheerful Haydn, or even into the plaintive discontent sometimes audible in Mozart, is sometimes explained in terms of a changed sociopolitical atmosphere. Haydn accepted the position of the musician as merely that of one of the higher servants of the nobility; Mozart, for all his nascent vision of democracy and brotherhood, was too gentle to be moved to anything approaching rage. But Beethoven was the child of a revolutionary era. He was less contented than either of his two great predecessors because he could not, like them, accept the status quo. Hence he spoke out violently with the voice of the genuinely committed rebel.

But whatever truth there may be in this picture, it is not the whole truth. The letters are said to confirm abundantly what some of the more recent biographers have maintained—namely, that the man whose utterances are so "noble" was in his own character and personality a sort of distressing parody of his musical utterances. It is not merely that he was quarrelsome, pettish, and given to throwing dishes at the cook. His relations with his scamp of a nephew—conventionally pictured as proof of his loving patience—actually included a dishonorable attempt to separate this nephew from his mother and to become in effect a mother himself. The lonely titan, aspiring toward fulfillment in the love of the several women he worshipped but was denied, seems, not entirely unlike Poe, to have seen to it himself that any promising relationship was broken off. All this, together with the grotesque possessiveness of his attitude toward the incorrigible nephew, invite the psychoanalyst to explore some pretty dark corridors. But even that is not all. Though it may seem odd to speak of a truly great artist as suffering delusions of grandeur, Beethoven seems to have been close to paranoid in both his sense of his own greatness and in what amounts to delusions of persecution. The fact remains that what were mere delusions in the artist are somehow transformed into convincing realities in the works which he created. Listening to them we believe what he believed about himself; reading the letters we still see a relationship between the man and his work. But it is by no means an identity.

Perhaps the best of the reviews I have read (that by Albert Goldman in *The New Leader*) puts it thus:

"No one who has read the Sterbas' book [*Beethoven and his Nephew*] will ever forget the terrible image it contains of the great Beethoven living constantly in a kind of emotional squalor, his imagination periodically inflamed by fantasies of a paranoidic order in which he figures as the noble and innocent victim of base and evil persecutors. And no one who knows Beethoven's music could fail to connect these dreadful distortions of reality with the mythopoetic content of his compositions—allowing, of course, for the idealization of fantasy in art."

This describes, perhaps as well as possible, what seems actually to have happened. But it does not answer the question (possibly unanswerable) how anything so improbable *could* have happened. Some critics dodge the question by insisting that in the case of any work of art one should always fix one's exclusive attention on the work itself; that all "background," whether biographical, historical, sociological or whatnot, is both irrelevant and misleading; that it not only tends to explain away rather than explain, but may also make it actually impossible to take the work in question at face value—which is the only way in which a work of art can profitably be taken. We must not let Beethoven the man get between us and the works. It is only they that we have any business concerning ourselves with. Too much biography and there is danger that we will hear in the "Ninth Symphony" only the paranoid ragings (which are not actually there) and miss the grandiose triumph of a joyously achieved victory over cruel fate (which very decidedly *is* there).

Such an attitude defines one approach to criticism and possibly the most fruitful one. But if—as seems to be the case—we must remove Beethoven from the category of the normal and healthy artist where we once pigeonholed him along with Haydn and Handel, then we must put him among the neurotics and raise again the question with which we started: What is the relationship between works of art and the neurotic afflictions of their creators?

What is the power, which Beethoven had and Poe did not have, of using but transcending delusions of grandeur and of persecution? Would this question lead to the conclusion (not too helpful, I admit) that it is wrong to say either that neurotic abnormality is genius or that, as Dr. Hinckle protested, it is merely a disability over which the artist triumphs? Would it enable us to grant that most geniuses are neurotic and at the same time explain why all neurotics are not geniuses? Genius, in this conception, does not consist in the abnormality but in the power to transform it, and Beethoven was a far greater genius than Poe just because he could make a sane image out of what was in itself not entirely sane. Such an explanation is perhaps no explanation at all. It leaves "genius" as mysterious as ever. But it does enable us to recognize the troublesome fact that great works are often created by men less great than they, while, at the same time, it removes the temptation to fall into the error of believing that art itself is not "sane" and "healthy."

Those who read Havelock Ellis in pre-Freudian days will remember that he was concerned with our problem in a rather old-fashioned way at a time when the "abnormality" of genius was most likely to be attributed to physical causes. Max Nordau in his once-famous, but now mostly unread *Degeneracy* argued that most modern literature was indeed neurotic and therefore simply bad art. But others were far from ready to accept this simple solution. Did the febrile excitement characteristic of the tubercular, contribute to the glow of Keats's poetry? Did a moderate colony of *Spirechaeta pallida* act as a stimulus in Swift, Neitzsche and Beethoven, all of whom were suspected of playing host to it? Were geniuses most likely to appear in families some members of which were mentally subnormal, and did this suggest that the creative spirit was more closely related to feeblemindedness than to insanity?

Any theory that the artist is in some sense sick (note, by the way, that Thomas Mann seems to have at least toyed seriously with this thesis) raises a practical problem that becomes more pressing as "planning" is more and more talked of and is coming to include artificial insemination in the interests of eugenics, as Sir Julian Huxley has only recently proposed. One of Havelock Ellis's theories might suggest that syphilis should not be stamped out completely; some psychological theories, that all neuroses should not be nipped in the bud. Perhaps Beethoven would never have written any of his major works if he had been psychoanalyzed in time.

For the present, most of these are, fortunately, only theoretical questions. But there is a related and very practical one. No age before ours has been so determined to give children "all the advantages" of a good education and a happy, normal childhood. Yet the lives of great men all (or at least in numerous instances) remind us that they frequently had none of these good things, and that overcoming difficulties was a stimulus, not a deterrent. Either God or Nature seems to work in a mysterious way.Whom the Lord [or Mother Nature] loveth he chasteneth.

Who is to take the responsibility for planning these difficulties and attempting, for the benefit of humanity at large, to thrust painful greatness upon some of those about to be born? Had I been asked, as I was reaching the age of discretion, whether or not I wanted to be Beethoven at the price he paid, I am afraid I might have said: "No, thank you. I'd rather be 'normal' or even just 'average.'" But think what the world might have lost had Beethoven been given that choice.

—*Saturday Review*
JANUARY 19, 1963

. . .　. . .　. . .

No hobbies for children

Did you know that hobbyhorses are now hard to come by? I don't mean the sort that you and I ride but the old-fashioned kind that have a head at one end of a stick and are very suitable for use either in the nursery or in the back yard.

Perhaps the fact is not very important in itself. But the reason why the toy shops no longer stock the horses, is. That reason—as given by S.H., *The New Yorker*'s shopper who keeps an eye out for the little amenities of life—is simply this: The play-school consultants have decided that a hobbyhorse "does not develop the group spirit." The youthful rider is likely to gallop off on an adventure of his own. He may even do something which he happens to want to do instead of adjusting himself to the common denominator of his group. And you know what that can lead to.

Here is a straw in the wind if there ever was one, and the warm winds (sometimes called hot air) which blow lustily around the child psychologists are full of straws. Against anything which suggests nonconformity, introversion, or even a desire to be alone with oneself now and then, they are dead set. "Too much reading"—and an awful little is too much—comes under the same head. The little boy I once saw astride a hobbyhorse *and* with a book in his hand was obviously perilously close to the category "delinquent." Nowadays even "self-expression" is routinized. My young friends tell me that if you don't want to finger-paint when the others do, that is just too bad. "Do what you want" is the rule. But you jolly well better want what you ought to want, and what you *ought* to want is what the others "at your age level" are supposed to want.

We Americans were once supposed to be admirable individualists, but it now seems to be taken for granted in some quarters that we oughtn't to be. If the school counselors—to say nothing of most of the peace-of-mind boys who ladle out advice to so-called adults—have their way, the rugged sort of individualism is not the only sort we will soon have got rid of.

Lives of great men may remind us that quite a few of them started going their own way while young. But then they didn't go to a nursery school where there were experts who knew what was good for them. And so they grew up so "unadjusted" that some of them were abnormal to the point of being geniuses. For all anybody knows, the whole unfortunate business may have begun with a hobbyhorse which did not "develop the group spirit."

"Look here, Wolfgang Amadeus, why don't you go out and

play baseball with the other boys of your age level instead of moping over that old harpsichord all day?"

This, it seems to me, is something which McCarthy might well look into. Too much conformity, too much group spirit, is exactly what a Communist never thinks anybody has too much of. The individual who has notions of his own, and doesn't like even what's good for him if he isn't consulted about it, is precisely the man who is hardest to sell on the idea of a democracy which is *for* the people without being *by* them. He doesn't care much for organized leisure; he doesn't march gladly in parades; and he doesn't always believe what he is told. Totalitarianisms of the right or the left are alike in fostering the most extroverted societies the world has ever known and they aim at producing the most "adjusted" individuals that it is possible to imagine—so adjusted indeed that they really believe that whatever is, is right, if only it is "for the group."

Most proponents of more and better adjustment at all age levels are like most Americans in thinking that they are strongly anti-Communist. In fact, and again like most Americans, they tend to be a little too jittery on the subject. But they do not always look under the right beds. As a matter of fact they have a strong tendency to a curious sort of schizophrenia: They hate Communism but they are strongly predisposed to admire many traits and many tendencies which, more consistently, the totalitarians also admire. Sometimes what they seem really to want is the kind of man and the kind of society which stop just short of the totalitarian. They may have no faith in Communism. But they have lost their faith in a good many things which would make Communism impossible.

I am not talking about "creeping socialism" or any of the other bugbears often raised in conservative quarters. I am not talking about anything which can be discounted as a defense of great economic inequality. In fact, I am not talking about anything economic at all. I am talking about character and temperament; about the kind of human beings we seem to want to produce; and about the methods we rely on in our effort to produce them.

We put more and more faith in "conditioning"—even, paradoxically, in "conditioning" as a method of creating "free" individuals. But we have almost as little faith in actual freedom, moral or intellectual, as the Communists themselves.

Some of our liberal leaders have an unfortunate habit of falling in with the current formulas without, perhaps, really accepting them. Mayor Joseph Clark of Philadelphia has an excellent record as a liberal. Yet he recently permitted himself to justify his hope for the future by remarking that in our schools and universities "Youth is *conditioned* [italics mine] to respond to a liberal program of orderly policing of society by Government, subject to the popular will, in the interests of social justice."

Now I am not objecting to "the orderly policing of society." But I *am* objecting to the fact that Mayor Clark permitted himself to speak as though he didn't pin his faith on education in any sense of that term compatible with a democratic society, but upon exactly what the totalitarians rely on. I repeat that I do not believe that he really accepts this philosophy. Probably what he meant to say was that school and college students are being— or should be—led to *think* about policing, about what kind and what extent of policing is necessary or desirable. But what he says is that they are being "conditioned" to respond to a liberal program. Yet he might be willing to agree with me that any program ceases to be "liberal" at the very moment when it becomes acceptable because we have been "conditioned to accept it."

Or take the case of a college textbook on psychology which it has recently been my dubious privilege to examine. It is called *Psychology and Life* and it describes itself as intended to "meet the needs of students without sacrificing scientific rigor." Though it runs to more than five hundred pages, only one of them is devoted to a subject called "morals" and this is the definition offered as meeting "the needs of students without sacrificing scientific rigor": "To behave morally is to behave in the way that society approves."

Is there anything better calculated to prepare a student to accept the morality of the totalitarians, or to weaken the impression likely to be made upon him by any protests against their violations of what we believe to be decent, than the conviction that moral conduct is "nothing but" what a particular society approves of? Sending Jews to the gas chamber, or forcing political opponents to confess treason, is, by this definition, obviously "moral conduct" just insofar as it is approved of by the society in which the things occur. And if the authors of that textbook believe, as they probably do, that they are wholeheartedly anti-Communist, then they are victims of the prevalent schizophrenia. On what basis can they possibly be "opposed" to any form of government or any kind of society if every society is just as "moral" as any other if it is equally acceptable to those who have been conditioned to accept it? And who, I wonder, is most likely to believe that something more than "group approval" is involved in the definition of right and wrong, of good and evil? Is it the child who has sometimes ridden away on a hobbyhorse or the child who has never done anything which did not "develop the group spirit"?

A good deal has been said about the weakness of all merely "anti" programs. We have been wisely told that we ought to promise more than the Communists promise—possibly, even, actually give more than they have ever merely promised—in the way of material welfare. And so perhaps we should. But isn't that at best a sort of "me-tooism?" Can anyone who is not himself so fanatically Marxian as to insist that nothing except material welfare counts for anything at all, possibly refuse to grant that it would be well if we could say also that the mental and spiritual world of democracy is preferable to that of any totalitarianism?

But in what way is it really better, unless it is because a certain amount of individuality, a certain degree of tolerance for the aberrant individual, perhaps even some conviction that "moral" can mean a bit more than "what a given society approves of" are better than the absence of them all? And how can we maintain that they are, if we act as though we distrust and wish to discourage every manifestation of individuality?

When the great "modern" architect Le Corbusier was criticized a few years ago because the Radiant City (which he was permitted to build in Marseilles) provided little privacy for its inhabitants and reeked with the odor of cooking, he replied: "What's wrong with the smell of food if the cooking is good? No privacy? My apartments are for young people who have a different ethic from the French or American bourgeoisie. Everybody will be in the saloon together or everybody will go to bed." That is perhaps the "new ethic" which we are trying to inculcate in the little totalitarian monsters which some of the play schools would like to turn out—without an idea, an impulse, or an interest of their own. It is the ethic of those who have "the group spirit," and nothing else but. Is it not also an ethic which would find it not too difficult to "adjust" to one of the totalitarian societies?

When we foster that ethic we justify the suspicion that our so-called opposition to the totalitarian philosophy is only a certain lack of consistency, an unwillingness to accept the logic of our own premises; perhaps merely a disinclination to move quite so fast as some others do. But will we really win if the most we have to say of our enemies is only that "they go too fast and too far"? What's the use of talking about the rights of the individual unless you at least tolerate individuals who are individualistic enough to want the right to choose? Or is the only right which a so-called individual really has, merely the right to want to do, and to think what everybody else does? And are we so afraid that he might develop some genuine individuality that we don't dare trust him to gallop as far from "the group" as the other side of the room?

Perhaps the best answer to totalitarian promises of material welfare is a chicken in every pot. But if we want to encourage a distaste for the atmosphere of totalitarian society, then maybe our first slogan should be: "*Two* hobbyhorses in every nursery."

—*Saturday Review*

JULY 24, 1954

· · · · · · · · · ·

English as she is spoken

English is a wonderful language, and in some respects, American English may be even better. No other is more precise and, at the same time, more flexible or more responsive to new needs, and that is because no other has more successfully struck a balance between stability and change. Pedants and purists are always trying to freeze it into a dead language like "good" Latin; the semiliterate are always tending to reduce it to an incoherent jargon only roughly comprehensible even to members within a small group. Each tendency has kept the other in check. If the nineteenth-century schoolmarm had had her way, it would be genteel and prissy; if the illiterate had had their way, it would be a barbarous jargon.

A publication like the *Saturday Review* tries to maintain the balance between pedantry and mere colloquialism. So, for that matter, do most publications addressed to the widest possible public. They are persistently more "correct" than their readers. On the other hand, radio and TV have leaned hard in the other direction and (to take a notorious case) have actually *taught* people to say "like a cigarette should." But the real enemies of minimum decent standards are now the members of a large and influential section of "educators," who have abandoned all faith in education.

They began by revolting against schoolmarm prissiness and then went on to talk about "acceptable English" as opposed to "literary English." That was only a beginning. Consider for example the following from a recent textbook called *The High School Curriculum:*

[English teachers] have suddenly discovered that many is the boy who says "I ain't got no" because his parents say it, his friends say it, and his community says it. Furthermore, these parents see no reason why they should change or why their sons should change. As the work of linguists has increasingly shown, there is no real absolute in language usage. Communication is the end result, and that language is good which facilitates communication and is inconspicuous.

To be inconspicuous, the language must conform to group conventions, and group conventions in some communities are often at variance with the conventions of others and of those of the English teacher. . . .

Though the tradition of presenting young people with the literary classics that "all cultured people are supposed to know" and trying to make them conform to a single absolute standard in their usage of language still maintains a strong grip on the English programs of the country today, individual schools and the national organizations of English teachers have been proposing different kinds of objectives from those stated above.

In other words, "national organizations of English teachers" now believe if their expensive schools take in a boy whose parents and associates say "Ain't got no" he should keep right on saying it. It will prevent him from being "conspicuous" and, as is now well known, it is just as bad to be conspicuously better than the average as it is to be worse.

He will "communicate" no doubt, but with whom? Not, for instance, with the group for whom the author of the textbook writes, since he himself sometimes talks gobbledegook but not usually illiterate grammar and syntax. Obviously, the answer is that he will "communicate" with the uneducated group into which he was born. Obviously, also, he is not to be encouraged to "communicate" with any other. "Social mobility" is supposed to be one of the glories of our civilization. What becomes of it if the school undertakes to confine every pupil to his own social level?

Elsewhere in the same book the author discusses at length the "social dangers" of special opportunities for gifted students. To group them with some regard to ability is to promote "a sort of intellectual caste system." It is, so he says, "undemocratic." Presumably, therefore, democracy implies not that everyone should be encouraged to rise to the highest intellectual, social and economic level he is capable of reaching, but that everyone should be told to stay right where it has pleased God to put him and to believe that no language, no literature and no level of intellectual development is better than any other.

If the purpose of classes in English is not to encourage pupils to speak and write in some fashion different from that which they bring into the classroom with them, then what are these classrooms for? You don't need to go to school to use language in the way your parents and your "group" use it.

American English successfully resisted the efforts of the Victorian schoolmarm to stifle its vitality. Whether it will be equally successful in maintaining itself as even reasonably articulate in the face of the contemporary educators' "democracy" is another question.　　　　　　　　　　　　　　　　　—*Saturday Review*

J U L Y 4, 1959

. . . .

Scholarship by proxy

There is a story (true, I hope) that back in the days when Lord Russell was only plain "Mister," he returned a very personal questionnaire from a professor at Western Reserve University with the following notation: "If this is a specimen of Western reserve, God protect me from Western impudence."

No one has ever shown much interest in my private life, not even in that now most publicized of privacies, my sex habits. To date I have never told anybody whether or not I have achieved "a mature and satisfactory sexual adjustment," and if I should ever be asked, I would probably reply that I am not sure I want what sounds a bit on the dull side.

On the other hand, I have been pestered for years by both private and form letters from so-called "researchers," one of whom sent me a list of two hundred American actors of the past and present with the modest request that I "arrange them in the order of my estimate of their relative artistry." About the same time I was visited by a so-called student from a New York institution of higher learning who asked me, with poised notebook, my "relation to contemporary literature," and then, after I had mumbled something-or-other, informed me with considerable enthusiasm that a collection of such opinions was to constitute his thesis, that it would be nice if I would sign his notes, and that perhaps when the collection was complete *The Nation* would like to buy it for publication. Shortly before that I had received from a Ph.D. candidate in a Middlewestern university, a request for a list of the most significant modern plays of all countries, accompanied by the charming admission that, as he was writing a thesis on the subject, he would like to be told which works it would be most worth his while to read.

I was, I am proud to boast, less appalled by the calm effrontery of the demand and the apparent assumption that I would be only too glad to spend a few weeks compiling such a list, than I was by the naïveté of the mind that could take it for granted that the proper way to investigate the significance of the modern drama was to read only the plays that someone else had decided to be significant.

About that time I wrote in *The Nation* an article called "Scholarship by Proxy," but it seems to have had little effect. The habit of writing doctoral theses that consist of a collection of the opinions and "evaluations" of other people seems to be growing, and I am afraid that my usual reply ("Why don't you do a little evaluating on your own?") produces no effect other than to convince the recipients that I am unwilling to assist the struggling scholar. "You say," I sometimes add, "that my eminence in some field or other will add great value to your work. I can assure you that this eminence (which of course I would be the last to question) was not achieved by asking other people their opinions concerning the subjects upon which I undertook to pontificate."

The method seems to be seeping down into the high school and even the elementary school. Fairly frequently I get carefully scrawled letters on ruled paper from children who usually confess that their teachers have put them up to it. They pose questions it would take a volume to answer. Typical are those that say something like: "I am told that you have written about Eugene O'Neill. Will you please give me your estimate of this writer and his importance." One (and I am not making this up) read: "I am told that you have criticized contemporary society. Please tell me what your ideas on this subject are."

There is now another development. Not long ago I said goodbye to the last (and I mean last, not latest) of five Tucson High School students, sent by their instructors in journalism to interview me. Before the last of them had had a chance to open her mouth I challenged her by asking if she knew anything about me or had ever read a line that I had written. "Well," she replied, "I have the impression that you are a sculptor."

This young lady got a lecture to the effect that an interviewer was required to know something about the person interviewed. I know that this is a whopping lie. In fact, I had only recently been questioned over the telephone by a reporter who called to inquire about something I had said publicly concerning Dostoevski and who began with, "By the way, who *is* Dostoevski?" Still, he probably never took journalism in high school, and those who have, should have been instructed that they can hardly ask intelligent questions unless they know at least something about the occupation of the person they are interviewing.

—*American Scholar*
AUTUMN, 1963

. . .   .

How to taste a book

When I was a beginning instructor in Columbia College, the common complaint was that freshmen couldn't write. Now it seems to be that they can't read either. And thus we dispose of Progress in Education.

In all seriousness, there is probably this much in it: As the number of technically illiterate people diminishes, the *proportion* of the technically literate who can read in the fullest sense of the word, has decreased. The proportion, that is to say, of those who are both capable of and willing to make the effort of attention required if one is to follow anything more complicated than the simplest statement, is smaller than it was when it was so difficult to get schooling that only those who really wanted it were likely to get it at all. Moreover, the present tendency of our society is to accept the fact of minimum literacy and to devise "visual aids" and simplified texts instead of trying to teach real reading to more than the select few.

For at least one hundred years—witness J. A. Etzler, with whom Thoreau was momentarily taken—prophets have been telling us that the Age of Universal Leisure was just around the corner and that, when it arrived, everybody was going to devote his life to art, science and philosophy. Actually, of course, most people really do have more leisure than they used to have, and they may be about to get still more. Just how much of their increased leisure they will spend as prophesied, is an open question, but I am convinced that it would be worthwhile for the schools they are compelled to attend to make a greater effort to teach as many of them as possible to do more than skim over newspapers and leaf through picture magazines.

Moreover—and on the basis of a few experiments I made many years ago—I believe that, within limits, it can be done, even as late as the college years. The process is rather hard on the dignified teacher who likes to think that he should concern himself with less elementary matters. If the assignment is, say, Arnold's *Culture and Anarchy*, this man wants to "supply the historical background," discuss the relation of Arnold to T. S. Eliot, or whatnot. But if he will stoop to taking a few sentences one by one, and ask a student just what the devil Arnold seems to be trying to say, he may be saddened to discover that said student hasn't the foggiest idea and doesn't really believe that Arnold is saying anything at all. But then our teacher may also be gladdened to learn that when the same student has had his nose rubbed into the text, he quite often begins to appreciate that from Arnold's wordy puzzles it really is possible to extract an intelligible meaning.

On their own initiative, a certain number of people, have always taught themselves to read in this sense. But the majority still do not. The process of learning is too strenuous for the lazy; they must be encouraged (often also forced) to the trough. But if they ever do learn to read (either of their own accord or not), then most of "the problem of leisure" is solved already.

Suppose, now, that a given individual really does know how to read. How shall he practice that skill to get the maximum of pleasure and profit out of it? One answer, I think, is that once the skill has been adequately developed he may trust himself to read what he likes and in the way he likes. But perhaps that statement will stand a little amplification.

Mortimer Adler, in his well-known *How to Read a Book*, describes a process which might better be called "How to Study a Book." He recommends much underlining, reviewing, etc. That is the way to learn to read and also the way in which certain books should be read by everybody. But not all reading should be study of that kind. Bacon's chestnut, "Some books are to be tasted, others to be swallowed," is still the most important thing ever said on the subject. As a matter of fact, more of this chestnut should be included: "Some books are to be read only in parts; others to be read but not curiously; and some few to be read wholly with diligence and attention. Some books also may be read by deputy, and extracts made of them by others."

Which books are to be read in which way is not a question to be answered once and for all. It depends not only upon the book but also upon the reader, and even upon the moment. It is a question of what we want to get out of a particular book, and no man who has never read any book, except carefully and all the way through, can possibly have time to acquire that acquaintance with the prodigious number of books every intelligent man should, for his own satisfaction, know something about. So far as the great works of the imagination are concerned, the best advice is often that of Samuel Johnson:

Let him that is yet unacquainted with the powers of Shakespeare . . . read every play from the first scene to the last, with utter negligence of all his commentators. . . . Let him read on through brightness and obscurity; . . . let him preserve his comprehension of the dialogue and his interest in the fable. And when the pleasures of novelty have ceased, let him attempt exactness, and read the commentators.

But this, of course, assumes that the reader already knows how to read. If he does not, then the first thing is to learn, or to be taught. And that may require—as the elements of most skills do—labor. The danger always is that in an Age of Leisure no one will want to labor, although without labor there can be no proper leisure.   —*Saturday Review*

SEPTEMBER 21, 1957

. . . .

The infatuation with the primitive

A few weeks ago I stood with a small group of other tourists at the mouth of the cave-sanctuary near Lascaux in southern France. Presently we were admitted through the iron doors which now close it. We walked down a concrete ramp and by the light of electric bulbs gazed at the polychrome zoo painted on the uneven walls, one picture sometimes superimposed upon an older one. The pictures date from the last ice age when glaciers covered most of Europe. The pictures are also, according to the pronouncements of many art historians, greatly superior to those executed by other races thousands of years later; so superior indeed that anthropologists were for a time reluctant to believe they could be as old as they actually are. And not only were the artists more accomplished than those who succeeded them in prehistoric times; their feeling, again according to the art historians, was more "modern" than that of the academicians of the eighteenth and nineteenth centuries. They were closer to Picasso than to Landseer.

At least, "modern" is what we now call it. But I could not help thinking that it was lucky for the reputation of these anonymous painters that their work was first discovered in 1940 instead of in, say, 1840. Had it come to light in the nineteenth century it would have excited anthropologists, but not critics of art. Ruskin for example would have seen in it no more than the faint beginnings of artistic ability, for the adjective "primitive" had at that time connotations entirely derogatory; whereas today it implies, as often as not, admiration and praise. "Primitive," said our grandfathers, "and therefore barbarous." "Primitive," say we, "and therefore beautiful."

Has anyone ever suggested that this preference today for what used to be called barbarism may have chilling implications? After all, it is one thing to say that "progress" in the arts is not, as in technology, obvious. It is another to accept as simple fact that in certain fundamental respects art regressed until only a generation ago, when it found again in "the modern" a true role. Could it mean that we are looking back in some far from desirable way; that we admire primitive art, not because it is like us, but because we are becoming more like it; that we are determined, not to go forward along a true road newly found, but back and back and back until we are wholly barbarous ourselves? In any case, all the recent enthusiasm for the primitive surely represents a revolution too startling to be merely accepted without further inquiry.

In painting and sculpture we seek our inspiration either in the very ancient, or among those living peoples who, like the African tribes, have remained in a primitive state. We admire and imitate the masks and other carvings of peoples who not too long ago would have been called hardly human. This taste for the primitive, either archaic or surviving, until recently would have seemed sheer perversity.

Yet if it actually is perverse, the perversity is, to at least a minor degree, widely shared even by those of us not wholly committed to the modern primitive. Though much of the latter does not please me greatly, I am—to take a very mild example—more moved by Giotto than by Raphael, which is usual enough today, but even a hundred years ago would have been generally regarded as merely silly. Nor is there any reasonable doubt that a great part of our best art—even though some of us are not entirely comfortable with it—does look backward for its inspiration.

As for modern literature, it is certainly not classical, and though some would say its tone is barbarous, its form does not, like that of the plastic arts, obviously suggest the primitive. Joyce's *Ulysses* does not immediately remind us either of the epic of Gilgamesh, or of some creation-myth still current in some primitive tribe—at least not as directly as a Modigliani portrait will now always remind me of a flattened statue of a Cycladic mother goddess (carved about 2000 B.C.) which I happened to see in Athens shortly after my visit to the Lascaux caves.

But if literature seems headed down some road which is neither that of the civilized nor the primitive, some of the other arts definitely look back to the barbarous. Jazz, which at least many take so seriously that they call it the only "modern" musical idiom, is mostly derived from savage Africa, and in its own way much "serious" modern music also reemphasizes elements once very prominent in the primitive. The graceful tinkle of sixteenth-century lute music is certainly far more "civilized" than the aggressively primitive "Rites of Spring," often taken as a landmark in the development of the modern idiom.

Consider also the case of the drum—presumably the most ancient of musical instruments, just as rhythm is presumably the most ancient of musical elements. As far back as the emergence of the classical orchestra, it played a role of increasing prominence. It first began to crash out in Beethoven and Berlioz, and in the late Romantics, it thundered.

Nevertheless, it was not until very recently that "percussive" came to be an adjective with usually favorable connotations. The piano was played "percussively," and composers either emphasized this quality in instruments not purely percussive or, more and more frequently, wrote music for whole groups of percussive instruments. As for popular music, of the more "advanced" sort, many of the best-selling phonograph records are now labeled only "percussive" this or "percussive" that. In the early eighteenth century, John Byron invented the terms "tweedle-dum" and "tweedle-dee" to ridicule what he thought absurd distinctions between one composer and another. Today it is more likely to be the difference between "bum-bum-bum" and "bum-*bum*-de-bum."

Is it possible that atonality is not a new freedom but merely a relapse into some pre-Greek period before any kind of mode of tonality had been discovered? And why has architecture, too, moved away from Greek grace and Roman dignity toward the great monolithic mass which suggests the Inca and the Aztec rather than either the classical or, for that matter, the Gothic? What in general is the origin of this feeling of kinship with the primitive, and why has its meaning been so seldom questioned? Perhaps it has, in writings with which I am not familiar, but I can recall only such casual references as that in Aldous Huxley's *Along the Road,* and the frontal attack made upon modernism some forty years ago by Wyndham Lewis in his queer (and queerly interesting) *Time and Western Man.*

Wrote Huxley:

Barbarism has entered popular music from two sources—from the music of barbarous people . . . and from serious music which has drawn upon barbarism for its inspiration. . . . Composers seem to forget that we are, in spite of everything, and though appearances may be against us, tolerably civilized. They overwhelm us not merely with Russian and Negroid noises, but with Celtic caterwaulings on the black notes, with dismal Spanish wailings, punctuated by the rattle of castanets and the clashing harmonies of the guitar.

Wyndham Lewis's thesis was that our eclectic culture—which is so proud of its appreciation of the art of various epochs, of a cosmopolitanism which permits us to turn with ease from Michelangelo to Hiroshige and from Palestrina to Rimski-Korsakov—actually means that we have no more than a hurried, tourist's familiarity with anything and that what he called "time-trotting" is as absurd as the globe-trotting some of us indulge in with so little profit. Some time after his book was published, Lewis asked me to meet him in Regent's Park where we would not be overheard by spies. He invited me to join him in a counter-conspiracy against all those who were engaged in propagating the primitive in art and thought—D. H. Lawrence and Sherwood Anderson being prominent among the villains—in order to undermine the basis of civilized society.

It seemed pretty absurd at the time, and the "conspiracy" is so typical of the fanatic (which Lewis certainly was) that it reminds me of an acquaintance who was unshakably convinced that the Kinsey Report had been subsidized by the Communist party in order to undermine the moral character of Americans and thus soften them up for conquest. But I am not quite so sure as I was then that there does not actually exist a drift in a somewhat disturbing direction, all the more alarming just because there lies behind it something much harder to deal with than a Machiavellian conspiracy.

To designate the feeling experienced by the American of another generation when he made contact with European culture, Edmund Wilson borrowed from Melville the phrase "shock of recognition." Is, then, the excitement with which moderns view the primitive a shock of recognition, an ominous sign that a barbarism that was, has made contact with a barbarism to be?

There are, of course, various other possible and less sensational interpretations, even if one rejects the simplest and most current, which is that Picasso is primitive or even prehistoric, rather than renaissance or classical, simply because all of what used to be called civilized art moved further and further away from its true aims and methods. We had learned all that could be learned from it and found that it had led us astray. We then sought true inspiration elsewhere.

At the other extreme from this prevalent interpretation, one might say that the more extravagant aspects of primitivism are no more than a fashion destined to pass because fashion always is, as Oscar Wilde said, "a form of ugliness so intolerable that we have to change it every six months." For this interpretation there are plenty of historic parallels. The aesthete in *Patience* objected to an artistic effort on the ground that "it isn't medieval; it isn't *even* Japanese." One of his present-day successors might similarly object that "it isn't prehistoric; it isn't even African." The nineteenth century did learn something from both the medieval and the Japanese, but it absorbed what it could learn and then returned to its own proper business, which was not to be completely either.

Somewhere between these two possible interpretations—the one which sees primitivism in the arts as self-justifying, and the other which dismisses it as a fad exaggerating a modicum of truth into a stupendous revelation—there is a third, which would call it a kind of neurotic syndrome, understandable but unhealthy and the consequence of the prevalent, not unjustifiable alienation of the intellectual and the artist from the world in which he finds himself. Technology has created a physical environment which he finds uncongenial, and modern thought has created a mental and spiritual environment no less repugnant to him. He rejects the civilized and the rational because he feels that both have betrayed him. He goes off in search of D. H. Lawrence's "dark gods" and discovers that the plumed serpent acknowledges important truths to which Socrates was as blind as Herbert Spencer, or as any of our own exponents of the rational and the utilitarian.

Under remotely similar circumstances the eighteenth century, weary of its tame virtues, invented the Noble Savage (not as artist, because it never admired except in literature any painting, sculpture or architecture more ancient than the so-called "Gothic") as an embodiment of benevolence and stern, simple virtue. The actual savage has long been known not to have resembled even remotely that innocent paragon; so far as I know, it is as artist only that the primitive man is now admired. He was, we admit, ignorant, cruel, dirty, and bedeviled by senseless taboos. But he created works of art unrivaled in modern times except by those who have sat humbly at his feet—as he still lives in Africa, in Polynesia and elsewhere, or as his ghost lingers in the caves at Lascaux.

Some years ago Gerald Heard propounded the ingenious theory that civilization, though always developing, rises along a spiral rather than on a simple upward curve. At different times it looks back with sympathetic understanding at this or that earlier stage of its development—now sensing a kinship with Greece and Rome, now with the Gothic, now with the Byzantine as it spirals over them. As a highly speculative explanation of a fact which might otherwise seem to have only the meaningless meaning of erratic fashion, this theory has its attractiveness. It is also somewhat reassuring. But I cannot help wondering whether this spiral may not be descending rather than rising and if, therefore, the "eternal recurrence" may be not so much an actual recurrence as a repassing from above.

I hope that my own fears are unfounded. But developments in the arts have often been paralleled in other fields and as I contemplate political, social and military events rather than those merely artistic and cultural, I find them suggesting the gloomier alternative. Hitler, Mussolini and Stalin represent phenomena which, before World War I, we believed to have been banished from the Western world forever. Now we know that they and their like are something the possibility of which will always face us. The anthropologists' pet theory, that customs are the only basis of a moral code, is very up-to-date, but it is also a return to the concept of the tribal god whose rules and regulations are valid only for his chosen people.

This Sunday morning, just before I wrote these lines, my radio, tuned to Tucson's FM station, played an hour of music built around the beat of drums and the thumps of bass viol strings. As I listened to it—and not without pleasure as I am somewhat ashamed to confess—I couldn't help wondering whether I was merely paying reasonable tribute to the dark gods whom it behooves us still to recognize; whether I was a time-trotting tourist in Wyndham Lewis's sense; or whether I was sliding down the spiral toward an African prehistory far more remote than even the caves at Lascaux, and was indeed experiencing a shock of recognition.   —*Saturday Review*
SEPTEMBER 29, 1962

. . .   .

Beauty and function

One of the most gratifying privileges of the essayist is that of expressing opinions on subjects he doesn't know much about. I hope I don't usually push that privilege as far as I intend to push it this time, but I am going to say that I find most modern architecture unpleasing or worse.

To begin more modestly than I propose to continue, I will say first of all that I have long been puzzled by the cult of functionalism when carried to the point where it despises as superficial ornament everything not serving the immediate purpose of shelter, comfort, convenience and so forth. Has any architecture that took itself seriously as art as well as utility ever before our time, been in this sense purely functional? I grant in a pinch that Gothic ornamentation like that atop the old Woolworth Building seems somewhat inappropriate, but I prefer even that to the glass box or the unadorned monolith. Even if the beautiful is always functional (which I rather doubt) it does not follow that whatever is efficiently functional must be beautiful. I have looked at least casually at many buildings, including Thai temples, Gothic cathedrals and Renaissance palaces, and except for a few fortresses and prisons I cannot remember a single impressive example anywhere of a beautiful building that was purely functional in its design.

Perhaps this last qualification should be itself somewhat qualified. Two years ago I saw for the first time the remains of the Crusaders' castle at Sidon. I presume that its builders aimed at security from attack first of all, and second at such meager comfort as could be made compatible with their primary purpose. Yet to me it was evident from the very considerable remains that however functional the building may have been it is not merely monolithic, and I do not believe that it seems to me dignified, even beautiful, merely because I have projected upon it romantic notions. Whatever the Lever Building in New York may be, it will never make an interesting ruin.

Like all medieval castles, the fortress at Sidon cannot have been a very comfortable place to live in. Given the choice, I should probably choose to take up residence in the dreariest modern apartment house rather than in the most picturesque medieval castle. But either one of two things must be true. Either there is some fundamental incompatibility between aesthetic effect and comfort as we understand it, or we have not found the way of making them compatible.

In the English magazine *The Countryman* I once saw photographs of three bridges across the same modest stream—one medieval, one seventeenth-century and one quite recent. Judged purely by the eye, the first was the most pleasing, although the simplest in its lines; the second, although deliberately ornamented, was less so. The third was not to me pleasing at all, however useful it may be. The same comparisons could be made over and over again where ancient and modern stand in close proximity. Modern gains in efficiency seem to entail almost always a loss of something that pleases the eye. I cannot help wondering whether or not this must inevitably be so. That modern bridge would get me across the stream; but unless I wanted to get across I would prefer not to have it there at all. And the same thing might be said of the freeways, underpasses and cloverleaves of our modern roads.

Functional and utilitarian are meant to carry different connotations, but I wonder if in actual fact the obsession with the functional is not merely an aspect of our all but exclusive concern with the utilitarian. Are not our architects merely making a virtue out of their inability to conceive any ornamentation that would be suitable to what they construct, and denying that beauty is its own excuse for being, just because they don't know how to create anything beautiful?

Of course, the blight is spreading. Not very long ago I had another look at London and Paris, and while neither has entirely lost its character, both are disfigured here and there by characteristic skyscraper apartment and office buildings. Even those who do not like them offer "necessity, the tyrant's plea." There are tentative plans to remake Paris almost completely, and it looks as though the time might not be far distant when to go from any city to any other would be merely to move from one group of glass boxes to another.

Even in the United States travel can still be rewarding outside cities and towns. But only a few of the metropolises still have individual character (New York and San Francisco, for example) and there is little to be gained from the lesser big cities, which are nothing except merely lesser. As to towns, they are more and more alike. There are no such things as local products. To travel from one to another is hardly to be aware that one has moved at all, and it certainly doesn't do much to "broaden the mind."

As long as vast hordes of people are concentrated in a small area, I suppose the mere overwhelming size of our buildings is inevitable, but this also strikes me as unfortunate; and necessity does not make them any less regrettable. Many things have conspired to make modern man seem little, and he must be overawed as he crawls antlike at the base of mountainous piles of steel, glass and stone. I have, in the past, accused him of both hubris and loss of self-respect, but the paradox is not unresolvable. He suffers from delusions of grandeur when he thinks of what he can do and from the sense of helpless futility when he thinks of what he is—or has been persuaded to believe himself to be. The engineer, the technologist, is proud; the philosopher, despairing. Gigantic structures dwarf man as an individual, especially when, as in the case of the great cubbyholed structures he so commonly spends his nights in, they represent no aspiration other than that toward the wealth and power of a community of midgets. Cathedral spires pointed upward toward an imagined Heaven; skyscrapers reach up into an empty sky.

Considerations such as these suggest only the beginning of my doubts and objections, for it seems to me that the most admired modern architecture, however purely functional it is thought to be, also expresses something and makes a comment on life, society, politics and ethics even beyond what I have just been discussing. I presume (and I confess again that my acquaintance with the recent history of architecture is very slight) that what distresses me most are the theories and intentions that came out of Germany between wars. Certain much-admired buildings are often called "monolithic," and I think it not fantastic to remark that this adjective, also in an approving sense, is very popular among totalitarians. Buildings that adopt or try to adopt the style seem to express the political ideal of both Nazi Germany and Communist Russia. They express the totalitarian idea in a variety of ways, including the scorn of anything that suggests either the joyful or the affectionate. They deny that beauty can ever be its own excuse for being, and they also, of course, remind the individual that he counts for nothing in contrast with the state—whose monolithic power is symbolized by the grim monolithic structures.

It is no wonder that on such structures any ornament in the style either of Greece or the Middle Ages seems inappropriate—not because it violates the principles of functionalism, but because such ornamentation suggests what the monolithic structure denies, namely, that the human spirit properly aspires toward joy and faith and freedom. Pose in a niche one of the huge heads from Easter Island and it would seem quite suitable—a reinforcement rather than an irrelevance in relation to the message of the building itself. Hence, the functionalist, when he does concede sculpture or bas-relief as an accessory, chooses something that imitates either pre-Columbian America or primitive Africa.

Such ornamentation is all too appropriate because it says what the whole building says: Man is small and helpless, the victim of evolving technology, if not of the dark, inscrutable gods of superstition.

Certainly if modern architecture, in this functional, monolithic style, does not imply anything about the ideals and opinions and intentions of our society, then it is unique in this respect. Surely there is some connection between the open-air grace of the Greek temple and the Greeks' aspiration toward a mental and emotional life that sought (and believed it could achieve) inner peace and a way of being at home in the world. No less certainly the Gothic expressed both the medieval sense of the darkness of this life and the promise of another one, while at the same time its ornaments found a place for both pious legends embodying the dark superstitions that haunted it and, in sly grotesqueries and obscenities, a satyric protest against excessive holiness. The this-worldly Renaissance believed in splendor and built splendid buildings at the height of its vigor, even if that splendor later degenerated into luxury and mere frippery.

What style of the past does the monolithic and functional seem most to resemble? Not that of Greece (or even early Rome), not that of the Middle Ages, and not that of the Renaissance. But it does remind me quite forcibly of certain non-European remains built to express societies untouched by Periclean Greece, thirteenth-century France or sixteenth-century Rome. The pyramids of Egypt and the pyramids of Yucatan are monolithic and functional—even though we do not believe in the reality of the functions they were supposed to perform. And from the very little I know about the Mayas and the Aztecs (who have been called the Nazis of pre-Columbian America) their societies also, I'd say, were totalitarian, so little convinced of the importance of the individual man that ten thousand were offered as human sacrifices at the dedication of a single temple to angry, rather than loving, gods. I cannot help wondering if the monolithic structures of our own cities may not do their bit toward persuading us that the death of ten million is not too large a price to pay for the ultimate peaceful uses of atomic fission. We also have our angry gods to be placated.

I know it will be said by some that architecture, like literature and all the other arts, expresses the mind, spirit and social condition of the time in which it was created. Hence, if the most characteristic buildings of today express function in a civilization that minimizes the individual and does not really believe in the possibility of freedom or beauty, then that is as it must and should be. I, on the contrary, have always believed that art not only expresses but also helps create the civilization in which it flowers, and I think it would be well if poets as well as architects would cease to rest content with expressing the dismal world in which they live (or think they live) and begin looking for a way out. I am convinced that jazz, for instance, not only expresses contemporary man's jitters but helps to make him jittery.

If the Gothic style for churches is merely imitation and pastiche, it is at least an imitation of something appropriate. I see nothing appropriate in the "modernist" churches that have begun to dot even Tucson—fantastic structures all with acute-angle roofs pointing in various surprising directions and intended to stress the tensile strength of modern materials rather than any faith in the spiritual realities that churches are supposed to be concerned with. They are beginning to give our city a Disneyland look, and at best they are only cute.

Most "modernistic" structures are as derivative (although not as purely imitative) as fake Gothic, and if we must draw inspiration from the past, I would prefer that we choose some past that is part of, rather than alien to, the mainstream of European culture which runs from Greece through the Renaissance on down almost to our own day.　　　　*—American Scholar*
WINTER, 1963-1964

. . .　　. . .　　. . .

Picasso versus Picasso

I am, I hope, not insensitive to any of the arts. I have spent happy hours in museums and I listen with pleasure to Bach, Mozart and Beethoven. But I have more confidence in my ability to understand what is said in words than I have in my understanding of anything which dispenses with them. Such opinions as I hold concerning modern music or modern painting are as tentative as those I have expressed in these pages about modern architecture.

Nevertheless, as I said then, it is one of the privileges of the essayist to hold forth on subjects he doesn't know much about. Because he does not pretend to any expertness those who know better than he what he is talking about, need be no more than mildly exasperated. His obtuseness and his misconceptions may give valuable hints to those who would set him right. If he didn't expose them, his would-be mentors wouldn't know so well just what the misconceptions are and how they arose. An honest philistinism is more likely to be teachable than the conscious or unconscious hypocrisy of those who admire whatever they are told they should.

In the case of modern painting, the very fact that I can take pleasure in some of the works of yesterday's avant-garde, but little in that of my own day, suggests even to me that I may be merely the victim of a cultural lag. But there is no use in pretending that I am delighted by what delights me not, and I find that much serious criticism of the most recent painting is no help. Those who write it are talking over my head; they just don't start far enough back.

For instance, I read in *The Nation* that what a certain painter I had never heard of had accomplished during the war might be summarized as "an unstructured painterliness—neither expressionist nor surrealist in character, and therefore out of keeping with available alternatives." Shortly after the war "he followed through with an intimation of the picture façade as its own reason for being, preferring a unitary sensation, by being irregularly blotted out by masses that kept on pushing at, and disappearing past, the perimeters. Executed on a vastness of scale quite unprecedented in easel painting (which he was in any event attacking), these paintings sidestep drawing and the illusion of spatial recession without ever giving the impression of evasiveness. The result was a sense of the picture surface— now extraordinarily flattened—as a kind of wall whereby con- stricted elements no longer had any exclusive formal relation- ship with one another."

When I read things like that my first impulse is to exclaim, "If that young man expresses himself in terms too deep for me. . . ." But then I realize the possibility that the words do say something to those whose visual perceptions are better trained than mine. Nonetheless I am at best like a second-grader still struggling with the multiplication table, who has wandered into a seminar at the Institute for Advanced Studies.

When, therefore, I happened to see an advertisement of the Book-of-the-Month Club which explains how the Metropolitan Museum of Art had been persuaded to prepare a twelve-part seminar on art which could be subscribed to for "only $60," I had the feeling that this might very well be getting down to my level. The advertisement was adorned by reproductions of two contrasting pictures: one of the Metropolitan's own "Storm" (or "Paul and Virginia") by Pierre Cot and the other a swirling abstraction. "Which of these is a good painting?" demanded the headline. My immediate answer was, "neither." And I was not too much discouraged by the fact that I was pretty sure this was not the right answer.

I think I know at least some of the reasons why "Storm" is not one of the great masterpieces—even though some sup- posedly competent expert must have once paid a whopping price for it. On the other hand, I had not the slightest idea why the abstraction was good or even just not nearly as bad as the sup- posedly horrid example facing it.

I confess that I did not subscribe to the seminars. But I did borrow a set from an acquaintance who had done so and I must report that I did understand what the Metropolitan people were saying, as I had not understood *The Nation* critic. But I was not by any means wholly convinced. Many years ago I read Roger Fry on "Significant Form" and the terrible-tempered Albert Barnes on "The Art in Paintings." I found nothing in the Metropolitan seminar which was not this doctrine somewhat updated, and I was no more convinced than I had been by the earlier critics that what they were talking about was indeed the only thing in painting worth talking about, or that significant form by itself (if that is possible) was as good as, if not better than, classical paintings in which equally significant form had been imposed upon subject matters themselves interesting or moving in one way or another. In that problem lies the real crux of the matter. Granted that "composition," "significant form," or whatever you want to call it is a *sine qua non* of great painting, is it also the one thing necessary? Is it *the* art in painting or only *an* art in painting? My mentors from the Metropolitan are by no means fanatical. They never themselves insist that subject matter or the communication of an emotion in connection with it are irrelevant in judging a picture. But unless my memory fails me, they never really face the question of the extent to which the painter who abandons the suggestion of a subject matter is to that extent lesser than one who at the same time tells a story, reveals a character, or communicates an attitude.

The hopeful student is confronted at the very beginning with what seems to me this unanswered question. He is warned that "Whistler's Mother" was called by the artist "Arrangement in Grey and Black"—and let that be a lesson to you. You may think that your enjoyment of the picture derives from its appealing likeness of the author's mother and from sentimental associations with old age" but "the *real* [italics in the original] subject is something else . . . We may ask whether the picture would be just as effective if we omitted the subject altogether . . . the abstract field of contemporary painting argues that subject matter is only something that gets in the way. It confuses the issue—the issue being pure expression by means of color, texture, line and shape existing in their own right and representing nothing at all."

Throughout the course stress is laid again and again on the comparison between two seemingly very different pictures said to be similar, though I don't think they are ever said to be identical. For instance, Vermeer's "The Artist and His Studio" is compared with Picasso's "The Studio." "Picasso," I am told, "had sacrificed . . . the interest inherent in the objects comprising the picture . . . the fascination and variety of natural textures . . . the harmonies of flowing light, the satisfaction of building solid forms out of light and shape. What has he gained? . . . Complete freedom to manipulate the forms of his picture. . . . The abstractionist would argue that the enjoyment of a picture like Picasso's 'The Studio' is more intense because it is purer than the enjoyment we take in Vermeer."

Is "pure" the right adjective? Is it purer or merely thinner? To me the answer is quite plain and the same as that given to the proponents of pure poetry who argued that poetry is essentially only sound, so that the most beautiful single line in French literature is Racine's "La fille de Minos et de Pasiphäe," not because the genealogy of Phaedra was interesting but just because the sound of the words is delightful. The sound of "O frabjous day! Calloh! Callay" is also delightful but I don't think it as good as "No spring, nor summer beauty hath such grace, / As I have seen in one autumnal face."

It is all very well to say that two pictures as different as those by Vermeer and Picasso are somewhat similar in composition, and that to this extent they produce a somewhat similar effect. But to say that the total experience of the two is not vastly different is, so it seems to me, pure nonsense and so is the statement that the two experiences are equally rich.

The author of the seminar session just quoted seems himself to think so when he writes, "But we also contend that a painting is a projection of the personality of the man who painted it, and a statement of the philosophy of the age that produced it."

If that is true, then the painter who claims to be "painting nothing but paint" is either a very deficient painter or is, perhaps, without knowing it, projecting his personality and making a statement of a philosophy of the age that produced it. He is doing that just as truly and just as inevitably as Whistler was doing more than an arrangement in black and gray. And if that also is true, then the way to understand what is most meaningful and significant in any modern painting is to ask what it is that the painter, consciously or not, is revealing about his personality and about the age which finds his philosophy and his personality congenial.

At least that much seems often to be admitted by admiring critics of certain painters not fully abstract, but who seem to be interested primarily in pure form. Take for instance the case of Ferdinand Leger and his reduction of the whole visible world, including human beings, to what looks like mechanical drawings. Are they examples of pure form, meaning nothing but themselves? Certainly they are not always so considered by admirers. When the painter died in 1955 the distinguished critic André Chastel wrote:

From 1910 on, his views of cities with smoke like zinc, his country scenes inspired as if by a woodchopper, his still lifes made as if of metal, clearly showed what always remained his inspiration: the maximum hardening of a world of objects, which he made firmer and more articulate than they are in reality. Sacrifice of color and nuance was total and line was defined with severity and a well-meaning aggressiveness, projecting his violent, cold Norman temperament. This revolution he consecrated himself to seemed rather simple—the exaltation of the machine age, which, after 1920 dominated the western world.

To me it seems equally plain that even those who profess to paint nothing but paint are in fact doing a great deal more, because they would not find anything of the sort to be the real aim of painting unless they had certain attitudes towards nature, towards society, and towards man. What that attitude is, cannot, I think, be very well defined without recourse to two words that I hate to use because they have become so fashionable and are so loosely tossed about. What these painters are expressing is the alienation of the existentialist. They no longer represent anything in the external world, because they no longer believe that the world which exists outside of man in any way shares or supports human aspirations and values or has any meaning for him. They are determined, like the existential moralist, to go it alone. They do not believe that there is anything inherently beautiful in nature, just as the existentialist moralizer refuses to believe that there is any suggestion of moral values in the external universe. The great literature and painting of the past have almost invariably been founded upon assumptions the exact opposite of these. They expressed man's attempt to find an appropriate beauty and meaning in an external world from which he was not alienated, because he believed that both his aesthetic and his moral sense corresponded to something outside himself.

Salvador Dali (whom, in general, I do not greatly admire) once made the remark that Picasso's greatness consisted in the fact that he had destroyed one by one all the historical styles of painting. I am not sure that there is not something in that remark; and if there is, then it suggests that in many important respects Picasso is much like the workers in several branches of literature whose aim is to destroy the novel with the anti-novel, the theater with the anti-theater, and philosophy by philosophies which consist, like logical positivism and linguistic analysis, in a refusal to philosophize. They are all determined, as the surrealist André Breton once said he was, to "wring the neck of literature."

Having now convinced myself of all these things, I will crawl farther out on a limb and confess that I have often wondered if the new styles created by modern painters—pointillism, cubism, surrealism, and the mechanism of Leger (to say nothing of op and pop) ought not be regarded as gimmicks rather than natural styles. And to my own great astonishment I have discovered that Picasso himself believes, or did once believe, exactly that.

The luxurious French monthly *Jardin des Arts* published (March, 1964) a long and laudatory article on Picasso, in the course of which it cited "a text of Picasso on himself" which had been reproduced at various times, but most recently in a periodical called *Le Spectacle du Monde* (November, 1962). I translate as follows:

When I was young I was possessed by the religion of great art. But, as the years passed, I realized that art as one conceived it up to the end of the 1880's was, from then on, dying, condemned, and finished and that the pretended artistic activity of today, despite all its superabundance, was nothing but a manifestation of its agony. . . . Despite appearances our contemporaries have given their heart to the machine, to scientific discovery, to wealth, to the control of natural forces, and of the world. . . . From that moment when art became no longer the food of the superior, the artist was able to exteriorize his talent in various sorts of experiments, in new formulae, in all kinds of caprices and fantasies, and in all the varieties of intellectual charlatanism. . . .

As for me, from cubism on I have satisfied these gentlemen (rich people who are looking for something extravagant) and the critics also with all the many bizarre notions which have come into my head and the less they understood the more they admired them. . . . Today, as you know, I am famous and rich. But when I am alone with my soul, I haven't the courage to consider myself as an artist.

In the great and ancient sense of that word, Greco, Titian, Rembrandt and Goya were great painters. I am only the entertainer of a public which understands its age.

Chirico is another modern painter who has said something very much like this. But enough of quotations. And to me it seems that Picasso said all that I have been trying to say—namely, that a picture somehow involved with the world of reality outside man is more valuable than one which has nothing to say about anything except the painter himself. What he calls painters "in the great and ancient sense of that word" were able to be such only because they were not alienated existentialists. —*American Scholar*

SPRING, 1967

. . .   .

Maybe it would be better not to know

Robert Southey once said that the two greatest mysteries in this world or out of it were: 1) the Holy Trinity and 2) what makes a book sell. Moreover (if my somewhat blurred recollection of this wise remark is correct), he then went on to express the opinion that God simply doesn't want men to know how the second question might be answered. I agree with God for what is possibly His reason: Many books that don't sell nevertheless deserve publication.

Some publishers would, on the other hand, like to be able to answer the question with that scientific accuracy now so much more in fashion than God's will. Some of them, no doubt, actually do have traffic with those practitioners of a dubious black art who predict on the basis of their samplings, just what the public acceptance of a new product will be. But it is just as well that even now they do not depend entirely upon any rating system analogous to that which the television tycoons submit to so abjectly. Had they done so in the past, *Moby Dick* for example would never have been published, since even the least dependable of opinion polls would have determined that the public acceptance of it would be nearly nil. Some publishers still rely upon a thing as unscientific as a hunch, and a few may even be reckless enough to accept a book just because they believe it to be a good one.

Not long ago there was a good deal of criticism of that most awesome of horses' mouths, the Nielsen Company, on the ground that its estimates were not accurate enough, largely because the samples were too small. My own objection to all the opinion polls and rating systems is not that they are not good enough, but that they are too reliable. However imperfect they may be, they tell those who use them more than they ought to know—from the standpoint of the public good, if not from that of those engaged in the exploitation of human weaknesses.

Too often they are encouraged to base their appeals on that low estimate of human nature and public taste which the polls seem usually to encourage. Considering many of the published results of various surveys, one is tempted to say that if what they seem to demonstrate is true, then it would be better if the truth were not known—for the same reason that ignorance of which books will sell is one reason why works above, rather than below, the average of tastes are not fewer than they are.

Consider for example the UP account of a report issued by NBC for the purpose of encouraging a certain type of very profitable advertiser to sponsor broadcasts in color. Here are some of the characteristics which are alleged to distinguish the average owner of a color set from those still making do in black and white. They tend to use "aerosol products over bottle versions of the same product; movie film rather than still-picture film; electric toothbrushes, and so forth" . . . They are "especially heavy users of shoe polish in spray cans . . . below average in the use of paste shoe polish." They are said to buy more new automobiles than the average citizen and they "have a tendency to buy products with a 'status symbol' aura . . . Have a high degree of interest in buying wall-to-wall carpeting . . . Are much more likely to use Scotch and Bourbon rather than Rye," which last is described as a "non-status" whiskey.

All of this sounds like parody but it isn't. What it actually is, may be well summed up in the words of Rick Du Brow, author of the UP dispatch from which the quotations were taken. "These statistics reflect . . . the most bourgeois sort of taste, the kind that indicates persons who worship status and material success, who try with all their might to keep up with the Joneses, who will settle for quick, mechanical products instead of the real item if they are easier to use."

Learning these facts, or alleged facts, can have only one result. It will encourage advertisers to intensify still further the practice of addressing almost exclusively just the sort of persons described and to use every effort to cultivate the same characteristics in those who have not yet developed them. Insofar as their audience is susceptible to appeals, subtle or blatant, to materialism, status-seeking, and a tendency to equate the good life with the gadget-cluttered one, to just that extent will the prevalence of these tendencies be increased. Ignorance may not be bliss but in cases like this it would (assuming the validity of the conclusions drawn from NBC's survey) be more wholesome than the truth.

Television has relied upon "ratings" more exclusively than any other quasi-artistic or intellectual enterprise (and that includes even the movies) ever has. And no other ever occupied so large a proportion of the public's time.

According to the *TV Guide*—said to have a larger circulation than that of any other weekly publication—the American home has a TV set in operation on an average of six hours a day, and whatever may be said about the alleged increase in the amount of reading done in the United States it is obvious that a household that spends six hours a day on television can hardly spare much time for any other leisure activity. At least sixty-five minutes of these six hours (still on the authority of *TV Guide*) are given over to commercial "messages," which means ninety separate pitches per day, 630 per week, or more than 32,000 per year. That such a bombardment would be stultifying no matter how honest and legitimate the appeals might be is evident, but in actual practice it becomes a sort of brainwashing when the messages are dominated by the determination to develop or accentuate the kind of vulgarity said to be most characteristic of the people who are sufficiently devoted to television to want to own the newest devices.

The point of *TV Guide*'s article is to raise the question, "Does Advertising Make You Buy?" It asks whether or not the advertisers who pay approximately two and a half billion dollars for those 32,000 messages "get their money's worth," and it admits that "oddly enough, nobody knows."

Some of us may hope that they don't and that their wiles were ineffectual. But the real point is something different. Not only the sixty-five minutes a day, but also nearly all the material offered during the remaining five hours was chosen almost exclusively upon the basis of the accurate or inaccurate reports of the actual state of the mass audience. A few more watchers report on one program than on another, and the slightly less popular program goes off to be replaced by one which, so it is hoped, will win a higher rating—and in neither the case of the program junked nor in that of the substitute is there any question raised concerning its intellectual, aesthetic, or moral level.

Marxism notwithstanding, the profit motive is both legitimate and useful, as long as it is not *the only motive*. Or to put it somewhat differently, the writer, the publisher, and the television company may quite properly want their respective enterprises to pay. In fact, the last two always, and the first very often, would simply have to turn to some other activity if theirs didn't. And on the whole, I think this economic pressure less unfortunate in its effects than the kind of bureaucratic pressure which sooner or later almost inevitably goes along with government-sponsored artistic projects—though I see no reason why such government-sponsored projects should not exist alongside those who do have to make money. But to say this is not to say that the writer, the publisher, or even the TV official need assume that the *only* question he will ever ask is not merely Will this be profitable? but Will this be more profitable than anything else I might write, publish, or produce?

It is discouraging to observe that the newest "media of communication" are the ones which come nearest to accepting the profit motive as the *only* motive, and the great difference between the television networks and the publishers is simply the fact that many of the latter do take some pride in being responsible for things which they themselves, as well as the public, will admire. The networks, on the other hand, and despite occasional boasts about this or that sacrifice in the public interest, come much closer in their admitted policies (as well as in practice) to saying simply: "We consider it our business to ask nothing except whether this or that program will win the largest possible audience and therefore most please the most profitable advertiser."

Here, for example, is a pronouncement from Mr. Julius Barnathan, now ABC vice president in charge of Broadcasting of ABC Operations and Engineering (as quoted in *Newsweek*, November 11, 1963): "What do you mean by 'caliber programs'? I'll tell you what it means to me. It means a guy sitting there in front of a TV with a hero sandwich in his hand and a glass of beer, saying 'That's a program I'd like to watch.' "

Remember that there is no free competition in commercial television. The national government has granted a few monopolies which it protects. No one would raise more agonized protest than these favored few if the government did not protect them —though of course they are horrified by any suggestion of a government intervention with free enterprise or free expression —except when such interference protects *their* monopoly.

Since the government does guarantee these fabulously profitable monopolies, would it be an unwarranted interference with what is actually a monopoly, not a business engaged in free competition, if in exchange for its protection the government demanded (on pain of revocation) that the monopoly should not operate on the assumption that the profit motive is the only motive and that the only criterion to be used in preparing programs is simply, "Will this or that item produce a larger profit than any other?"

After all, there is a sizable body of citizens with at least minority rights in the airways who are not completely typified by "a guy with a hero sandwich in his hand and a glass of beer." (Incidentally, I don't know what a hero sandwich is though I have seen them advertised in the windows of lunch counters; but if they are anything like the "Poor Boy Sandwich" which I did once meet, I don't think I would want to eat one while watching any program whatsoever.)

There is, moreover, a regulation which has often been proposed and which a government agency might impose without exercising any actual editorial control. It would certainly relieve the pressure of the advertisers and it opens no possible objections other than the fact that it might well make broadcasting somewhat less profitable—while leaving it quite profitable enough. That often-proposed regulation is simply the requirement that the advertiser should sponsor the network's program as a whole, not any one hour or half-hour of its choice.

Utopia? Perhaps—now that the sponsor has become so thoroughly accustomed to dictating and the broadcaster to accepting his dictation so supinely. But if this is true it is simply another example of the way in which the newest commercial enterprises tend to be those which are the most crassly opportunist, and the most abjectly determined to play only in terms of what they believe to be the lowest common denominator—which, alas, the all-too-good rating systems enable them to do, with what they regard as an adequate degree of accuracy.

Can you imagine a newspaper or a magazine run in this way—with each story, article or editorial individually sponsored by the advertiser and not printed until such a sponsor could be found? Some magazines and some newspapers are accused (justly, no doubt) of being subservient, to some extent, to their advertisers. But no publication of any kind, above the very lowest level, has ever operated as the broadcasting industry does. Even its news broadcasts and public service programs are likely to be sponsored if only a sponsor can be found for them. But what newspaper would dare to interrupt both its news stories and editorials with the all-too-familiar "and now a word from . . ."? Would any be willing either to so annoy its readers or so advertise the fact that its advertisers are everywhere in control?

No one ever went broke by underestimating the taste of the American public, said H. L. Mencken, and he has been often quoted. If that is true, then it would be better for all of us if we didn't know just how low it actually is. If we didn't know, some chief of programming might overestimate the public taste enough to raise the level of his network a bit, and give his audience something a little better than what it would choose.

Moreover, if there is anything in education, he might even raise the level of the public taste an equal amount. None of the major networks is so near bankruptcy that it is in the public interest to have it do whatever will bring the very largest possible profits. And if ignorance of the true state of public taste would persuade them to give it something better than what it now gets, that would be all to the good.

Classical scholars have held different opinions concerning the question cynics sometime ask, "Would the audience of fifth-century Athens really have liked less-exalted dramas better than the works of Aeschylus, Sophocles, *et al.*" Audiences certainly did flock to them but they had no choice, except insofar as the satyr plays, which followed the tragedies, were an alternate. And even these, though they certainly were less exalted in sentiment, are still considered to have been in their own way no less admirable as literature. So far as I know, the question was never asked in Athens door-to-door.

But even if, as some scholars argue, the very exceptional audience of Periclean Athens would have turned up its nose at the works offered by anyone who believed what Mencken said was true of them, the fact remains that a few centuries later the Roman emperors decided to try to keep the populus docile by giving it precisely what it wanted. The drama then gave way to the musical vaudeville and, finally, to gladiatorial and wild-beast combat.

John Stuart Mill (certainly not one to look with favor upon government interference with either business enterprise or free speech) once wrote, in an essay not sufficiently pondered by those who urge us to have unbounded faith in "the people," and who identify "the people" primarily with those who like to settle down in front of a TV set with a hero sandwich and a glass of beer:

Capacity for the nobler feelings is in most cases a very tender plant, easily killed, not only by hostile influences, but by mere want of sustenance; and in the majority of young persons it speedily dies away if the occupations to which their position in life has devoted them, are not capable of keeping their higher capacity in exercise. Men lose their high aspirations as they lose their intellectual tastes, because they have not time or opportunity for indulging them; and they addict themselves to inferior pleasures, not because they deliberately prefer them, but because they are either the only ones to which they have access, or the only ones which they are any longer capable of enjoying.

In any case, it is certain that if those who cater to the lowest possible public taste insist upon eagerly following that taste downward, then it will continue to descend as a sort of Gresham's law begins to operate, and the worse drives out the less bad.

Perhaps Mencken's statement was true in the past tense he employed; perhaps no one ever *has* gone broke by underestimating the taste of the American public. But that doesn't prove that it can't be done or that nobody ever will go broke for exactly that reason. Given the attitudes and the methods of the television tycoons, they may succeed in descending below the level of all but an ultimately unprofitable minority.

And at least there is one hopeful sign. The Nielsen Company itself recently made public a very encouraging discovery. This year one million fewer people were watching television than were watching it a year ago. This is certainly not because the level of programs has been raised above their level. It may just possibly mean that Mencken's pronouncement will have to be updated. Even the man with the hero sandwich and the glass of beer is beginning to get bored.   —*Saturday Review*

MAY 17, 1966

. . .   .

The highbrows are not always right

Two articles in two magazines have drawn my attention to the existence of a Literary Establishment described as rather more distinct than anything of the sort that existed in my day. Members of this Establishment are said to be primarily concerned with talking to (and impressing) one another, although they also have great influence upon that section of intellectual youth that dutifully likes what it is told it ought to like and turns up its nose on cue from the noses of Establishment members. Some, at least, of the members seem tacitly, and sometimes explicitly, to accept a criterion of literary merit that seems to me highly unreliable: "Wide popularity is *prima facie* evidence of inferior quality." To me it seems that "Popular, therefore inferior" is almost as likely to mislead as "Popular and therefore excellent."

It is of course a commonplace of the textbooks that, by the middle of the eighteenth century, literacy—in England at least —was sufficiently widespread to make it possible for a writer to appeal from the patron to the public. Some persons have always regarded this as an unmixed blessing; others have pointed out that it made a great deal of trash profitable. The thesis propounded by some now seems to be that the emergence of a large public was an unmixed calamity and that since the time when it appeared High Culture has been squeezed out by Mass Culture on the one hand and Middlebrow Culture on the other; also that of the two latter, both of which now flourish exuberantly, the Middlebrow is the worse because it competes directly with the High and is likely to be mistaken for it by that large public that believes itself to be cultured when it is only vulgar.

Hence the importance of the Establishment. It alone can accomplish the task of separating the sheep from the goats or, in more elegant terms, of pointing out to the few outside the Establishment who are capable of appreciating High Art which books belong in this category and which are mere vulgar pretenders.

Now I certainly do not believe that all best sellers are masterpieces or that a novel or a play must be great if it is much admired for a month or two by what is called the educated public.

On the other hand, history will bear me out that there are many instances where time has reversed the contemporary judgment of the most solemn critics. "Who reads Cowley now?" The answer was, "Nobody," only a generation after he had been the darling of the highbrows. And of course the most notorious example is Shakespeare. If popularity damns, then there is no hope for Chaucer, Shakespeare, Dryden, Pope, Fielding, Byron, Dickens, Thackeray, Trollope or Tennyson, every one of whom (except possibly the first) not only enjoyed a public larger than the elite of his day, but catered unconsciously or consciously to the large public by making concessions to it. All had at least some of the stigmata of the middlebrow: They were definitely not *avant-garde;* they appealed to the masses; they were in many respects imitative of their predecessors; and, in the case of several, definitely chauvinistic.

It is of course as easy to idealize the populace as it is to idealize the aristocracy, but to assume that the aristocratic patron necessarily had good taste is to succumb to the "good old days" fallacy. Suppose that the reputation of Gibbon's *Decline and Fall* had depended, not upon the public which hailed it as a masterpiece, but upon that prince of the royal blood who accepted a copy of the second volume with the immortal words: "Another damned, thick, square book. Always scribble, scribble —eh, Mr. Gibbon?"

Petrarch, who admired the unread and now unreadable works of Boccaccio, referred contemptuously to *The Decameron* as "Published, I presume, during your early years." But the middlebrow public of his day had given it a warm reception. In the prologue to *Don Quixote,* Cervantes says that his aim is to write so that "the simple shall not be wearied, but the grave shall not despise it." Yet for all that, he seems to have been unhappy about this masterpiece and wrote thereafter only the unreadable *Persiles and Sigismunda,* which was clearly intended to meet the standards of High Art as defined by the serious critics of his day.

I doubt that popularity or accessibility is a reliable criterion of either worth or worthlessness, especially since books perhaps not intended for the general public, and perhaps not at first accepted by it, sometimes turn out to be exceedingly popular in the long run.

Swift, it should be remembered, said that he wrote *Gulliver's Travels* to vex mankind, not to please it. That is something that the Establishment would approve of highly. He had as great a contempt for the brains, taste and integrity of the average Englishman as any member of the Establishment has for the brains taste, and integrity of his contemporaries. But *Gulliver's Travels* was soon one of the most widely-read books in the language. As Chesterton said, there is only one thing worse than being afraid to disagree with the public and that is being afraid to agree with it.

Do members of the Establishment get nervous if a new book from their typewriters sells more than any of their previous books? Would they refuse to write for a magazine whose circulation grew beyond a certain point? And if so, then what, precisely, is that point? How widely can a book be read and still escape damnation as "middlebrow"? How does a member of the Establishment feel when he gets a favorable review in the *New York Times Book Review?*—which happens to be, of all organs of literary opinion, the one that members of the Establishment hold in greatest contempt.

Many years ago, the woman editor of what was at the time the most widely respected highbrow monthly told me that her writers, unlike those who wrote for *The Nation,* could be sure that what they said would be understood. "We have," she explained, "succeeded in whittling our circulation away until we reach only those genuinely interested in aesthetics." Not long after this remark the magazine succumbed to its success. I wonder if those members of the Establishment who occasionally contribute to such magazines as *Esquire* and *Playboy* have ever advised the editors to "whittle away" their circulation.

It has been explained to us very often (sometimes apologetically and sometimes with complacency) that ours is an age of criticism and this is, of course, one reason why the critics tend to assume that the nonprofessional reader is necessarily wrong. But the Alexandrian Age also was an age of criticism and there is something Alexandrian about much contemporary critical analysis. It seems to be assumed that poems exist in order to be explicated and that, therefore, the best poem is the one that provides the explicator with the best opportunity to exercise his ingenuity.

Similarly, novels exist in order that critics may lay bare their symbolic or mythological content (often unsuspected by the novelist himself). Thus Mark Twain certainly did not know that *Huckleberry Finn* was, as one of the best-known contemporary critics has recently demonstrated to his own satisfaction, a homosexual novel. Indeed, the tendency to discover various other hidden complexes where they have previously been unsuspected may remind some of us of the story of the psychiatrist who told a patient who had just submitted to the ink blot test that he was obsessed by sex. "I'm obsessed by sex—I am the one who is obsessed by sex!" the patient exclaimed. "Who has been showing me all those dirty pictures?"

And when a critic, instead of merely pointing out that *Huckle-berry Finn*, or some other great novel, has been admired for the wrong reason, undertakes the complementary demonstration that some nearly unreadable work is really a masterpiece because its author has so obviously understood that the true function of the novel is to be ambiguous, mythic, or involved with the castration or some other complex, I am reminded of what a seventeenth-century French reader remarked when the author of an epic poem called attention to the fact that he had scrupulously "obeyed all the rules of Aristotle": "I am grateful to him for having obeyed the rules of Aristotle but I am very angry at Aristotle for having compelled him to write so dull a poem."

Even the ideal of pure poetry, pure painting and pure music seems to me to lead nowhere. So does the stated determination of the modern poets that every word shall be inevitable, indispensable and profoundly significant—that there must be, above all, no uninspired lines. If Homer sometimes nods, why should not a modern poet be granted a similar indulgence? Byron is full of commonplaces, so are Wordsworth and Tennyson. But are they destined to be regarded always as lesser than Ezra Pound and Robert Lowell? What we demand in the long run is not perfection but a rewarding whole.

Serious critics (in the special but familiar sense of the term) have never taken me seriously. Perhaps, then, it is only sour grapes to say that they have, in one sense, taken themselves too seriously—not because they are (as I have often found them) acute, conscientious and illuminating, but because they vastly overestimate their own influence upon the fate of literary works. The members of the Leavis school (who represent this kind of seriousness at its most serious) sometimes state explicitly, and they imply almost continuously, that they are aware of a tremendous and almost dreadful responsibility. Just insofar as they prevail, just thus far will righteousness prevail. On them and on other serious critics falls the task of making the proper discriminations and arranging in their proper order the hierarchy of writers past and present. Just to the extent that they do so, will the genuinely great get their due and the inferior be prevented from enjoying the attention and esteem they do not merit.

It is, these critics say (and to this extent I agree with them), tremendously important that excellence be recognized and vulgarity discountenanced. But I don't agree with their corollary that righteousness will prevail just to the extent that serious critics champion it. No man, said Dr. Johnson, was ever written down except by himself. That, I think, is about nine-tenths true; and so is what Johnson might have added but didn't: No man is ever written *up* except by himself.

Criticism is an interesting activity for the critic and often makes interesting reading for the reader. It is a stream that flows parallel to the great stream of creative writing. But in the end it will be the writer, not the critic, who determines what is High Art and what is Middlebrow Vulgarity. Not even Professor Leavis can exercise much influence upon the ultimate reputation of those whom (with such a sense of his awful responsibility) he attempts to write down or write up. Whether or not D. H. Lawrence is ultimately established as the greatest English writer of the twentieth century will depend upon what Mr. Lawrence wrote, not upon what Professor Leavis has said about it.

In favor of the outmoded and now despised impressionistic, or adventures-of-the-soul-among-the-masterpieces, kind of criticism which T. S. Eliot damned as the expression of the weak creative impulse rather than the genuinely critical, at least this much can be said: It recognizes the secondary role of the critic instead of seeming to elevate him above the creator.

Shortly after the end of the First World War a Columbia University professor published an enormously successful novel. As is so often the case when an academic or a highbrow achieves popular success, he was so delighted that he was unnecessarily insistent upon calling the attention of his colleagues to the fact that he was famous. The following story, which I believe to be true, was told: The wife of the best-selling author met on campus one of his professorial colleagues and demanded excitedly, "Have you read John's book?" "Not yet," was the reply. "Oh," she said, "it is a great book; you must read it right away; it will endure." "In that case," replied the possibly envious colleague, "there is no hurry."

Critics who are too much concerned with undeserved popularity or undeserved neglect might bear this anecdote in mind. I don't say that criticism may not hasten or retard, but I do say that serious critics need not wake up in the middle of the night in terror lest they have damned some great book to eternity or enthroned some faker. —*American Scholar*

WINTER, 1966-1967

. . .   .

What is modernism?

There are not many nations given so indefatigably to honoring their men of letters that a cabinet minister would preside over a ceremony in which the principal speaker eulogized a *poète maudit* upon whose newly erected monument was engraved the poet's own clarion call to his fellows: "We have set out as pilgrims whose destination is perdition . . . across the streets, across the countries, and across common sense itself."

The cabinet minister was André Malraux; the sculptor was Picasso; and the poet, Guillaume Apollinaire—successively the champion of cubism, of dada, and of surrealism. His own best-known works are a volume of poems called *Hard Liquor* (Alcools); a novel, *The Assassinated Poet*; and a play, *The Breasts of Tiresias*. The twentieth century, so he predicted, "will be the century of de Sade" and that prophesy seems well on the way to fulfillment.

Even if we had a Minister of Arts in this country, we cannot quite imagine him officially honoring a poet who urged painters, as well as men of letters, to set out resolutely on the road leading to that pit of Hell, of which an elder poet said the descent is easier than the road back. No, one can't imagine an American Minister of Culture doing that and, in fact, the pro-ponents of government support to the Arts are most likely to fear that, officially at least, we would be oppressively pure, genteel, and middlebrow.

But if we are not yet quite up to the French in this respect, there is no doubt about the fact that the avant-garde, even when perverse and sadistic, is no longer without honor even in rather surprising quarters, and that mass-circulation magazines give their most frequent and extensive treatment to movies, plays, novels and poems which in one way or another—extravagant concern with usually abnormal sexuality, violence and cruelty, or at least the nihilism of the absurd—seem to be headed along the road which Apollinaire bid them take.

Earlier this year (March, 1966) Cyril Connally, a leading English critic, was commissioned by the certainly ultra-respect-able London *Sunday Times* to make a list of the hundred literary works which best presented various aspects of Modern-ism in intellectual literature. He headed his list with that same Guillaume Apollinaire whom the French Minister of Culture was so eager to honor, and though it is true that his list does include certain works which are neither beatnik, sadistic, existential or sexually perverse, at least a half, or perhaps two-thirds of them, might, I think, be classified as guideposts to perdition. Among them (and remember these are not merely offered as striking works of literature but as typical of the modern spirit) are *Nadia* by the surrealist André Breton; *Journey to the End of Night* by the pro-Nazi and violently anti-Semitic Celine; Gide's *The Immoralist*; Huysman's *Là Bas*; Villiers de L'Isle-Adam's *Cruel Stories*; Rimbaud's *Les Illuminations*; and many others more or less in the same spirit of world weariness, world hatred, or perverse indulgence. And he finds the quintessence of modernity in Baudelaire as translated by Robert Lowell.

> Only when we drink poison are we well—
> We want, this fire so burns our brain tissue,
> To drown in the abyss—heaven or hell.
> Who cares? Through the unknown we'll find the new.*

Commenting on the list and Connally's explanatory notes, *Time* magazine (which certainly does not appeal to minority interests only) remarks that, though to many the list will seem perverse, it is nevertheless "an achievement in taste and learning."

Readers curious enough to consult the full text with Connally's own comments on individual works will find that he calls Baudelaire's poetry "a beam of light glowing for posterity," even though, it would seem, the poet himself declares that he does not care whether it points the way to a heaven or a hell; also that André Breton, one of Connally's heroes, proposed to "wring the neck of literature" and that Connally himself quotes with apparent approval the following sentence of

---

* Reprinted with permission of Farrar, Straus & Giroux, Inc. from *Imitations* by Robert Lowell. Copyright © 1958, 1959, 1960, 1961 by Robert Lowell.

which it is said "nothing more surrealist has ever been written": "Beautiful as the chance encounter on a dissecting table of an umbrella and a sewing machine."

I do not believe that more than a very small fraction of *Time*'s readers really shares the convictions or admires the enterprises of such writers. Yet they are obviously much interested in them and timid about expressing any doubts. If they give deserved praise to, say, Tennessee Williams for his theatrical skill, they are half afraid of not taking seriously enough the implications of his extraordinary notions concerning sexual abnormality, and they are half convinced that their own normality needs to be apologized for. If a whole school of novelists (now a bit démodé) defines its conception of the good life as driving a stolen automobile at ninety miles an hour after a revivifying shot of heroin, almost nobody says merely "Pooh" or "Don't be silly."

Those of us who read not only the mass-circulation magazines but such highbrow weeklies as *The Nation* or *The New Leader* have come to expect a curious contrast between the front and the back of the book. The opening pages are full of schemes for improving the condition of this or that; but the section devoted to the Arts is occupied mostly by reviews of books, movies, paintings, and musical compositions, most of which are bitterly cynical, pessimistic, and by old-fashioned standards, obscene. Moreover, this seems to reflect truly a similar contrast in taste and preoccupation between the two groups of what we still call intellectuals. Most of them are either do-gooders or, on the other hand, ready to entertain the possibility that the road to perdition is the wise one to take. If you are not a potential member of the Peace Corps, you are almost certainly a devotee of The Absurd. You want either to rescue the underdeveloped countries or explore once more the meaninglessness of the universe or the depravity of some vision of the *dolce vita.* If *Time* (as it recently did) puts Sartre and Gênet on its "best reading" list for a single week, neither of them can be said to be, by now, attractive only to the few.

Do I exaggerate either the violence, perversity or nihilism of most of the most discussed modern writers, or the tendency of even the mass magazines to select specimens as either the best or, sometimes, only the most newsworthy books? Let us look at a few excerpts from two or three publications to illustrate what I am driving at. Let us look first at the leading review in an issue of *The New Leader*. It concerns James Baldwin's newest so-called novel and was written by the magazine's staff critic Stanley Edgar Hyman who, though far from approving of the book, writes as follows:

As an enthusiastic admirer of his two earlier novels, I am sorry to find this, his most ambitious effort, a very mixed bundle.

The protagonist of *Another Country*, a young Negro jazz drummer named Rufus Scott, kills himself on page 88, and the rest of the book is taken up with the adventures and misadventures, mostly sexual, of the half dozen people who had been close to him. Of the important characters, only Rufus and his sister Ida are Negro, but almost everything in the book that is powerful and convincing deals with Negro consciousness.

That consciousness, as the novel shows it, seethes with bitterness and race hate. Let the liberal white bastards squirm is Rufus's most charitable feeling towards Vivaldo, his best frinend; his less charitable feelings is a passionate desire for the extinction of the white race by nuclear bombs. Ida is even fiercer. She regularly affirms, in language not quotable in this family magazine, the total sexual inadequacy of whites, as well as their moral sickness and physical repulsiveness. . . . The other Negroes in the book share this bitterness and hatred without exception. A big Negro pimp who lives by beating up and robbing the white customers of his Negro whore clearly does it out of principle; before robbing Vivaldo he stares at him with a calm steady hatred, as remote and unanswerable as madness. The Silenski boys are beaten up by Negro boys unknown to them out of simple racial hostility and Richard, their father, automatically comments: Little black bastards. Rufus's father, seeing his son's mangled corpse, remarks only: They didn't leave a man much, do they? A musician who had been Rufus's friend, finding Ida out with a white man, calls her "black white man's whore" and threatens to mutilate her genitals twice, once for himself and once for Rufus.

Though *The New Leader's* critic is by no means favorably impressed, the jacket of *Another Country* is able to cite the even better known and academically very respectable critic, Mark Shorer, as calling *Another Country* "powerful." Is that the adjective he would have chosen if this almost insane outburst of racism had been the work of some Southern Klu Kluxer—as it might easily be made to seem by reading "white" where Baldwin says "black" and "black" where he says "white"? Why is black racism "powerful," white disgusting?

Now for a movie, as admiringly described in *Time:*

Naked Prey spills more beauty, blood and savagery upon the screen than any African adventure drama since *Trader Horn*. Squeamish viewers will head for home in the first twenty minutes or so, when producer-director-star Cornel Wilde swiftly dooms three last century white hunters and a file of blacks, attacked and captured by a horde of warriors from a tribe they have insulted. One victim is basted with clay and turned over a spit, another is staked out as the victim of a cobra.

The only survivor is Wilde. In a primitive sporting gesture, the natives free the courageous white man without clothes, weapons or water—and with ten stalwart young spearsmen poised to track him down. Hunted now, the hunter begins to run, and *Prey* gathers fierce momentum as a classic, single-minded epic of survival with no time out for faint-hearted blondes or false heroines.

It used to be said that the theater was often more searching, more bitter, and more "adult" than the movies ever dared to be. Today it can hardly keep up with them. But it tries, as witness an account of the latest play by the man generally regarded as Britain's leading playwright:

A Bond Honoured, British playwright John Osborne's adaptation of an atrocious horror show by seventeenth-century Spaniard Lope de Vega, has a hero who commits rape, murder, treason, multiple incest and matricide, and blinds his father—after which he is crucified in precise imitation of Christ. London's critics cast one look at the tasteless mayhem at the Old Vic and held their noses. Whereupon Osborne, 36, flipped his Angry Aging Man's lid, firing off telegrams to the London papers. Osborne declared an end to his "gentleman's agreement to ignore puny theater critics as bourgeois conventions. After ten years it is now war, open war, that will be as public as I and other men of earned reputations have the considerable power to make it."

This account is again from *Time* but its pooh-poohing of Osborne's masterpiece got an angry reply from Kenneth Tynan, the drama critic who was for a time the regular reviewer for *The New Yorker*:

Of the twelve newspaper critics, at least four held their breath. Herald Hobson in the *Sunday Times* said of Osborne: "He is not only our most important dramatist; he is also our chief prophet." According to Randall Bryden of the *Observer*, "The effect of *A Bond Honoured* in performance is marvelously theatrical." Allen Brien of the Sunday *Telegraph* thought it "a serious, ambitious and valuable play which matures in the memory and fertilizes the imagination," while for Milton Shulman in the *Evening Standard* it was "a stunning parable with a magnificent theatrical impact."

Having glanced at a conspicuous American novel, a conspicuous movie, and a conspicuous play, let's look now at two serious American critics, taking Leslie Fiedler first. His contention that the best American fiction from *Huckleberry Finn* to Hemingway and Faulkner is always concerned with a repressed homosexuality, is well known. In his most recent book, he comes up with the following opinions:

[On the suicide of Ernest Hemingway]: One quarry was left him only, the single beast worthy of him; himself. And he took his shotgun in hand, probably renewing his lapsed allegiance to death and silence. With a single shot he redeemed his best work from his worst, his art from himself.

[Of President Kennedy and the Arts]: John F. Kennedy, as Louis XV, seemed up to the moment of his assassination the true symbol of cultural blight; not only our first sexually viable president in a century, after a depressing series of uncle, grandfather and grandmother figures, but the very embodiment of middle-brow culture climbing.

I have been leaning heavily on *Time* because it seems to be the publication which best gauges the interests if not necessarily the opinions, of the largest number of literate Americans. But for a second critic, and incidentally an excellent example of the schizophrenia of the liberal weeklies, I will choose an essay by the most "in" of contemporary avant-garde critics, namely, Susan Sontag published in *The Nation*, which has been for long the very paradigm of do-goodism. The article takes off from a discussion of Jack Smith's film *Flaming Creatures*, which she describes thus:

A couple of women and a much larger number of men . . . frolic about, pose, posture, and dance with one another. Enact various scenes of voluptuousness, sexual frenzy, romantic love and vampirism—to the accompaniment of a sound track which includes . . . the chorale of flutish shrieks and screams which accompany the group rape of a bosomy woman, rape happily converting itself into an orgy.

It also, says Miss Sontag, includes "close-ups of limp penises and bouncing breasts . . . shots of masturbation and oral sensuality." "Of course," she continues, "*Flaming Creatures* is outrageous and it intends to be. But [or should it be, therefore] it is 'a beautiful film.' . . ." [It is] "a triumphant example of an esthetic vision of the world—and such a vision is perhaps always, at its core, epicene."

Just why an aesthetic vision of the world is perhaps always at its core homosexual is not explained, and it suggests the same reply which Chesterton made to the aestheticism of the Nineties. The art of those who professed it, so they claimed, was morally neutral. But, said Chesterton, if it really were neutral it would often find itself dealing favorably with respectability, virtue, piety and conventional behavior. The fact that it never does treat of any of these things in a neutral manner was sufficient proof that the art of its practitioners was not morally neutral but actually (to come back to Apollinaire again) an invitation to take the road to perdition.

If Miss Sontag does not explain why an aesthetic vision must be epicene (i.e., homosexual) she does undertake to explain why modern art must be "outrageous." "Art is always the sphere of freedom. In those difficult works of art we now call avant-garde, the artist consciously exercises his freedom."

That argument is obviously the same as that favorite of some existentialists, namely the contention (a) that the unmotivated act is the most positive assertion of freedom, and (b) that the best unmotivated act is one of arbitrary cruelty. Why this should be so, I have never understood, and I understand no more why the freedom of the artist can be demonstrated only by the outrageous. In the atmosphere of the present moment, the boldest position a creative or critical writer could take would be one championing not only morality but gentility and bourgeois respectability. Even this article which I am writing at this moment will probably be more contemptuously or even vituperatively dismissed than it would be if I were defending sadism, homosexuality, and nihilism.

How square and fuddy-duddy the management of the American Telephone and Telegraph Company must be to take, as it recently has, full-page advertisements in mass media to ask and answer a question in headline type: "What can you do about obscene, harassing, or threatening phone calls?" Doesn't AT&T

know that one of the easiest ways to demonstrate one's freedom in a splendidly unmotivated act consists in making an obscene telephone call? From that, one can easily work up to the various vandalisms now so popular among teen-agers and, finally, to unmotivated murder. Who else demonstrates so triumphantly an existentialist freedom as the killer for kicks?

What precisely is the road, or roads, which have led to the state of mind illustrated by the quotations which make up so large a part of this article? I do not think that any analysis ending in a satisfactory answer to that question has ever been made. Someone with the stomach for it might undertake a study as nearly classic as Mario Paz's *The Romantic Agony,* which traces so brilliantly the origin and destination of 1890 decadence —to which last, Modernism is more closely paralleled than is usually admitted, and of which it is, perhaps, only another phase. Cyril Connally (in the discussion already quoted) has this to say:

[It] began as a revolt against the bourgeois in France, the Victorians in England, the Puritanism and materialism of America. The modern spirit was a combination of certain intellectual qualities inherited from the Enlightenment: lucidity, irony, scepticism, intellectual curiosity, combined with the impassioned intensity and enhanced sensibility of the Romantic, their rebellion and sense of technical experiment, their awareness of living in a tragic age.

All that is true enough and familiar enough without going far enough. It does not explain why the most obvious and unique characteristics of the current avant-garde are not any of the characteristics of the Enlightenment or of any except the decadent Romantics. How, for instance, do lucidity, irony, scepticism or even intellectual curiosity become preludes to "the century of de Sade"? How did an assault upon Victorian complacency and hypocrisy end by practicing a sort of unmotivated vandalism?

I suppose that anyone who undertook to trace that development would have to begin by asking whether or not there is a single dominating characteristic of this latest development of the modern spirit, any thing which by its frequent emphasis seems to distinguish contemporary Modernism from the movement out of which it is said to have grown. This Modernism seems, indeed, to be compounded of many simples and not all who represent it include all of them in their mixtures. Is the distinguishing characteristic a tendency to elevate raw sexual experience to a position of supreme importance so that the Quest for the Holy Grail has become a quest for the perfect orgasm? Is it homosexuality, nihilism and the impulse to self-destruction as typified in the cult of drugs, or is it that taste for violence which, as in the case of Baldwin, becomes unmistakably sadistic?

If I had to answer the question, I would be inclined to say that this taste for violence, this belief that it is the only appropriate response to an absurd world is indeed the one element most often present in any individual's special version of the moment's avant-gardism. Psychiatrists say that suicide is often motivated by the desire for revenge against some person who will be made to suffer by it. They are inclined to call this motive irrational, but in modern literature and modern criticism it is sometimes accepted as the ultimate rationality—as in the following two examples. In Friedrich Duerrenmatt's much discussed play *The Visit* the principal character explains her conduct by saying: "The world made a whore of me, so I am turning the world into a brothel." In *The Nation*, the reviewer of a novel calls the self-destruction of its hero "an alcoholic strike against humanity." In commonsense terms all such retaliations and revenges come under the head of biting off one's nose to spite one's face, but that seems to be what some modernists advocate.

Seldom if ever before have any of the arts been so dominated by an all-inclusive hatred. Once the writer hated individual "bad men." Then he began to hate instead the society which was supposed to be responsible for the creation of bad men. Now his hatred is directed not at individuals or their societies, but at the universe in which bad men and bad societies are merely expressions of the fundamental evil of that universe itself.

It was once hoped that the iconoclasts who flourished during the early years of our century would clear the ground for higher ideals and truer values. Somewhat later it was argued that existentialism, having demonstrated that the universe was in itself morally and intellectually meaningless, now left man free to construct meanings and morals for himself and in his own image. What that has come down to, the Baldwins, the Burroughses, and the Jack Smiths have demonstrated in our language—the Apollinaires, the Gênets in theirs.

Of course there is always the literature of social protest to which one may turn if one has had enough of sadism and the absurd. But sometimes the reviewers sound as though they were getting the same sort of sadistic kick in a less open way. Here, for example, is the way in which a recent novel is praised in (of all places) *Vogue:*

The Fixer, a brilliant new novel by Bernard Malamud, is harrowing. It is a dreadful story that cuts and lacerates without relief; it is a drama of ferocious injustice and then more injustice.

If anything except unrelieved violence in one form or another is "escapism"; if human nature, the world and even the universe itself are what so many esteemed artists declare them to be, then what can any reasonable man choose to do, except escape in either life or literature—if he can.

Perhaps that is why in London recently, thousands crowded an exhibition of memorabilia of the creator of Peter Rabbit.

—*Saturday Review*
MAY 6, 1967

. . . . IV

As I Like It

How real is the ego?

James Boswell believed that life had no value unless you kept a diary. "I should live no more than I can record," he wrote, "as one should have no more corn growing than one can get in." For him, making a record was neither an amusement nor a means toward an end, but the only meaningful portion of life. Other men (Johnson, notoriously) might write to live; Boswell lived to write, and one may guess that Samuel Pepys felt much the same. Marcel Proust, of course, elaborately defended his similar conviction—that the conscious experience of living is the only thing worth living for and that one cannot fully grasp an experience except in retrospect.

Perhaps all great diarists are alike in this, and although their attitude strikes most of us as odd, I wonder if it should. That young men spend their lives anticipating the future, old men in remembering the past, is a platitude. But I don't see why the first should generally be regarded as so much more satisfactory than the second. After all, neither the past nor the future is present, and to that extent both are shadowy. And at least the past did happen, while the anticipated future may not —and probably won't.

Why then can't most of us, like Boswell and Proust, take

more pleasure in saying with Horace and Dryden, "What has been has been and I have had my hour," than in dreaming of a future that will never come? Is it because, as Johnson said, "The natural progress of the human mind is not from pleasure to pleasure but from hope to hope"? Now that my meridian is receding farther and farther into the past, I will be in a better and better position to examine the phenomenon. To tell the truth I began quite a few years ago.

At least one thing is clear. We couldn't find either our own past or our own future any more gratifying than other people's unless we were convinced that the "I" to whom remembered things happened, and to whom an anticipated future belongs, actually is continuous with the "I" of the moment. Yet a denial that any such unified and persistent *persona* does exist is as old as Heraclitus and is one of the many popular assumptions upon which doubts are persistently cast by both modern fiction with its stream of consciousness, and psychology with its tendency to think of motive and character as a shifting configuration of stimuli and conditioning factors, so that man becomes merely the sum of temporary happenings rather than a persisting "I" to whom external things happen. It used to be simple to say that "the self" is the soul and as such persists not only through time but through eternity also. But many theologians have given up "the soul" in that sense, and the philosopher is faced with the problem of what is left of the "I" after "the soul" has ceased to have a definable meaning.

Not very many years ago, when I was giving some lectures on modern drama, I devoted one of them to "the dissolution of the ego," with Pirandello obviously the playwright most persistently concerned with this theme, and Proust as a contemporary novelist almost equally obsessed by the conviction that our sense of being the same person from year to year is delusion. John Doe, so they both say, may be a label supposed to refer to some continuous entity which it follows from birth certificate to tombstone, but that entity is only a fiction.

Hume says somewhere that introspection has revealed to him only a series of sensations, never any continuous "I." Bertrand Russell ridiculed Descartes' "I think, therefore I am" for naïvely assuming a nonexistent ego when even Descartes himself was no more than a series of events. And just the other day I came across a quotation attributed to Buddha, which says precisely the same thing. "There is this or that passing idea, this or that transitory emotion, this or that image, but no organized whole behind them which can be called an ego." Perhaps I am merely a Dr. Johnson refuting Berkeley by kicking a stone, but I wager that although Buddha may have been indifferent in the face of death, both Hume and Russell have found it impossible to contemplate with complete detachment the ending of that series of events to which we stupidly give their names. If Proust really believed that he was not the same person who wept when his mother delayed kissing him goodnight, then I fail to see why he should have found his own past any more interesting or vivid than that of others, and I suggest (as cross-examining lawyers say) that all the volumes of *Remembrance of Things Past* are really an attempt to convince himself of something Bergson had taught him to doubt— namely, that Marcel Proust was an entity, not a series of disparate events.

An ancient Greek joke turned upon the case of a wrongdoer who protests that he should not be punished today for what he did yesterday because, as Heraclitus had demonstrated, it is not the same he. At the time of my drama lectures I was most interested in pointing out that this joke is no joke since all classical, Christian and, indeed, all rationalist ethics depend upon the assumption that there is a persistent "he" to get his just deserts and possibly to be made a better man tomorrow. Hence,

I argued, it seems that if the *persona* is indeed a fiction, it is a necessary one. I was not able, however, to say much in its defense beyond remarking that in ordinary life we obviously live by it; as when, for instance, we say of someone, "that is not worthy of him," or, slangily, "be yourself," both of which locutions imply that, although men are often inconsistent, there is nevertheless some self against which the inconsistency of an act or an attitude can be measured. Neither would mean anything at all if some individuality did not persist.

Just the other day some reference to Freud and the "pleasure principle" started me thinking about the whole problem again, and I came up with what seemed to me a fresh proof that the persisting ego is indeed a reality, not a fiction. Even the pleasure principle, although supposedly something that the mature individual must get beyond, could affect no one unless the "I" at this moment were the same "I" who is to get some pleasure in the next moment, and we could not get beyond the "pleasure principle" if we did not believe that the "I" who sacrifices the present for the future is the same one who will reap the future benefit. Heraclitus himself would have been confounded unless he was prepared to admit that a future threat to someone else would disturb him as deeply as the same threat to himself. With the possible exception of a few saints, there is not and never has been anyone whose concern for others was precisely the same as his concern for himself. Unless we were sure of the fact that there is some continuing reality in us, we would be no more disturbed to be told that we must die tomorrow than we are by the knowledge that many somebodies certainly will die today, and every day thereafter.

If the future of everyone else actually did concern us as much as our own, then we would all be either completely indifferent to everything except the moment, or we would have achieved that perfect selflessness that is sometimes presented as an ideal. But if we really did achieve this state, life would be intolerable because daily we should be dying a thousand deaths and suffering ten thousand agonies. That the starving millions of Asia and the tortured victims of the concentration camps are relatively unreal to us is, in one way, a blessing. Egotism, in the sense that we are aware of a persisting *persona* and that therefore its future is somehow of more concern to us than the future of others, is necessary if human existence is to be tolerable.

One of my Tucson friends is an electrical engineer now cooperating with a biologist at the Massachusetts Institute of Technology on some novel experiments. These involve the use of tiny electrodes inserted into the brain of a frog, and the purpose is to discover what happens in an individual nerve cell when it receives, and helps react to, an external stimulus. They are discovering wonderful and surprising things, but I judge after asking some questions that these investigators (unlike some working in similar fields) are well aware of the fact that if you expect in some such way to understand what the connection is between a biochemical process and a conscious sensation of color or sound or smell—to say nothing of thought—you never get even close to realizing your expectations. All that you actually succeed in doing is to describe in fuller and finer detail the processes that accompany sensations. So far as an ultimate explanation is concerned, you are following a will-o'-the-wisp. It is still impossible to imagine what kind of connection there could be between a physical fact and consciousness. The two remain discontinuous universes between which no bridge can be built. We can never be sure, even, that the one world receives correct reports from the other. It may be that the sense and the consciousness that seem to interpret this external world give a totally false picture of it. Perhaps the material eludes the consciousness, perhaps the consciousness invents the material. When I think my consciousness makes me aware of something outside myself, it is only an assumption that this something is really there. Perhaps I am only wrapped in a dream, and in either case only the awareness (or dream) is indisputably real.

If, as I feel sure, the solipsist cannot be refuted in the laboratory, neither, I think, can the nature of the *persona* be revealed there; although one kind of scientist will of course insist that the laboratory does, on the contrary, make perfectly clear the limited sense in which the organism that begins in the womb and ends in the grave is continuously one thing. That one thing, he will say, is simply the soma which the infinitely complex mechanisms of heredity have made unique and which the stimuli that it happens to have received have modified. But even assuming the accuracy of this statement as far as it concerns physiological facts, it does not explain why we care more about what will happen to us tomorrow than we do about what will happen to someone else; and it cannot explain that, because it cannot explain the always and perhaps eternally inconceivable connection between physical fact and consciousness.

What we do know with special urgency is that we do care what happens to us tomorrow and do feel that what happened to us yesterday happened to us and not to someone else. Having called upon science, metaphysics and theology to explain and justify both this conviction and the complementary conviction that our consciousness is not the only reality in the universe, and having got no answer from any of them, we are compelled to fall back upon Santayana's Animal Faith. Ultimately, it is by that that we live and act. Even if it deludes us with appearances while science gives us facts, we can only reply that as far as the experiences of living are concerned appearances are realer than reality. In fact it may be that the concept of an eternal life for the soul became so widely accepted in so many religions partly because man could not imagine that the most indisputable reality he knew—namely, his own enduring self—could cease to exist.

. . .

Those who despise both "the literary mind" and "the metaphysical mind" are fond of pointing out that great writers and great thinkers have a way of disagreeing so completely with others equally great, that where one sees white the other sees black. That distinguished writers and thinkers do indeed do just that was brought to mind while I was writing this very piece and happened to come across a recent essay by François Mauriac, where (the lame translation is my own) he writes: "When I observed the other evening a little group of friends reunited about the table of Francis Poulenc I was struck, as I often am, by the fact that human beings change hardly at all. What they were at the beginning is what I find them later and what they remain to the end. . . . Whenever I meet again those whom I have known in the past and see again only after a long interval, I am struck by the immovable, immutable presence of something which duration does not change and which is not concerned with time."

Obviously this is not only a flat contradiction of the principal thesis expounded in many volumes by Mauriac's contemporary, Marcel Proust. It is also, by implication, a denial of what Buddha, Hume, Russell, and many other metaphysicians have proved to their own satisfaction. How different this is, say many, from what one finds among scientists who are almost always in substantial agreement with one another! But the truth is that even when a consensus does exist at a given time, what that consensus agrees upon, changes from decade to decade as completely as do metaphysical or literary opinions.

Consider the case of what might be called the orthodox eschatology of science. Just about the time when I was first reading Proust, Sir James Jeans (along with some others) was making the Second Law of Thermodynamics as fashionable a topic of intellectual conversation as "alienation" is today, and we all took it as a proved fact that increasing entropy would inevitably extinguish all life in a universe where no difference in temperature between one place and another could exist. Yet Jeans was hardly safe in his grave when his biographer, the late Professor E. Milne, ended his book with a beautiful British understatement: ". . . I am now convinced that an unconditional prediction of a heat-death for the universe is an over-statement." That was published in 1952, and now we are being assured that the real end of our world will be by fire not by ice. I am not quite sure why, but I think the demonstration runs something like this: The white dwarf stars are now supposed to represent a late stage in the life of a sun that has fallen in on itself. Our own little private sun is still in its youth, but someday it will turn into a white dwarf and be so hot that everything on earth will be quickly consumed.

If the literary mind believes incompatible theories simultaneously, the scientific mind accepts them successively, and I am not sure that that is anything to boast about. It was a poet who observed:

> Some say the world will end in fire,
> Some say in ice.

—*American Scholar*
WINTER, 1964-1965

. . .   .

Life, liberty and the pursuit of unhappiness

In my heyday (which was the Twenties), most of my contemporaries took the Declaration of Independence seriously—especially that phrase in it which declares that the pursuit of happiness is an inalienable right. Among all too many of today's intellectuals this is no longer a respectable opinion. According to them, every thinking man must be, and every decent man should be, thoroughly miserable—the decent man because the world is unjust, the thinking man because the whole universe is, and must remain, "absurd."

Perhaps there is more concrete misery than usual in the world today and I'll go along with the "decent man" far enough to agree that it should concern us. But I fail to understand what good it does anybody to say, like the character in one of Koestler's novels. "In an age of transition no one has the right to be happy." And I am even less persuaded by the existentialists who try to convince me by dubious abstract arguments and bold dogmatic assertions that I must think myself into some sort of abstract despair.

In the currently most admired novels and plays there is a terrible monotony. Becket, Ionesco, Sartre and Gênet repeat with little variety of method and no novelty of doctrine the same things: The universe is meaningless, without rhyme or reason; or as their endlessly repeated shibboleth has it, "absurd." Good and evil are empty words. One thing is as valuable as another. Though man is, in some inexplicable way, free, and thus exempt from the necessity that governs everything else, he can demonstrate this freedom by being either a saint or a monster. Most people choose the latter alternative and it is logically no less admirable than the other. Hence the truest picture of life consists almost exclusively of unhappy but usually cruel and debauched people, behaving irrationally in an irrational universe.

When I first met some of these specimens of the most serious and characteristic works of our time, and first learned how greatly they were admired, I supposed that I must be misunderstanding what they were really intending to convey. Since I have read the explications furnished by their many sympathetic critics, I realize that I understood only too well. By one analyst I am assured that even Camus, "the most traditional, the gentlest and the wisest" of the lot, really did wish us to understand that a motiveless atrocity serves admirably to demonstrate human freedom; and that Gênet, "the wildest and loveliest," invents a new morality in which "dishonesty is better than honesty; cowardice is better than bravery; betrayal is better than loyalty; homosexuality is better than heterosexuality, and so on." Simone de Beauvoir declared that the Marquis de Sade was "the freest man who ever lived" and presumably she must find intriguing such of his reasonings as that which exalts incest on the ground that it promotes family affection! Since Sade spent a considerable portion of his life in jail and Gênet would be serving a life sentence as a habitual criminal had it not been for the intercession of literary admirers, to call Sade the freest man who ever lived must be to take very literally the doctrine that "stone walls do not a prison make."

Whatever else may be said of either the novel or play "of the absurd," it is evident that both its creators and their characters are devoted to the pursuit of unhappiness—which may be an inalienable right but is certainly not the one the rest of us are compelled to exercise.

The *poète maudit* has, of course, often been with us. Oddly enough, we had at least one—Edgar Allan Poe—who appeared most improbably in mid-nineteenth-century America. France has had the most of them and they run the gamut from Baudelaire to Rimbaud and Apollinaire, on to the nadir of Sade. But have they ever before been taken seriously as exponents of the only truth which a generation of intellectuals found it possible to recognize?

That the works of the current crop have a certain shock value is obvious—both as propounders of paradox and (especially in the case of Gênet) as purveyors of effective, if perverse, eroticism. Some of their admirers tacitly minimize the latter. The men they most admire are described as great writers who just happen to be often exercising their gifts in the treatment of gaudily erotic themes. But at the risk of being dismissed as hopelessly Philistine, I am bound to register my opinion that they would have a much smaller audience if they were not pornographic.

Even their shock effect soon loses its effectiveness because they repeat the same shock over and over again and are condemned by their very dogmas to monotony. An endless variety of meanings can be, and has been, read into the universe and human life. But meaninglessness is always the same. Once you have said that life is absurd, it is absurd (in a simpler sense) to say it again and again. You have reached the end of the line. There is nowhere to go from there—except perhaps to a further exposition of that unhappiness to which a belief that nothing is better than anything else inevitably leads.

The beatnik and the existentialist may seem far apart, but the professed convictions of each lead easily to the same messy, unrewarding conduct. Their lives are likely to be as much a failure from the standpoint of the hedonist as from that of the most conventional moralist. They don't even "have fun." And that, by a prevalent system of values, is the ultimate failure.

All this, so they tell me, is inevitable. Nihilism is the only possible modern philosophy. For the first time in history we know the facts and have the courage to face them. The literature of the Absurd is the only literature the future will tolerate, and despair the only mood intelligent men can ever know. The race of human beings has wandered for many thousands of years from delusion to delusion, but it has come to rest at last. There is no God and we are His prophets.

I doubt it. Existentialism is merely a creed no more solidly founded than Calvinism—which it resembles in the gratuitous assumption that human nature is vile and the majority of men damned before they were born to torture, either in this world or the next. The premise that the universe is meaningless is merely a premise, not a demonstrated fact. The contention that man is capable of freedom and value judgments, although he is the product of natural forces which know nothing of either, is singularly improbable. Either of the alternate assumptions makes more sense. If he is indeed unique in nature, then something transcendental made him so. If he is something which Nature herself has produced, then Nature must be in some way responsible for capacities he inherits from the universe itself.

Neither literature nor any of the other arts merely reflects the times. They create as well as record convictions and moods. If a sizable audience now believes that life is absurd, existence a continual misery, and human beings almost without exception vile, it believes it in large part, not because of its own experience, but because poets of talent have convinced it of the alleged fact. I risk the bold prediction that sooner or later—and rather soon, I think—it will awake from its nightmare, and the "theater of the absurd" will be as outmoded as the proletarian "art-is-a-weapon" drama of the thirties which many critics of the time described as the only drama of the future. One of the advantages—perhaps there are not many—of having lived a long time is the fact that it inevitably makes one something of a square. We know by experience what those who know the past only through history can never believe—namely, that those eternal truths which have been newly discovered turn out to be mere fashions after all.

Perhaps it is a sign of the times that the only drama of the Absurd to achieve a great success on rather than off-Broadway —Edward Albee's hideous masterpiece *Who's Afraid of Virginia Woolf?*—is one in which surrealism is abandoned in favor of what comes pretty close to old-fashioned naturalism. It is understandable, even bitterly funny, no matter what your intellectual convictions may be. Unlike most of Becket, Ionesco and Gênet, it makes sense whether you are an existentialist or not. And you don't even have to believe that it is typical; only that some human beings, not all, are like the doomed quartet which constitutes its *dramatis personae*. That is at least a step back toward sanity.   —*Playboy*

DECEMBER, 1964

. . .   .

On not keeping young

A recent English book was entitled *Mediatrics, or the Characteristics, Importance and Proper Care of the Middle-Aged.* Its subject, so the author said, is shamefully neglected in this day when we are so excessively concerned with pediatrics and gerontology that we forget the largest, most important, and most overburdened class.

Along with much other relevant material, the treatise included a section on the criteria for determining when middle age has set in. But it failed to mention what seems to me the most dependable of all. Middle age (if I can remember that far back) begins when the individual ceases to believe that the newest opinions are the truest and begins to hold that the good old days of his youth really were good.

When this moment comes, the practical question is this: Should the aim be to "grow old gracefully," or to "stay young"? Contemporary prejudice being what it is, the how-to books all assume that the second alternative is obviously the more desirable and the stress is usually on "staying young mentally"— perhaps because self-deception is easier to achieve in that department than in any other. The group with which I am most concerned—namely, college professors and other professed or professional intellectuals—often pride themselves on keeping up-to-date. Its members read the latest books, take part in debates concerning the latest critical theories, cultivate a taste for jazz, expound the doctrines of existentialism, and "understand," if they don't exactly defend, the beatniks.

My own opinion is that all this is usually a mistake. In the first place, they do rather badly what the young do much better, and the old fellow who tries to dance the frug is not much more ridiculous than the one who gives classroom lectures on Ginsberg, Kerouac, Jean Paul Sartre or even Salinger. In the second place, such writers as these are the ones whom the brighter students will discover for themselves and are more likely to over- than to undervalue. The professor's business is to see to it that his charges make the acquaintance of those they are less likely to find out for themselves and, especially, to hear what can be said in their favor.

We know that the future belongs to the young, and even the present, to those well that side of middle age. But the chief business of the liberal education—so it seems to me—is to brief the inheritors on their past and to bring them up-to-date rather than to design their future. Moreover, what the student learns today ought to be something that will not be merely of "historical interest" a decade hence; and no contemporary writer is ever as sure to be still interesting then as are those who have already (if I may use an old man's phrase) stood the test of time. I am not asserting that no contemporary writer will endure; only that we can't possibly know which ones will. The student who devotes himself to Chaucer and Shakespeare has a gilt-edged investment. If he has spent all his time on some of the bright stars of today it is just possible that within his lifetime they will be as out of fashion as Masefield and Galsworthy are now.

These points seem to have been largely overlooked in the controversy concerning our graduate schools of English that ran rather hot in the pages of the *Scholar* a year or two ago. The dispute was mostly over the question of whether or not these schools actually are "modern," not whether or not they ought to be. One critic objected that T. S. Eliot was not sufficiently attended to, and the respondent replied that he was, on the contrary, extensively explicated and written about. But no one seems to have noticed the irony in the fact that Eliot himself has stated categorically that, in his opinion, neither his poetry nor that of any other contemporary has a proper place in the academic program—which should be devoted to the classics exclusively. If Eliot is so important, why not ponder his opinion? The fact that in the 1962-63 academic season nearly one third of all dissertations were on twentieth-century literature, and that more concerned William Faulkner than any other subject, seems to me to suggest a possible imbalance not in favor of the ancients. While the old-fashioned dissertation on "The Major Influences on the Style of Peter Pindar" does not strike me as usually very fresh or important, I am not sure that the currently fashionable subjects like "The Unity of Henry James's Minor Novels," or "Patterns of Imagery in Faulkner's Short Tales," are always much better.

A recent and rueful experience of my own exemplifies how quickly novelty wears off and the sensational becomes old hat. Only one book of mine has ever been widely assigned as required reading, and my pride in the fact that it is still being so used, thirty-six years after publication, was considerably tempered by a letter from a professor in an American university. Because, so he said, this book (called *The Modern Temper*) had quite bowled him over when he read it as an undergraduate, he recently tried it out on his own students. I might be interested to know that the typical reaction was well stated by one of them who said that while the book had a certain historical interest in being, he presumed, rather advanced for its time, it could not be expected to impress those who had been brought up on Sartre, Becket, *et al.* "To us, Mr. Krutch's pessimism seems quaint and rather sweet." Since my own frame of mind is somewhat more cheerful in 1965 than it was in 1929, and since to be modern is to be much less cheerful than I was at my worst, regret at being dismissed is somewhat tempered by the realization that I could not be up-to-date without being thoroughly miserable. Moreover, I have no doubt that several of my betters have produced a similar reaction. Does not O'Neill also seem quaint and sweet if you put him beside, say, Tennessee Williams?

If I understand correctly the contemporary terminology, a Square is not quite the same as what used to be called a Philistine. The latter is either non- or anti-intellectual and either indifferent to, or scornful of, all the arts. A Square, on the other hand, is a kind of middlebrow who defends the hopelessly passé in literature, art, philosophy and morals, and who has answers to important problems that those who are hep discovered long ago to be no answers at all. Few want to be put into that category and I certainly do not, but what the young readers of *The Modern Temper* were saying seems to be that while I was not Square by the standards of the late Twenties, that is precisely what the 'sixties have revealed me to be.

What I still have to say in this disquisition will confirm them in their opinion. It is simply this: The doubts and agonies that the contemporary avant-garde emphasizes and exploits most persistently do not and never have troubled me very much. I have plenty of old-fashioned ones of my own. I am not at ease in any Philistine Zion. But, to take two simple examples, the sense of lost identity and the problem of the unmotivated act do not paralyze my will or alienate me from society, the universe and myself. They seem, to put it bluntly, rather farfetched, and when I read a novel by Camus (generally regarded as the least "far-out" of the Existential novelists) I simply do not recognize myself in the characters or recognize my experience in theirs, and I cannot help wondering if the same is not true of many of those who nevertheless profess to find this literature the most interesting.

Whether to congratulate myself on this fact or to wonder uncomfortably if I am merely a Square after all, I do not know. In any case, my reaction to much of the most-admired avantgarde writing is very much like that to, say, the theological writings of Jonathan Edwards. His desperate attempts to convince himself that he would be willing to be damned throughout eternity if that would contribute to the glory of God seem to have been the result of a genuine conviction that he was lost forever, unless he could acquiesce gladly in the possibility that he might be. I have no doubt that the dilemma was agonizingly real to him. But it is not to me. I wonder how many of my contemporaries find that the avant-garde books really do speak to their condition. I can pity Edwards and Camus, although the problems are certainly not real to me and my relation to the metaphysically-founded sufferings of both seems to me equally remote.

The solutions at which so many of our writers arrive do not seem to me wholly valid. In even the middle-class magazines, one reads more or less sympathetic reports that the Marquis de Sade is a writer so definitely "in" that familiarity with his works is a *sine qua non* to the aspiring intellectual; and that the most admired contemporary is Jean Gênet, whose most-admired work, *The House of Flowers,* is said to be a record of the fantasies that accompanied his masturbations while serving his term in prison. Sartre calls him St. Gênet because, if I understand him aright, Gênet had the courageous sincerity to act out in his own life the essential vileness that is the most characteristic feature of human nature and thus wins a position in the hierarchy of atheistic existentialism almost as high as that of Sade, who demonstrated the complete freedom of the human will by doing precisely what religion, law and social custom had most insistently forbidden us to do.

If these ingenious paradoxes were new, there might be some excuse for those who are dazzled by them, and for concluding that they must represent an analysis of the human predicament to a depth never previously equalled. But they are not new. Rasputin's injunction, which is said to have been "Sin because without sinning you cannot repent, and only those who repent attain the state of grace," is somewhat similar, and he probably borrowed it from the Manichaeans of the early Christian centuries whose doctrines were so similar to those of Sartre that they were led to call the betrayer of Jesus "St. Judas" nearly two thousand years before Sartre canonized Gênet. If the students were to dig deeper into the past, they might find their current heroes at least as much "old hat," and almost as quaint and sweet, as the author of *The Modern Temper*.

One reader of this department complained that I quoted Dr. Johnson so often that I gave the impression of never having read anyone else. Only a Square, I suppose, would find in Johnson or in most of his contemporaries anything other than merely antiquarian interest. For the most part, they are not paradoxical and not much inclined to consider novelty a recommendation where morals, prudence or the pursuit of happiness is concerned. In fact, there is some appropriateness in the phrase used by Aldous Huxley when he spoke (without meaning to be wholly derogatory) of "the kindly superficiality of the Eighteenth Century." But for that very reason I think its writers might well have a place in the graduate schools of English at least as prominent as that of our contemporaries whom the student is much less likely to overlook. Their kindly superficiality might suggest "adjustments" to the human condition at least as satisfactory as those proposed by our own makers and thinkers, who may not be superficial but are seldom kindly.

In many respects I am even more of a Square than I once was, partly because I have found in Johnson and others of his century problems much like my own and solutions more congenial than those offered by our avant garde. The eighteenth century was reasonable, rather than fanatically devoted to reason; and it would not have been much impressed by the argument that Sade and Gênet are supremely great writers and teachers just because ingenious paradoxes could be developed to prove that they are. If that century makes everything too simple, too orderly and best examined in the light of common day, we tend on the contrary to see everything as complex, whether it is or not, and to blur every distinction. The indispensable century may have had too much faith in common sense, but we have too little. If it was almost too completely at home in its daylight world, we are too hopelessly alienated.

Although I realize that I am now about to tread upon dangerous ground, I will risk even the suggestion that our alienated and tortured youth might learn from the eighteenth century a solution of the so-called problem of sex that is at least preferable to the nonsolutions now commonly arrived at in the new literature. That solution many eighteenth-century men found in what might be called "the gallant game of life," and the Victorians found this solution very shocking. But the alienated modern is not likely to become Victorian in one step, and gallantry is surely preferable to the homosexual and sadistic perversions now so often sympathetically described as the most acceptable escape from the modern dilemma. I am not quite sure what that dilemma is, but it seems to be the result of two things: on the one hand, a conviction that practically everything is somehow sexual; on the other, a positively medieval distaste for the physiological aspects of normal love-making. John Donne (in some respects a century ahead of his time) once wrote:

> Whoever loves if he does not propose
> The right true end of love, he's one who goes
> To sea for nothing but to make him sick.

That is certainly not Victorian, even in the assumed fact or in the poet's attitude toward it. It is a very simple way of reconciling love and sex, and even if it is not the best way, it does describe an attitude likely to provide an "adjustment" at least more satisfactory than any that seems to have been achieved by the most esteemed literary exponents of what they assume to be the inevitable modern dilemma.   —*American Scholar*

W I N T E R ,   1965-1966

· · ·   · · ·   · · ·

Honor and morality

Some years ago a distinguished playwright told me how he had taken his East Side mother-in-law to see Maurice Evans in *Richard II*. The old lady—whose experience with both literature and the theater was extremely limited—listened intently in silence for half an hour, then waved a derisive thumb in the direction of the mellifluously complaining Richard and announced firmly: "I don't sympathize."

Now this was, of course, a fine tribute to the purely dramatic skill of Shakespeare. He had provoked the reaction he aimed at without any direct indication of what his own attitude was. I remember the anecdote at the moment for a simple reason. "I don't sympathize" vigorously sums up my own response to certain modern Richards, namely those who enlarge with too much self-pity upon their "alienation" from modern society, modern man and, indeed from the universe as a whole. On the one hand I find myself ready to agree with a good deal of their criticism; on the other I am irritated by their chronic reaction to the things we both abhor.

To take the most obvious and least significant case, consider the beatniks. I dislike—almost if not quite as much as they do— the dominant middle-class and organization-man concept of the Good Life. Although we can't all be philosophers, scholars, artists or monks, I agree that too many moderns aspire to nothing more than the "status symbols" that money can buy, and far too few to what George N. Shuster recently defined as the ultimate aim of education: "sharing the life of the scholar, poet and saint." But to respond to this situation by taking a shot of heroin and driving a car at ninety miles an hour seems unlikely either to improve society or, what is more relevant, lead to a Good Life.

Sympathetic interpreters of the beatniks have described them as "taking a revenge on society." For example, the hero of a recent novel is described by a reviewer thus: "Seeing too well in a world dazed by the bomb, Renaud undertakes an alcoholic strike against humanity." But the phrase "an alcoholic strike," like "a revenge on society," seems to me merely comic. It suggests the popular saying about "biting off your nose to spite your face," that being precisely what some intellectuals (including many somewhat above the beatnik level) are doing—as though turning into a dope addict did not hurt oneself even more than it hurts anyone else. It seems only slightly less obvious that the more respectable intellectuals who devote themselves exclusively to exploring and exploiting their "alienation" are doing much the same thing. Surely it is more productive of personal happiness and even "more useful to society" to be a candle throwing its beams into a naughty world than a beatnik crying "revenge, revenge" from the gutter. We hear a great deal about the responsibility of society toward the individual. The individual also has a responsibility toward society. And if things are as bad as the alienated say, the only way one can discharge that responsibility is by being an honorable man.

. . .

I presume that this thesis hardly needs elaboration and is not likely to be contested outside beatnik circles. But a considerable number of the most talented novelists, poets, painters and composers of the present day reveal, even if they do not proclaim, their alienation; and it seems to me that their most frequent response is only less grotesque, not more fruitful, than that of the beatniks. Even granted, as most of them proclaim in some version of Yeats's often quoted words, that "Things fall apart; the center cannot hold," is there still nothing for a wise man to do except take heroin with the beatniks or, as is usual among the alienated squares, elaborate in more and more complicated phrases their dark convictions?

To this question the hearty do-gooder will of course reply: "Why obviously the thing to do is to work for social improvement. Join the party of your choice and the church of your choice; be sure to register for all elections and attend the meetings of your local P.T.A." Without entering into any question concerning the ultimate effectiveness of such a method of employing one's time, it must be admitted that your alienated artist or philosopher is no more likely than a beatnik to undertake it. Let us suppose, therefore, that he has, like Thoreau, both "signed off" from the church and wished that he could as easily sign off from society as a whole. Of course he will be thoroughly disapproved of almost everywhere outside the circle of the completely alienated; but he might, like a few others besides Thoreau, find in this determination to stand alone the possibility of making for himself a private world from which he was *not* alienated, instead of devoting himself exclusively to the task of saying just how alienated he is. He could even find a few justifications formulated in the past for doing just what he has done.

I seem to remember somewhere in Plato the opinion that when times are thoroughly bad a wise man will merely stand by the wall. Similarly, it would appear from the *Meditations* of Marcus

Aurelius that although the emperor was no less aware than Yeats of a world in which "things fall apart," he spent relatively little time in either elaborating or bemoaning the lack of wisdom or virtue in society. He determined instead to cultivate them in himself. Then there is even a wholehearted defense of the mere slacker, which is quoted by Montaigne from one Theodorus who held that "it is not just that a wise man should risk his life for the good of his country and imperil wisdom for fools."

As I see it, the question is not so much whether the alienated would do better to imitate Marcus Aurelius rather than Baudelaire and Apollinaire, for it is a larger and, so many will think, an outrageous question. Is it possible that present-day civilization would be, in some important respects, better than it is if more people had thought less about how to improve society and more about how to improve themselves?

No doubt the medieval monk was too exclusively concerned with his private salvation. But we have gone to the other extreme and are so obsessed with the idea of society as a whole that it no longer seems quite respectable to seek even intellectual or spiritual self-improvement. I am not saying that we are, in actual fact, excessively unselfish. But the cant of the time requires that we should always be asking of any proposed good, "Can everybody have it?" or "Is it an answer to the general problem?" With astonishing regularity I get letters from people who comment on something I have written with a "Well, that's the answer as far as you are concerned; I guess it could be the answer as far as I am concerned. But only the privileged, or the lucky, or the well educated, or the intelligent, or the whatnot, can do what you and I can. So what is the answer for society as a whole?"

No doubt it would be fine if we could find a universal formula for salvation. I would welcome a convincing one if I ever heard it. But I never have, and I see no reason why, this being true, the individual should not save himself so long as he is not doing so at somebody else's expense. After all, society is composed of individuals. It cannot be "saved" except insofar as the individuals who compose it are.

I am not preaching universal indifference to society and social action as the highest wisdom. I am saying simply that if and when one individual feels (as so many articulate people do seem to feel) that the world is hopeless, then it is wiser to see what one can do about oneself than to give up all hope of that also. "I came into this world," said Thoreau, "not primarily to make it better but to live in it, be it good or bad." If you insist, you may soften that a little by substituting "exclusively" for "primarily," but the meaning will still point in the same direction. Or as the same argument was recently discussed in that excellent "little magazine" called *Manas:* "If an artist can find nothing but bad brushes to paint with, he will not dissipate all his energies leading a revolution against bad brushes—but will develop techniques which make it possible for him to paint with bad brushes. He may even discover things that bad brushes do better than good brushes. It is one thing to fight the good fight for good brushes, and another to start to paint."

During the Thirties, when most intellectuals moved leftward, quite a number of those who confessed (at least to their friends) that they had embraced Communism were nevertheless engaged in writing movies for Hollywood or advertisements for Madison Avenue, while at the same time professing to regard both the movies and advertising as poisonous exhalations from a deliquescent society. Often (and I report from my own experience) they justified themselves by saying that there was no use trying to be anything but rotten in a rotten society. Come the revolution and we will all be decent. Meanwhile, since we live in an evil society, we submit to it without any bourgeois nonsense about merely personal decency.

Such an attitude is only a logical extreme of the one taken by those who may not completely renounce either personal integrity or personal happiness, but insist upon our duty to think primarily in terms of what can be done for society, and who sink into despair if we do not know an answer. I will even go so far as to suggest the possibility that society may be in a bad way partly because we have laid so much stress on public education—to take one example—and so little upon self-education. (Perhaps it also has something to do with the fact that I have met "educators" who were not, and made no effort to be educated themselves.)

Thoreau wrote: Philanthropy is almost the only virtue which is sufficiently appreciated by mankind. . . . The kind uncles and aunts of the race are more esteemed than its true spiritual fathers and mothers. I once heard a reverend lecturer on England, a man of learning and intelligence, after enumerating her scientific, literary and political worthies, Shakespeare, Bacon, Cromwell, Milton, Newton and others, speak next of her Christian heroes, whom, as if his profession required it of him, he elevated to a place far above all the rest, as the greatest of the great. They were Penn, Howard and Mrs. Fry. Everyone must feel the falsehood and cant of this. The last were not England's best men and women; only, perhaps, her best philanthropists.

This is a tough-minded opinion. It is stated with characteristic exaggeration. But at least there is something to be said for those who do their best even though they do not see at the moment just what practical good it is going to do "for the common man."

After all, the medieval monk did perform a service. Neither the God he served nor the learning he preserved counted for much in the world from which he had retired. But he did exemplify in himself virtues that might otherwise have ceased to exist entirely, and he did preserve learning that without him would have been lost.

What it all comes down to in practice is simply this: If you despair of the world, don't despair of yourself. And it is because so many of the alienated critics of our society, with whose criticisms I agree, seem unable to do anything of the sort that I find myself alienated from them also.

Thirty years ago, when I published a book much more pessimistic than I could possibly write now, I received a good many letters that might have been boiled down to a sentence in one of them: "If these are your convictions why don't you go hang yourself?" The answer was, and has continued to be through all such changes of opinion as I have undergone, that there is a private world of thought and endeavor which society has never been able to take away from me.   —*American Scholar*

SUMMER, 1960

. . .   .

Legs are coming back

I am, I believe, the first historian of culture ever to point out that the modern male lost interest in his own legs about the time that he developed an ardent concern with those of his female companions. A proper Victorian gentleman used his to walk with; and although he might so far forget himself as to make sly allusions to "a neat ankle," he was expected to assume that respectable ladies, like the Queen of Spain, had no legs. Then skirts went up, and until the most recent revolution in taste transferred his attentions to certain other conspicuous secondary sex characteristics, he was so absorbed in an aesthetic contemplation of the now obvious fact that ladies did have them that he naturally forgot even the practical uses he could make of his own. Now, after a generation or two, the novelty has worn off, and walking is coming back into fashion.

I am aware, of course, that there are rival theories to explain the decline of pedestrianism for pleasure, or as a means of getting from one place to another. Some say that it was due merely to the fact that the invention of the automobile, plus our fanatical concern with gadgets, encouraged us to use this vehicle to the near exclusion of the devices supplied by nature. Those who follow the lead of that sour sociologist Thorstein Veblen have a different explanation. They attribute the phenomenon to the alleged fact that members of the leisure class refused to use their legs, in order to demonstrate that they did not have to. In China, the deformed feet of female aristocrats were a status symbol proudly exhibited by those who wished to make it evident that if they wanted to go anywhere there would always be someone to carry them. In the West, high-heeled shoes served the same purpose, although the fact that they could be taken off indicated a less absolute confidence. Senior executives can't very well wear crippling shoes but many of them now play routine golf by riding from shot to shot in motorized carts, just to avoid the exercise once supposed to be the excuse for the game.

The one moment that anyone who has ever seen Shaw's *Pygmalion* is sure to remember is that in which the newly-made lady, who has just been asked by an admirer if he can walk her home through the park, demonstrates her sense of newly-acquired status by exclaiming in words more appropriate to her former station in life: "Not bloody likely. I am going in a taxi." This is strong support for the Veblen theory; but I naturally still prefer my own—that walking went out of fashion when female legs became erotic rather than utilitarian—and came back when they had been exposed so long and so abundantly that the sight of them was no longer a treat. Now men can remember their own and the uses to which they may be put. This theory may be a bit farfetched but it is at least my very own.

In any case, there is no doubt that the tide is turning. Any accurate observer stationed in the neighborhood of Madison and Park will notice a novel phenomenon. A group of young executives bound for two or three martinis and a bit of lunch somewhere in the East Fifties has spent ten minutes trying to get a taxi which would carry them at a snail's pace across town. One says to the other, "Let's save time by walking." And once the astonishment at the novel suggestion has worn off, there is a general agreement with this original idea. Our young executives are learning an important lesson. Labor-saving devices sometimes increase labor, and rapid transit is often the slowest way of getting somewhere.

This is only a minor example of a cultural revolution. We have a Secretary of the Interior who not only walks but climbs, and a Justice of the Supreme Court who writes books, shamelessly describing his pedestrian exploits. It may be that the other official who recently insisted that a fifty-mile walk would do us all good is going to extremes, but extravagant reactions are a usual phenomenon associated with social changes. It looks as though walking, not riding, is about to become a status symbol.

Notoriously, Americans tend to extremes. They have been more exuberantly committed than any other people to whatever is thought of as modern—whether it be gadgets, clothes or even social manners. And walking tended to be more completely outmoded here than anywhere else. As many a visitor to Los Angeles (where some aspects of the American way are carried to their ultimate extremes) has discovered, the police regard with suspicion any pedestrian on the sidewalk who does not appear to be waiting for a taxi. And even in New York most of the natives have forgotten how to *flâner* in the Parisian fashion. In England, on the other hand, country walking never went completely out of fashion, and the public right-of-way along traditional paths across private property is jealously protected to this day. The German student's *Wanderjahr* never completely ceased to be a respectable tradition, and within the last decade the youth hostels (not patronized by youths only) have become increasingly familiar all over Europe. More recently American college youths have discovered them, and the European tour conducted at least partly on foot has become, among the rich as well as the poor, an increasingly popular substitute for the old-fashioned grand tour. The significant fact is that such partly pedestrian tours are not merely *faute de mieux* for those who cannot afford anything else—their advantages as well as their economy have come to be what count. Even within this country nothing is more fashionable at the moment than "garden tours" or "visits to stately homes," which must necessarily be conducted on foot.

One reason for all this—and one that some may be inclined to take rather more seriously than my opening suggestions—is simply this: We have begun to recover just a bit from our obsession with the automobile and the airplane for their own sakes and to realize that the motorcar (and, of course, *a fortiori* the airplane) is a method of locomotion rather than an end in itself—that if you travel for the sake of seeing something rather than simply to get from one place to another, you might almost as well stay at home. From a jet flying at forty thousand feet you see so little that luxury consists in watching a movie while traversing India or Japan; and from an automobile you see little except superhighways and cloverleaves, which are the same everywhere. Yet, as I have observed in my own exploration of our continent, many people value the national parks because they are somewhere to go in a car instead of valuing the car because it can take them there. In many an American family the week-end conference begins, not with the question, "What would we like to visit?" but "Where can we go for a drive?"

For obvious reasons, all producers of the gadgets encourage the idea that even acquiring the latest model dishwasher or deep freezer is less in order to enjoy its supposed usefulness than a way of being one-up on your neighbors. And the manufacturers of automobiles outdo all others in reliance upon this not always subtly conveyed suggestion. For instance: One widely exhibited

TV commercial shows the head of the house arriving in a brand-new car midst gasps of admiration from wife and kiddies, who immediately summon the neighbors to see what Daddy has done to make the neighbors feel envious and inferior. But since nearly everybody has a new car nowadays, its value as a status symbol is declining, and gadgetry has reached an ultimate absurdity in battery-operated swizzle sticks. Why-not-dazzle-the-neighbors? is a ploy already beginning to lose its effectiveness.

Meantime another recent phenomenon operates positively in the same direction. Americans have rediscovered nature. Books about animals, plants, mountains and oceans pour in an unprecedented stream from the presses because they are being bought in unprecedented numbers. No doubt this is partly because we can no longer take nature for granted; because a beautiful world is disappearing under the impact of an exploding population and the "progress" it makes necessary. Birdwatchers, once eccentric figures of fun, are now too numerous to be laughed at. The Audubon Society estimates that there are some ten million of them in the United States. The head of one of our largest corporations has published a splendid book about hummingbirds, and it has even been suggested that on a fine weekend there are more people out with binoculars than in the football or baseball stadia.

But you can't observe nature from an automobile—especially if, like most automobilists, you confine yourself to superhighways, because you are more concerned with your car than with yourself and don't much care where you are if only you get there quickly. You may ride out of the city, but once you get into the country there is no substitute for legs. And that is equally true whether your taste is for the ambitious hike or climb or merely for what I like to call windowshopping in nature, which means strolling about in no matter how leisurely a fashion but keeping your eyes open for the violet by the mossy stone or for one of the little creatures who share the earth with us. Thoreau is more widely read today than ever before, and one of the things we are learning from him is that nature is as wonderful in the small and the near-at-home as in the grandiose and the remote. One evidence that we really are learning this is that the series of five walks, inaugurated a few years ago by the Museum of the City of New York, proved so popular that the walks are now scheduled for every other week except in winter.

Even those (and there are still many of them) who boast that nature puts them out and who are uncomfortable as soon as they leave what an ultra-urbanized acquaintance of mine used to call "God's concrete" will find that city-walking also affords delight. You can't get the best of a city from a taxi or a bus (to say nothing of a subway) because much of it, like much of the best in the country, is made up of little things. Two hundred and fifty years ago the London poet John Gay wrote a descriptive poem subtitled "The Art of Walking the Streets of London," and he knew something that is equally true today—you learn a city only by walking it and you find the most rewarding areas those not too modernized, where what Miss Jane Jacobs called in her recent book "the life of the streets" still flourishes.

Whether you walk in the city or the country, the motion of the legs stimulates both the tongue and the brain. Precious little good talk is ever originated in any rapidly moving vehicle. *The New Yorker* magazine often reports absurd fragments overheard on a bus or in the subway, but it has never, as far as I can recall, recorded anything wise. Advertising slogans are thought up by men sitting at desks in offices they rode to, and the gobbledygook of sociologists and bureaucrats originates in the same way. But even Samuel Johnson, that hater of the country, said some of his best things while walking with Boswell in London or Scotland, and there are more impressive examples. Demosthenes composed his orations while walking the beach. Plato taught in a grove. Aristotle, who founded modern logic and modern science, was known to his contemporaries as the Peripatetic Philosopher.

"The road," said Cervantes, "is always better than the inn." That is profoundly true and implies the most fundamental of all reasons why it is better to walk than to ride. We walk in order to enjoy, literally or figuratively, what the road has to offer. We ride in order to get quickly to the inn. If walking were a recent technological marvel and legs a new invention, we would realize that they are more remarkable than the automobile or even the wheel. They can negotiate a wider variety of terrain than any vehicle. They can go places even a jeep can't. And they last much longer. Hurrah for what our fathers used to call shank's mare! If wishes were automobiles, beggars would ride. But nowadays "the man who has everything" is using his legs.   —*American Scholar*

                                    AUTUMN, 1964

. . .   .

Too short to save

One of my notebooks borrows its label from that of the famous box found among the effects of a New England spinster: "Pieces of string too short to save."

Some of the items it would be flattery to call *pensées*, and others are *obiter dicta* not likely to be of great interest to the general reader. As for example: "When I was a child, garlic was eaten only by low-class foreigners. During my lifetime, I have (and it was a sad change for me) seen it first become smart, and then quickly achieve middle-class respectability, so that to-day it is almost ubiquitous and turns up in surprising places like dressing for fruit salad." Others are merely advertising slogans copied down because they amused me for one reason or another. On a San Francisco restaurant: "Hamburgers with Dignity." On the barn of a California dairy: "Our cows are not contented. They are constantly striving to produce better milk."

Other items make note of additional support for some thesis I have labored previously. For example again: "Because of my stubborn conviction that sociological explanations of conduct are usually convincing only *ex post facto,* and couldn't have been used to predict, I was delighted by an item in a Tucson paper about two girl high-school students who confessed responsibility for making obscene telephone calls to a fraternity house. Would you expect them to be products of 'broken homes' or daughters of respectable families? You would be wrong whichever answer you gave. One was the child of a divorced couple, the other of a clergyman." Along the same line is an item supporting my conviction that if the present trend continues, "the worker" will soon be the only man who has any leisure. At least a survey made by the Chase Manhattan Bank reports that since World War II, the average worker now works a forty-hour week, while forty percent of all managers, executives, proprietors, and so forth, put in more than forty-eight hours. (N.B. I don't trust surveys except when the results are on my side.)

My excuse for making such things public is that I am often astonished to get, from readers from whom I have never heard before, animated responses to some casual remark, while my most profound discourses pass unnoticed. The same thing often happens when I meet an old student who says, "I have always remembered what you said in class one day," and then proceeds to quote something that I have no memory of having ever said and that is, at best, not one of the things I would most like to be remembered for. When this happens, I am, if in a complacent mood, reminded that arrows shot into the air will fall to earth we know not where and that, if I remember the poem aright, they are sometimes found in the heart of a friend. At more flippant moments, I am reminded instead of the old burlesque bit in which the comedian fires a gun at nothing in particular after which, half a minute later, a stuffed duck falls at his feet.

At any rate, here goes.

Like Mr. Khrushchev, I have never visited Disneyland. An acquaintance who is also an avid reader of science fiction tells me that it is too good for children and that he made his first inspection alone in order not to have his aesthetic pleasure disturbed by the antics of his young boys. I doubt that my own reaction would be the same as his. I often approve of mechanical contraptions if they do something that nothing else can do, or at least never did before so expertly or conveniently. But I hate them when they are merely mechanical substitutes for something real—like Disney's mechanical birds, synthetic jungles, and so forth. One of the greatest glories of his phony fairyland is, so I am told, a replica of Grand Canyon, and I have no doubt that it is much admired by people who have traveled farther to see it than they would travel to see the Canyon itself— and in some cases, no doubt, admired especially by those who have seen the real thing. For what is probably the same reason, child visitors to the Desert Museum outside Tucson are most impressed by creatures they have seen on the Museum's TV show. They are not interested in TV because it shows them animals, but interested in animals because TV has made certain isolated individuals into celebrities. Grand Canyon must be a wonder, say the visitors, if Disney spends all that money as well as all that ingenuity in reproducing it. And I wager that more people standing at the Canyon's rim remark to a fellow, "I saw the Disneyland replica," than say at Disneyland, "I once saw the real thing."

Not many years ago, various jungle plants began to be widely used in offices because they grow in very little light.

Nowadays they are being rapidly replaced by quite skillful imitations that require no light at all, no water, and no care. These fakes are also invading homes. In fact, I have even seen them mixed with a few living plants in so-called gardens. I fear that the time is rapidly approaching when all the plants will be plastic, all the animals stuffed, and all the scenery in Disneyland. This will be called evidence that man has finally come fully into his inheritance.

From the English, I think, our advertisers have borrowed the trick of beginning an elegant soft sell with a quotation from some respected writer. If I were in the business, I would suggest to, say, Merrill Lynch, Pierce, *et al.*, this clincher from Dr. Johnson: "There are few ways in which a man can be more innocently employed than in getting money." But I am not in the business. I am, on the contrary, a mere consumer and as such, more concerned to bolster my sales resistance than to sell myself or others, either the hard way or the soft. Accordingly, I have collected wise sayings to counteract the blandishments of specific persuaders. Here are a few of them:

For Chanel, Houbigant and the rest: "The best way for a woman to smell is not at all." (*Montaigne*)

For the book clubs: "Books of the true sort, not those things that moderns club for at book clubs." (*Charles Lamb*)

For *Vogue, Harper's Bazaar* and the rest: "Fashion is a form of ugliness so intolerable that we have to change it every six months." (*Oscar Wilde*)

For *House and Garden, Country Life* and so forth: "Adam and Eve were prisoners in a garden until, with Promethean courage, they sinned themselves out of it." (*Lamb, again*)

For the correspondence schools that teach you how to succeed in business: "Trade could not be managed by those who manage it if it had much difficulty." (*Johnson, again*)

For chambers of commerce: "Many people have the erroneous idea that a city must be large in order to be happy." (*Aristotle*)

For Schenley, Seagram and the rest: "Nor do I wish to improve the art of making poison pleasant." (*Dr. Johnson, explaining why he did not inquire into the Scottish methods of distilling whiskey*)

For airlines, ship companies and other promoters of tourism: "I cannot but regard it as a kindness in those who have the steering of me that, by the want of pecuniary wealth, I have been nailed down to this my native region. . . . What would signify in comparison the thin and diffused knowledge and love of the whole earth . . . got by wandering?" (*Thoreau*)

These will have to do for the present unless a theologically inclined friend was not pulling my leg after all when he informed me many years ago that Tertulian had written: "He who has been bathed in the Blood of the Lamb need never bathe again." That ought to put even Lever Brothers and Procter & Gamble out of business.

I wonder if any of my readers have recognized one characteristic of this department (now in its eleventh year) * that makes it very nearly unique—the fact, I mean, that it has never (well, hardly ever) mentioned sex. Lest anyone suspect that I am either prudish or pathologically uninterested in the subject, I will explain that I haven't said much about sex because it seemed to me that everything that could possibly be said about it had been said too often already. Nevertheless, there is one phenomenon that, as far as I know, has never been commented upon; namely, the change that during the last couple of decades has come over the prevailing intellectual attitude, and constitutes a revolution as complete as that accomplished by the earlier anti-Puritan revolt. The 'twenties were very much inclined to regard, or at least to pretend to regard, sex as what they called "merely (though sometimes delightfully) biological." Nowa-

* "If You Don't Mind My Saying So," *The American Scholar*.

days it is not *merely* anything. It has become highly mystical again, at least in the sense that it is again far more than either a mere incidental pleasure or a mere biological necessity. In the view of our leading novelists and critics, it has become a *sine qua non* of mental health, moral sanity and artistic sensibility—in fact, the essential mystery of life and the only key to its meaning. The Fiedlers, Mailers and most of the other "serious" novelists and "serious" critics, to say nothing of our Gênets, Burroughses, *et cetera,* are certainly not romantic or sentimental. They are likely to refer to the Mystic Rose by way of a four-letter word, but the four-letter words have come to have a ritual and magical significance so that the object referred to is again a Mystic Rose, nevertheless.

Toward the end of the 'twenties, I myself called one chapter of a book "Love: or the Life and Death of a Value." How absurd that would seem today when sex is again a value that most of our writers seem to believe no one else values sufficiently. Or consider Aldous Huxley or even T. S. Eliot in the days when the latter was just in the process of transforming himself from an *enfant terrible* into a classicist, royalist and Catholic. Commenting in *The Waste Land* on the visit of the young man to his girl friend, he wrote:

> When lovely woman stoops to folly and
> Paces about her room again, alone,
> She smoothes her hair with automatic hand,
> And puts a record on the gramophone.*

In any respectable novel, poem or play today, she would not put a record on the gramophone. She would write a book discussing at length how she had or had not been "fulfilled," and how all of us should make it our first business to see to it that we had been. I suppose that Lawrence was the first to turn

* Reprinted by permission of the Publishers, Harcourt, Brace & World, Inc., New York, N.Y.

against the "merely biological" cliché, but few writers have failed to follow him.

Everybody has his own explanation of the obvious fact that nothing intended to attract the attention of the public can now get along without introducing a seductive female into the picture somehow, even if she is not more appropriate than the one who is buying the latest "decorator color" toilet paper in the supermarket, or looking on while somebody demonstrates a bulldozer. Some say that this is because ours is a sinful age; others, that it is, on the contrary, because we no longer think it sinful to admit what has always been true, namely that nothing else interests the civilized human being so much as the members of the female sex. They interest men because men desire them and they interest women because women hope to learn from their most attractive sisters the secret of their attractiveness.

Being myself neither a Puritan nor an anti-Puritan, but one who tends to see man's alienation from the natural world as the explanation of many things, I have my own explanation. It is that sex is, for many people, the only remaining link with that animate world to which they really belong. Life, in other words, is being reduced more and more to an affair in which only machines and sex count. We certainly overemphasize the first, so perhaps the moralists are right when they say we are overemphasizing the second also.

While we are on this subject (and it is always a difficult subject to get off) permit me a few other observations on a somewhat different aspect of it. During the 'twenties, it was a universal belief that they ordered these things better in France. Formerly, they did at least order them differently. But times have changed so much that we have recently had unbelievable cases where the French courts prohibited the sale of books freely offered in the United States; and we are now accused of corrupting the morals of the very nation against whose supposedly corrupt literature Americans defended themselves for a century or more.

As readers of the *Scholar* do not need to be told, the French Academy revises its dictionary on the same system that we use here for painting the Brooklyn and Golden Gate Bridges: When you reach the end, you start over again at the beginning. Now it happens that it recently reached (for, I don't know, how many times) that word which must be one of the first that the French child learns if he hears it in the nursery rhyme *"Il est cocu le chef de gare."* The definition read formerly, *"celui dont l'épouse manque à la fidélité"* (he whose wife is not faithful); but according to *Figaro Littéraire*, the phrase has become *"dont l'épouse ou la compagne."* In other words, a Frenchman may now be cuckolded by either his mistress or his wife and, if very unfortunate, by both.

The anonymous conductor of the department *"Usage et Grammaire"* in *Figaro Littéraire* analyzes the full implication of this change and raises some puzzling questions or objections. His chief objection is one that all feminists will applaud. The Academy definition does not recognize that wives (and presumably mistresses) can be as truly cuckolded as their husbands or lovers. And yet, so he goes on to say, this is not only contrary to the contemporary acceptance of equality between the sexes but also constitutes a refusal to go along with other almost equally weighty authorities. The *Grand Larousse* has recognized since 1869 the feminine form of the word, *cocue,* and it cites the illustration: *"Les femmes sont bien plus souvent cocues que les hommes.* (Furier)" But it does follow this with the phrase "little used."

Doubtless it will be more often used in the future unless, as seems more probable, the epithet comes to be so little opprobrious that it falls out of use almost entirely in both the masculine and the feminine form. The *Figaro*'s grammarian also wants to know whether or not a man can possibly be appropriately classified as *cocu* if his wife but not his mistress is unfaithful, or if his mistress is unfaithful and his wife faithful, or does he perhaps not deserve the appellation unless both *"manque à la fidélité"*?   —*American Scholar*

AUTUMN, 1965

. . .   .

Owning is not always possessing

Almost all of us have friends wealthier than we are, who have finer houses, more or better automobiles, more expensive clothes. And nearly all of us have said at one time or another that these wealthier friends did not get from their possessions as much pleasure and satisfaction as we got from ours. Sometimes we go so far as to say that they have more than they can use or enjoy. But we don't usually go on to ask if the same thing may not be true, in a smaller way, of us. We assume that when we buy a thing we possess it. But often we don't. Ownership is not the same thing as possession and it doesn't come automatically.

The distinction is really plain enough and we never fail to see it in other connections. We know that we do not necessarily possess a man or a woman because we are married to him any more than we necessarily possess a child just because we begot him. The law says that we are married and the law gives us certain powers over the child. But the fact may remain that we possess neither the child nor the person to whom we are married. Perhaps neither one wants to belong to us and, therefore, does not. But the fault is also often ours. They cannot possibly belong to us unless we also belong to them; unless, as we say under the circumstances, we love them.

What is true of a wife, a husband, or a child is true of everything else we can "have" or "own" in any significant way. Of course it is true of a cat, a dog, or a horse. And it is also true of any other intimate possession. Once we have bought or in any way acquired it by legal title, we have taken only the first step. We must take possession of it later.

First of all, that means of course that we must somehow be aware that it exists and that we do own it. Ridiculous as the fact may be, many people do not even get that far. They buy so many pictures or books or suits and dresses that they actually do not remember what they have. And there are few of us who own so little that we have actually taken possession of all that we do own.

Actually to do that implies a great deal more than simply having the knowledge that it is said to be ours. We have to get into some kind of relation with it. We must love it—not in quite the same way that we love a wife, a husband, a child, or even a pet—but in a way that is not entirely different either. A home which is not loved, for which we ourselves do not do something, is not a home at all. And the same thing is true to some extent of every so-called possession. We cannot really own any part of it unless at the same time we give it some part of ourselves.

But how do we learn to do that? How can we get into the habit of possessing the things we own? What does "learning to love" really mean?

It means first of all that we must get into some sort of *active* relation with the thing to be loved. Mere ownership can be, and often is, entirely passive. We take one short step in the right direction if we merely actually use the thing we own, if we merely occupy the house or drive the car which we have bought. But, of course, that is only a very short step indeed. The next is to assume some sort of responsibility for it, and that means doing something *for* it as well as doing something *with* it.

Even in the case of a mere mechanical convenience it means not taking it for granted, but understanding something about how and why it works. In the case of a house—which is a mere material thing as long as it is nothing but a house, yet becomes a spiritual thing when it has been made into a home—it means more. It means some personal concern with the way it is built, furnished, and run. It means doing something for it oneself and, in the case of things one cannot do oneself, it means an active concern in what is being done for one. Decidedly it does not mean simply saying to an architect, a decorator, a housekeeper, or a maintenance staff: "Do what you think best; I leave it in your hands." One would hardly expect to be able to love a wife, a husband, a child whom one treated in that way. And in that way one cannot learn to love anything else either.

One of the good things about having less is just that it encourages, sometimes even forces us, into that active relation with things owned, which is the beginning of love. We are compelled to do more things for ourselves and, therefore, we find ourselves truly possessing or truly loving the things we have made, planned, or operated. They have become truly ours because we have become vividly aware that they exist, because we actually use them, and because we have assumed some sort of responsibility for them—in a word because we have permitted ourselves to belong to them as well as demanded that they should belong to us.

What is true of a house is true of every other useful material thing. It is doubly true of what we actually make for ourselves whether the thing is made with hammer and saw, with needle, or with paint brush. It is true also of food that has been prepared, cooked, or even merely supervised by oneself. The essential thing is to break the habit of taking for granted—and no one was ever unaware of what he himself had created.

Next to "doing," the greatest aid to loving and possessing is "knowing." Good wine, for example, is not usually a household product. But one gets a great deal more out of a good wine if one knows something about it. And the principle is infinitely extensible. You cannot be really interested in nature, music, or in the plastic arts unless you know something about them. Without such knowledge you may own pictures, buy the finest phonograph, and even endow orchestras. But you will not possess much of the beauty of any art. Knowing is really a form of activity and without it there is no participation. With it one may do the next best thing to creating. One may, to that extent, participate in the creative process and follow Mozart or Leonardo, at least at a distance.

Most of us realize by now that we must buy less than we used to buy and that means that we need more than ever to practice genuine economy. But genuine economy does not necessarily mean doing without what we need or even without what we genuinely want. It does not necessarily mean restricting ourselves to common necessities unless one includes under that head the necessities of the soul. It does imply buying only what we can really possess, which is the same as saying what we can really enjoy as well as really use. Sometimes it means also learning how to take possession of what we already own. If we cannot build a new house, perhaps we can, for the first time, learn how to live *with* not merely *in* the one we already own.

No doubt individuals differ as to the number of things they really need or can really possess. What is luxury for one may be austerity for another. There is no virtue in doing without what we may legitimately have, just for the sake of doing without. But we can learn to know ourselves better, learn to recognize those things which we as individuals are capable of loving. And there are many of us who will discover that when we have felt dissatisfied with our lot, it was lack of possession rather than lack of mere belongings that was the cause of dissatisfaction.

—*House Beautiful*

MARCH, 1953

. . . .

In defense of prejudice

"Prejudice" is the dirtiest word in the modern vocabulary. So perhaps it ought to be—if only we were quite sure what it meant. But at least this reader of contemporary discussions is getting bewildered. He doesn't know what the writers mean and he wonders if they do either.

Take the case where the "liberals" protest that we are "prejudiced" in favor of the Western conception of democracy as opposed to the Russian. They seem to imply that a really "unprejudiced" man would necessarily agree that one is just as valid as the other. But just how unprejudiced can you get if you are going to think at all?

To clear the air let us put the word "prejudice" alongside the word "preference" and ask if there is really no difference between them. It can hardly be said that we ought to be completely free of preferences. If we were, then we would be incapable of making what the philosophers call a value judgment. And a society in which nothing seemed preferable to anything else would be more barbarous than any which anthropology has ever discovered. Yet as the word "prejudice" is frequently used it is difficult to see how we could give up what it is taken to mean, without giving up preferences too. Is there really anything so shameful about preferring the Western concept of democracy to the Soviet?

Ever since the Renaissance the course of Western civilization has been determined by our preferences—or prejudices, if you insist—in favor, let us say, of investigation as opposed to dogma, health as opposed to disease, liberty as opposed to conformity, kindness as opposed to cruelty. No technique ever invented to undermine that civilization was ever more subtle than that which seeks to convince us that every preference is a prejudice, that all prejudices are wrong, and that, for example, we are only "prejudiced" in favor of our own mores when we find the Western concept of fair play more attractive than the doctrine that class interest alone determines the meaning of "justice" or that policy, not a respect for truth, should determine what we will promise or say.

Any man so unprejudiced as all that is a monster. If his condemnation is not that he chooses darkness rather than light, it may be something even worse—that he perceives no distinction between them. Yet a reviewer who is pretending to praise a group of recent books about the Soviet Union finds it necessary to interject the remark that "All the writers . . . assume that our way of life is mysteriously right and that the other side is evil." Why that adverb "mysteriously"? What is so mysterious about the assumption that one thing is better than another? How can one possibly indulge in any meaningful comparisons unless one does assume that a choice between them is legitimate? Is it really necessary to invoke a "mystery" to explain the feeling that judicial assassination is "somehow" not right?

Unfortunately, the "liberal" to whom all preferences except his own are wicked prejudices, had the way prepared for him by the so-called "impartiality" of the kind of history and sociology which was written during the second half of the nineteenth century and the first half of the twentieth. When a Lecky popularized the conviction that there is no distinction between mores and morals, the whole disastrous paralysis of judgment, as a legitimate function of thinking man, set in. Soon the sociologists with their "objective" studies followed, and shortly after them came the anthropologists with their "cultural relativism." The one was soon telling us that the only criterion for what men ought to do is what it has been discovered they are doing; the other, that the civilization of the European is not better than that of the Plains Indian but only "different." By the premises of either it is only natural to conclude also that Western democracy is only "different" from what the Kremlin has stolen the word to describe.

Such convictions three fourths of the "intellectuals" firmly hold. By now they have also seeped down until they have begun to permeate not only the middle class but almost every stratum of society, until the strongest preferences begin to waver when those who entertain them are reminded that they are "mere prejudices" after all.

It is not likely that "our way of life" can be preserved by those who would like to preserve it unless they believe that it is preferable whether "mysteriously" or not. Perhaps the time has come to realize this fact and to re-establish the first line of defense where logically it has to be. In one of his saner moments Nietzsche declared that "All life is a dispute about taste"—and tastes are preferences. To assert their legitimacy is to take a position midway between: "Right is right because God so ordained it" and "Nothing is right or wrong except as custom makes it so." It is to assert that if there are no absolutes in the universe then the only escape from anarchy lies through those "preferences" which man himself asserts when he chooses honor rather than treachery, love rather than hate, beauty rather than ugliness, light rather than darkness. If they

are all the same to the universe they are not all the same to
him. If to find them not all the same is "nothing but" a taste
or a preference arbitrarily chosen, then such arbitrary choices
are among the most fateful that a man or a civilization can
make, and nothing is more inappropriate than to talk about
"mere tastes" and "mere preferences."

A society without what are commonly called prejudices is
unthinkable. Obviously the "liberal" is aware of that fact when
he defends his own set of preferences and is a relativist in
respect to everything except his own. To be prejudiced even
within a reasonable meaning of the term is not quite as bad as it
would be to have no preferences at all—if such a thing were
possible. A prejudiced man may sometimes be a bad man; a
man without preferences would not be a man at all. To every
human being some things are better than others. To have many
preferences and to consider them important is—no matter what
some may call them—something to be proud of, not ashamed.

—*The Freeman*

JUNE 28, 1954

. . .　. . .　. . .

Who defines the American way?

Nineteen-hundred and fifty-eight may go down in history as
the year when many Americans first expressed dissatisfaction
with two of the things they had been proudest of: their automobiles and their schools. Some of the chrome will probably
come off both. But it would be a pity to have the reform stop
there. This looks like a good year to ask a fundamental question: What are schools (and automobiles) really for?

To the first of these questions the professional educators have a ready answer: "Preparation for life." That has a persuasive sound. But what kind of life should they prepare for? Is it for life as it is, or for life as it might be?

Once, the school, like the church, embodied a protest (or at least a countervailing influence) against what most of the other forces in society tended to make of that society and of man himself. The church held that man, undisciplined by religion, was wicked; the school, that unless he was educated he would be ignorant and crass. Both seem now to have fallen in love with the world as it is. They talk more and more about "adjustment" and to mean by that "adjustment to things as they are."

The one half-heartedly, the other with real enthusiasm, gives up the attempt to direct society and is content to follow it— like the political leader who watches where a mob is going, puts himself at the head of it, and cries "Follow me." Don't teach "literary English"; teach "acceptable English." If, as a New York Commission recently proposed, schoolchildren are not interested in the classics, don't waste time trying to arouse their interest but give them something they *are* interested in. Teach them how to drive automobiles, how lipstick is best applied, and how (one actual course in a Midwestern "institution of learning") to order groceries over the telephone. These are the things they will be doing; these are what their lives will be made up of; and the business of education is "to prepare for life."

If they won't read, then show them some pictures. As the public-opinion polls have proved, most of those who follow the American Way (and you are not against that, are you?) seldom read a book. Movie appreciation is a much better preparation for life—if you mean preparation for the kind of life the un-educated lead. From the advertiser (either directly or via his sponsored TV programs) most Americans learn far more than they ever learn in school about the prevailing mores and standards of value, about current tastes, beliefs, and preferred activities. If what we most need to learn are the obvious external aspects of the American Way and how to follow it, then advertising is the best teacher.

Not long ago a Western Senator, addressing a meeting of advertising executives, was reported to have congratulated them on how much educating they were already doing and to have urged them to do more, specifically, as he put it, "to participate actively in the classroom situation"—which I take to mean to minimize still further the extent to which education stands for any interests or ideals other than those which the advertiser finds it profitable to cultivate.

Just how ready *are* teachers to welcome such "participation in the classroom situation"? Not all of them, one may be sure. But the National Educational Association, which is, I believe, the largest and most influential organization of schoolmen, seems quite enthusiastic. Two of its recent projects are a pamphlet called "Using Consumer Credit" and an elaborate project called "Outdoor Education." The pamphlet includes a cartoon (high-school pupils cannot be expected to read) captioned, "Don't Be Afraid to Use Credit," and the "project" is built chiefly around the use of the fishing rod and the gun. The pamphlet offers profuse thanks for the "generous assistance" to two men whom it fails to identify, a couple of fellows who have been doing public-relations work for the National Consumer Finance Association, which turns out to be an organization devoted to promoting the interests of a group of small-loan companies. As for the Outdoor Education Project, its "advisory committee" includes a president and a secretary-treasurer of the "Sporting Arms and Ammunition Manufacturers Institute" as well as the secretary-treasurer of "The Associated Fishing Tackle Manufacturers." If there is any distinction between education in a democracy and the propaganda of special interests, is it likely that the distinction will be very carefully maintained by either the authors of the pamphlet on consumer credit or the directors of the outdoor "education" project? Of course, if the prevailing educational philosophy is sound there is no reason why the distinction should be maintained. If it isn't sound. . . .

The school curriculum needs the revision many have begun to talk about. Perhaps a required course in algebra would be a good thing. But it is more important to ask what schools are for. And the question can be put very simply: Should they follow or should they make at least an effort to direct? Should they adjust men to society or try to adjust society to man?

—*Saturday Review*

JULY 5, 1958

. . .　. . .　. . .

But I wouldn't like to live there

Every schoolboy (well, let's say every graduate student of English) knows that Samuel Johnson added the following four lines at the end of Goldsmith's *The Traveller:*

> How small of all that human hearts endure,
> That part which laws or kings can cause or cure!
> Still to ourselves in every place consigned,
> Our own felicity we make or find.

Victims of Hitler or Stalin, or even anyone who has ever heard of these victims, may find it hard to believe that Johnson's contemporaries could accept his pronouncement as a tenable thesis. It is as clear today as it was at any other unhappy time in the world's history that kings and laws can cause a good deal of "all that human hearts endure."

If Johnson could write the lines and readers could admire them, that proves, among other things, that the Englishmen of his day had far less reason than we to know just how much unnecessary human misery kings and laws can cause. No government of which they had any intimate knowledge had ever been as bad as a dozen governments have been in the course of the twentieth century. In that respect the world has become, for a great many people, a much worse place to live in than it was in Johnson's time.

What he said was a half-truth, and since it seems that we can never believe more than one-half of a truth at a time, today the assumption—almost everywhere tacit and often explicit—is that all, or almost all, that human hearts endure is somehow traceable to laws, rules, or—to use the most conveniently vague and inclusive term—society, or better yet, "the system."

It may be that extreme situations created by bad laws and bad rulers are tending to develop more and more frequently in more and more parts of the earth. But it is still true that in the United States we make or find most of our own felicity. Despite the Depression and despite our laws, most of this generation (with the exception, of course, of combat soldiers) has owed its most intense moments of happiness and its deepest moments of sorrow to causes that had little to do with the personalities or policies of our government. We may have fretted over them. We may, in other words, have borrowed trouble. But borrowing trouble certainly comes under the head of infelicities we make or find.

A cheerful view of our private situation, of man's destiny, and of the universe he lives in, is certainly one of the things— perhaps the most important single thing—that makes for happiness or its opposite. But such a cheerful view does not always depend upon any of the things that society increasingly (and I think properly) tries to provide us with. In the Middle Ages, when life was hard and suffering was the common lot, it was generally agreed that God is good. The more secure and comfortable we became—until recently, that is—the more this conviction faded away. We are now assured that God obviously doesn't exist and the universe is meaningless.

We plan to abolish poverty, and of that determination I approve. But I remember nevertheless that the suicide rate is higher among the rich than among either the poor or the moderately well-off; that it is, according to the California statistics, almost unknown among the destitute. I do not conclude that we should undertake to reduce the suicide rate by increasing the number of the destitute. Kings and laws can indeed have a good deal to do with creating the conditions under which it would seem reasonable to suppose that people would be happy. But kings and laws cannot actually make them so, and it is my conviction that in today's society, where affluence touches a majority of Americans, economic inequality is responsible for far less unhappiness than are the weaknesses and follies of many of those who share its benefits—such as keeping up with the neighbors, spending beyond income for superficialities, and false values of various sorts.

Irving Howe, one of the most often quoted commentators on the contemporary social and political scene, is fond of insisting that our thinking is not sufficiently Utopian. The preceding paragraphs may have helped to explain some of the reasons why my opinion is precisely the contrary. Utopian thinking assumes that perfect justice can be achieved, and that man not only *can* be almost perfectly happy but also that he can be *made* so—whereas nothing in human experience justifies any such assumption. To make it, leads simply to frustration because so much is expected of every improvement or reform that even the benefits that result seem to amount to no more than a failure. Another statement made by Samuel Johnson comes nearer unqualified truth than his addition to *The Traveller*. It is: "The remedy for the ills of life is palliative rather than radical." And to "of life" he might have added "or government."

To the Utopian, of course, any such conviction means too

ready an acceptance of the status quo. But that it should do so is no more necessary or inevitable than is the frequent tendency of Utopianism to end in an exasperated recourse to a dictatorship that proposes to drag people into felicity by the scruff of the neck.

No system of government, no matter how Utopian the thinking that plans it, ever achieves more than amelioration. In the eighteenth century, the proponents of democracy were sure that it would abolish war because only kings wanted war. A generation or so ago one of the commonest arguments in favor of Communism was that it, in turn, would bring the reign of peace that democracy had failed to establish. "The capitalists" were the creators of war, and the reply that individual Communist states might war with one another even if all the world were Communist was brushed aside, until the rise of Chinese Communism. Socialism still promises to destroy the power of money, but all it could really accomplish would be what Russian Communism did accomplish—the substitution of the power of political position for the power of wealth. Power of one sort or another vested in a few individuals persists.

The first completely developed outline for a Utopia known to come from Western Europe is Plato's *Republic*. And it is, of course, totalitarian, because even the least cynical realized that nothing short of compulsion could ever make men behave with complete rationality.

The law of compensation works both ways, and the blessings, even when very real, always turn out to be mixed. To give women the vote was an act of simple justice. No doubt it had one good result: It removed one source of female resentment—though I am not sure that women did not immediately discover another to make up for it. But the claim that politics would be purified and wiser; that more generous, and more compassionate laws would be passed was based upon the false assumption that women voters as a whole would be as earnest, as socially conscious, and politically enlightened as the feminist leaders. But—as the feminists themselves used often to proclaim most unguardedly—"women are people," and female people are so much like male people that it would be difficult to demonstrate that there has ever been any major decision made through the ballot box in which the results depended upon the women's vote.

When women's rights had just recently been achieved in England, G. K. Chesterton described their triumphant struggle in these words: "A million women rose up to say 'we will not be dictated to.' Whereupon most of them became stenographers." That is so gloriously funny that in laughter one is likely to overlook its core of typical truth. When women became free they not only became free to earn a living, but, far more often than not, they were expected to do so.

The society now established in England was certainly the product of Utopian thinking. It assumed that to abolish all special privileges and to guarantee equality of opportunity would create an ideal situation. But before that ideal is quite achieved, it is declared to be far short of Utopia by a new wave of Utopian thinkers. In a book called *Culture and Society,* Raymond Williams, who is said to speak for a growing segment of Utopian opinion, has declared: "A stratified society based on merit is as objectionable . . . as a stratified society based on money or birth." Apparently the only real Utopia would be one in which every citizen, no matter how stupid, improvident, or even vicious, enjoyed precisely the same privileges and advantages as the most intelligent and the most virtuous. Any reward for merit implies something far short of Utopia.

It was only a few centuries ago that men began to think of the Golden Age as a day about to dawn, instead of an irrecoverable paradise lost long ago. As a part of that shift, Utopia came to mean not "that which exists nowhere" but "that which will exist tomorrow." Nevertheless, the determination to settle for nothing less than perfection has been at least as often a curse as it has been a blessing. Without Utopian thinking neither Nazi Germany nor Communism would ever have come into existence. Russia and Nazi Germany are the only two modern nations in which a government had the absolute power to decree whatever was necessary to realize an abstractly formulated ideal; and the similarity between the two is real and significant, however strongly you may believe that one ideal is noble and the other depraved. Both turned into nightmares for the very reason that anti-Utopians had predicted.

Some thirty years ago I wrote a book called *Was Europe a Success?* that protested against the then-growing tendency of liberals to surrender all their previous convictions in exchange for the Utopian promise Communism held out. Lord Russell replied: "I do not disagree with Mr. Krutch as to what I like and dislike. [But] we must not judge the society of the future by considering whether or not we should like to live in it; the question is whether those who have grown up in it will be happier than those who have grown up in our society or those of the past."

The specific question to which Lord Russell refers seems to me to have received a definite answer in the fact that few of those who grew up in our society would change it for the Russian, whereas so many would like to move from, say, East Germany to West Germany.

But that is not the most important comment to be made on Lord Russell's pronouncement. Perhaps the rule, "Do unto others as you would be done by," is not always applicable. As Bernard Shaw's revolutionist said: "Don't do unto others as you would they should do unto you. Their taste may be different." But as a general rule, the scriptural advice is safer. You are more likely to please people by giving them what you would like to have than by giving them what you think they can be made to like.

The political reasons why Utopian thinking—even when it does not lead to a dictatorship—never achieves more than a questionable amelioration are all familiar truths. Though it may be obvious that the best and wisest men should rule, no one has ever proposed a workable method by which they may be chosen. The oldest—hereditary power—is based upon so obvious a fallacy that it has been abandoned in nearly every part of the Western world. Democracy was the panacea proposed by the eighteenth century, and though it seems to be pragmatically justified by working tolerably well—or at least better than the assumption that the descendants of great men will be equally great—no one has ever answered the embarrassing question: "How can the less wise be expected to recognize the superiority of the superior?"

In those countries which are supposed by many to be now pointing the way to the future, both hereditary and elected leadership have been discarded in favor of what is the most primitive of all methods of choosing rulers—a struggle for power in the course of which the public waits to see who will come out on top. That came to be the method by which the Roman emperors were chosen, and it is certainly that which put a Stalin, a Khrushchev, and his nearly anonymous successors at the head of what is either the first or the second greatest power in the world today.

But the deepest reasons for the inevitable failure of Utopian thinking lie not only in man's political incapacity but in general human nature. And that is perhaps the reason why the most modern of Utopias, the one imagined by some students of the behavioral sciences, proposes (like Professor B. F. Skinner) to begin by dehumanizing those who are to be conditioned into perfect virtue and perfect happiness.

That man cannot conceive of anything that would make him

perfectly happy and perfectly content is proved by the fact that his imagination has invented a variety of hells, all of them full of horror, but never a paradise in which he would want to dwell for eternity, or even for very long. The best that any thoughtful man is likely to say of any of the seriously intended pictures of a perfect state—from Plato through Sir Thomas More and down to Samuel Butler's *Erewon* or Shaw's *Future as Far as the Eye Can Reach*—is only: "It would be an interesting place to visit but I wouldn't want to live there."

Only the naïve are able to imagine a Utopia which they themselves could accept. In the United States one of the best-sellers of the 1860's was *Gates Ajar*, by Elizabeth Stuart Phelps. In it is described a future life in no way different from that of the upper-middle-class families of her day except in the absence of certain difficulties and frustrations. The blessed gossip with neighbors and look after the children, who have a very human tendency to seek out a celestial cookie jar. Her public, which certainly would not have found Dante's Paradise very attractive, was so delighted to be promised a future life that would be only more of the same, that she wrote three sequels.

Are there many today who are so naïve? Not, perhaps, in quite the same way, but there are many more highly placed than Miss Phelps's readers who are equally uncritical. I doubt that the most popular kind of Utopian thinking current today is actually much superior to Miss Phelps's. It is obvious that most people really believe they would be much happier if they could enjoy that better world which differs from ours in nothing more than a still more complicated technology, and is described daily by one prophet or another. Henry Kaiser put it into these words:

Atomic power will be harnessed . . . unlimited foods and raw materials will be synthesized . . . automation will create new opportunities and more jobs . . . there will be developed a still more dazzling array of new products, new uses of metals, new breakthroughs in chemistry . . . medical science at last will conquer cancer, heart disease, and maladies of the mind and emotions, and old age. . . . The opportunities ahead of us are limitless. . . . Why, we haven't seen anything yet.

—*Saturday Review*
AUGUST 20, 1966

• • • •

Still innocent and still abroad *

During the ten years just past, Americans have been going abroad, and Europeans have been staying at home. Most of the relatively few Englishmen, Frenchmen and Germans who have come to our shores have come to transact a specific piece of business, and it is only we who have, in any considerable numbers, crossed the ocean merely to see what we could find on the other side. Never before in the history of the world has so large a part of the population of any nation gone sightseeing in strange lands, and many secondary causes doubtless helped to occasion this new sort of *Volkswanderung*. There was, of course, the war, which for the first time made Europe seem real to thousands; and there was also prosperity, which made a margin of wealth and of leisure more common than it had ever been before. But behind these secondary causes lay another not always fully understood by those whom it affected. The time had come when America felt the need to compare its new world with an

* Author's Note: This essay was written thirty-five years ago while I was spending a year in France. I think it may now have some interest as illustrating the fact that "a certain condescension in foreigners" has not changed its character very much even though these foreigners are now imitating almost all of our vices and a few of our virtues much more actively than they did when it was written.

older one, to see itself as others saw it. The feeling that our country was essentially an outlying province of Europe—that feeling against which even the golden age of New England struggled in vain—had largely disappeared. American civilization had differentiated and detached itself from the older ones, and the time had come to check our accomplishment against them. The time had come, and we took it.

Satire has represented the returning pilgrim hailing the Statue of Liberty as the most welcome sight he had seen since leaving home and proclaiming his renewed conviction that God's country is some one or another of these United States. But satire seems to have forgotten that the majority of all the travelers of all nations have always said the same thing in the idiom of the locality from which the traveler happened to come, and that the remarkable thing about our tourists is the number who have expressed exactly contrary convictions. Perhaps most of those past middle age merely heaved a sigh of content when they found themselves once again in a familiar world, but an amazing number of the younger ones—and they were far better able to express themselves—felt very different indeed. Some liked the cathedrals and some liked the bars, but their observations helped to swell the tide of self-criticism which was sweeping over the United States and which constitutes a phenomenon almost unparalleled in the history of a culture. America, they said, had much to learn: to build, to write, and to paint, said some. To eat, to drink, and to make love, added others—with even greater fervor.

Meanwhile (and despite the fact that Europe stays at home) Europe thinks about America more often, more gravely, and with less favor than America thinks about her. The fact may some day be of considerable importance to us, and it is not worthwhile either to disguise it by taking too seriously the official speeches made by committees of reception or to fail to understand some of the reasons why it should be so. To us the Old World is a place to be visited; it is a museum of art, a repository of strange and sometimes delightful customs. But there is no fear mixed with our interest. Europe is a place we come to, not a place which comes to us and establishes itself in our midst. Our habits, our customs, and our ways of life are not threatened. Our country is not being rapidly interpenetrated with the goods, the manners, and the aims of a different civilization. But Europe sees our hordes debark upon her shores to rush here and there examining, judging and buying. She sees, to take simple examples, the American movies with their foreign scenes and foreign faces all but driving native actors and native themes from her theaters. She sees our automobiles traversing the roads which our machines are keeping in repair. She sees our harvesters reaping her crops and she hears our voices sounding from thousands of phonograph records in thousands of middle-class homes. And Europe not unnaturally wonders what in the end we shall do to her.

She does not know us as well as we know her, and indeed many of her most cultured citizens seem to have formed their ideas of the American at home almost exclusively from translated rehashes of the most sensational of our Sunday newspaper stories. But her ignorance is only one more reason why she is haunted by a distorted image of a great new world rising on the other side of an Atlantic which is no longer very wide. She imagines us as even larger, richer, and more powerful (as well as more barbarous) than we really are. She feels us alien and yet she fears that we are irresistible. No wonder that while the word "Europe" suggests to us a pleasant holiday, the word "America" suggests to her an unknown and terrifying future. It is hard to like an alien but it is impossible to like a conqueror, and Europe does not like us because it is, in part at least, as a conqueror that she sees us. Moreover, for that very reason, the theory that international misunderstandings would disappear as peoples came to see more of one another breaks down in this case. The more Europe sees of us the less we are liked.

II

Consider in particular the case of France. No other European country has been so frequently visited and no other has been regarded with such an excess of sentiment. References to the charm of "a little town in southern France" have become as platitudinous as references to the delights of Montparnasse. To her people such discordant virtues have been attributed that she has, on the one hand, been hailed as the promised land by disorderly bohemians and, on the other, held up as a model by the most respectable and patriotic of old ladies. Yet no one who has seen below the surface of French life can maintain that all this sentimental affection has been repaid with any considerable amount of genuine liking on the part of the French. Official delegations are welcomed with speeches, and gifts are received with something which often seems more like complacency than gratitude; but it is hard to escape the conviction that even the tourist business is regarded as a disagreeable necessity and that most at least of the leaders of intellectual opinion would prefer never to see an American again if they knew how to get along without him.

One may, of course, disregard mere travelers' tales. A dispute with a taxi driver is enough to produce in some Americans the ineradicable conviction that all Frenchmen are thieves, and no one need be surprised that certain of our tourists are cordially hated. But more easily controlled sources of information are not lacking. To read the chief Parisian newspapers day after day is inevitably to feel, in the very tone of the many references to America and Americans, the pressure of an almost universally diffused dislike; and to deduce from, for example, the gleefully exaggerated accounts of the current economic depression, the fact that nothing would please a French journalist better than the total collapse of American power.

An equal amount of ill feeling is, probably, not cherished by the simple private citizen, and undoubtedly there exists a con-

trary current in certain smart circles as well as in that section of
the youth which does not feel strongly the effects of the extraordinary cultural solidarity of France. Cocktails and jazz are
fashionable. Not a few young men and women admire what
they have heard of the splendor and speed of New York. But
though one may find their point of view expressed in a book
like Morand's *New York*, it is far less characteristic of articulate
French opinion than the vehement contempt of George Du-
hamel. When one reads current speeches on Franco-American
amity one feels sometimes that Lindbergh must be the only
contemporary American whom the French ever liked and Lafa-
yette the last Frenchman who liked America.

Nor can one fail to get an uncomfortable, almost an alarming,
sense of the strength of the resentment always ready to break
forth, if one observes how eagerly the newspapers seize upon
any pretext which can give an occasion for a general and un-
measured attack upon things American. The wave of anger which
swept over France during the discussion of the debt question is
well known, but a more recent incident is more significant for the
very reason that the provocation was slighter. A few months
ago several American fashion buyers were accused of stealing designs from the great dressmaking houses. The accusation was
spread over the front pages of the newspapers and it was made
the occasion of numerous vitriolic attacks, not merely upon the
accused persons or even the industry which they represented,
but upon American character and taste as a whole. All the old
wounds were industriously probed, all the old rhetoric was re-
furbished, and the round statement of one editorial writer that
"America is a nation of parvenus" was one of the least sweeping
of the unfavorable judgments passed.

One can hardly imagine even the most irresponsible of American newspapers seizing upon the alleged misdeeds of a few
private individuals as an excuse for denouncing the whole civilization of France or of any other country (unless, perhaps, it were
Russia); and one cannot imagine it for the simple reason that

America does not regard any nation (Russia again excepted) with a mixture of fear and dislike comparable to that with which France regards America. Ten years have passed since the war in which the two countries were allies. During those ten years Americans and Frenchmen have seen more of one another than the natives of any two widely separated countries ever saw of one another before; but the result has not been a happy one. Cocktails, jazz, and Charlie Chaplin may have conquered the world, but there can hardly be any doubt as to the opinion held in France by both the intellectuals who write the books and the semi-intellectuals who run the newspapers. To them America is a half-barbarous country whose inferior culture threatens the morally and intellectually superior civilization of Europe in general, and of France in particular.

III

We Americans are not unfamiliar with this judgment. Indeed, it is not very unlike that which has been expressed by the members of a dominant school of our writers, certain of whom have been widely read in translation and who may even have helped Europe in forming its opinion. But one who has lived through the age of Mencken and Sinclair Lewis, who has himself made some unflattering remarks concerning his native land, and who has, besides, visited France often enough to have replaced an idealized picture of that charming country by some knowledge of French life may be moved to wonder if the case against America is either so simple or so completely black as it is sometimes made out. Listening to the statements of French opinions about himself, he has been led to form certain opinions of his own concerning the mentality of those who formed the adverse ones and, in his own defense, has been led to observe virtues in his fellows which European eyes seem little inclined to see.

Our civilization suffers, to be sure, from defects enough. But if

the American intellectual is to maintain with his country a contact close enough to make his criticism effective, he must take
care that the criticism is just; and he had best guard himself
against the tendency, already rather widely manifest, to accept
without question the criticism of a Europe which is actually
neither very well informed nor, because of its own natural
prejudices, capable of an unbiased judgment. Hundreds of young
Americans have used France as the country from which to gain a
perspective upon the life amidst which they grew up. But little
is gained if they merely substitute one set of prejudices for
another; and few if any seem to have remarked what ought to
be a sufficiently obvious fact—namely, that France of all the
great nations of Europe is the one which has always been the
most completely self-contained and, for that reason, the most
incapable of understanding any culture except her own.

In the eighteenth century the injunction "Let us cultivate
our garden" formulated for her a historic principle which has
been reiterated in different words by some leader of every
generation since. Undoubtedly there is much to be said in favor
of the line of conduct which it recommends. To the fact that
she has remained relatively indifferent to the social and intellectual movements taking place outside her borders, she owes
the solidarity and the homogeneity of her civilization. Thanks
to it also, she possesses a cultural tradition probably more consistent and more continuous in its development than that of any
other Western nation. But no one could maintain either that
such determined self-sufficiency is calculated to develop the
catholicity of taste necessary for the judging of a foreign civilization or that, in actual fact, the French have ever manifested it.
They have been—and not without reason—proud of the part
which France played as a center of enlightenment and refinement, but they have always tended to regard the foreigner as
admirable only in proportion to the extent to which he showed
himself capable of absorbing French culture.

Moreover, that tendency to regard the outside world as a region which has much to learn but nothing to teach is manifest everywhere today—in great things and in small. It is manifest both in the amazing indifference to foreign literature and in the attitude adopted toward the foreign visitor, who is generally regarded as a barbarian to be tolerated (even made comfortable if necessary) primarily for the sake of the profit he brings and secondarily as a part of a burden necessarily imposed upon the nation chosen by destiny to civilize the world. For some two hundred years at least, Paris has been more frequently visited by strangers than any other city in the world, and yet even a few years ago when the tourist crisis was at its most acute, few if any Frenchmen ever thought of anything except the money which the stranger brought as an extenuating circumstance. Nor is it possible to discover in the articles now frequently published concerning the best methods of developing the tourist trade, a sign that any other point of view is ever considered. At his most generous the Frenchman regards the visitor as the possible re-cipient of the benefits of French culture. It would never occur to him to suspect that he had anything non-material to gain from contact with the representatives of other civilizations.

Even at the height of the uncritical enthusiasm produced by the war, Americans were sometimes a little startled by the calmness with which they found the French assuming that the interests of France were naturally the first concern of her allies as well as of herself. No one else seemed ever to have taken quite so literally the saying about every man's having two countries, which was, for the French, not merely a graceful compliment but a natural and reasonable fact. And when, a little later, there arose a "Party of the Intelligence" (composed of quite respectable French intellectuals) which calmly proposed— without the least suspicion that the phraseology might by others be considered insolent—"an intellectual union of the world under the leadership of Victorious France, guardian of all civilization," we had a glimpse into that abyss of national complacency that in France is so familiar and so nearly universal that it is never even rebuked. American complacency, so often satirized, is, as a matter of fact, unsure and merely blustery by comparison—conspicuous chiefly because it is neither universal nor very skillfully articulate. The better-educated an American, the more likely he is to develop a spirit of self-criticism and a tendency toward cultural internationalism. But in France, on the contrary, exactly the reverse is true. It is the intellectual classes which are most arrogant, most provincial, and most sure that France alone is the guardian "of all civilization."

So early is the educated Frenchman indoctrinated with the conviction, so little does he care to learn what others say and do, that to assume the superiority of all things French becomes with him second nature, and he reveals quite unconsciously a prejudice which he genuinely believes to be shared by the entire civilized world. For him Paris is the City of Light in an otherwise lampless universe; and it might be instructive to collect from the works of even the most cultivated French writers, an anthology of those complacent stereotypes which are seldom absent for long. Logic is "that virtue peculiarly French" and so, for that matter, is wit. The "supremacy of France in things of the spirit" is universally recognized, and Paris is, of course, "the capital of elegance." When one adds that "French cooking is everywhere recognized as the best" and that "the solidarity of the French family gives an example to the world," it begins to appear that the sum of these individual claims amounts to the assertion that all the virtues are merely national traits, and such is, at bottom, the opinion of the French intellectual. When he observes in a foreigner any signs of rationality, of wit, or of taste he attributes them, in all sincerity and innocence, to a veneer of French culture which the said foreigner has been fortunate enough to acquire by the reading of French literature or, perhaps, by residing for a time in Paris.

Nor does there (outside the Communist press) exist in France any organ of dissent. An *American Mercury*, a *Nation*, or a *New Republic* even would be unthinkable there where even such so-called liberal newspapers as *L'Oeuvre* are in everything except politics as chauvinistic as *Figaro*.

And it is certainly Point One in favor of the future of American civilization that at least its development is taking place to the accompaniment of perpetual self-criticism. However full the country may be of "bunk," there are always at least a few people to call it by its name. No intellectual American can grow up without being familiar from the time of his first serious reading with opinions highly unfavorable to the peculiarities of the culture of which he is a part. He has heard every national idiosyncrasy of temperament or manners contrasted unfavorably with the tastes or habits of foreigners; he has seen every native development subjected to the most rigorous criticism; and he has acquired the habit of examining with suspicion every novel institution. But the Frenchman is taught from the beginning that whatever may be justly described as French is unquestionably superior. It is no more possible to get behind his faith in France than it is possible to get behind one of the dogmatic convictions of a sincere and well-trained Roman Catholic. To question fundamentals is simply not permitted, and whoever attempts to do so is merely met with vituperation.

Thus when, for example, some two years ago, Gemier told the International Congress of the Theater that the stages of Russia and America were more interesting than those of France, the public indignation was expressed by Henri Bernstein, who replied in the pages of *Comoedia* that the director of the Odéon was certainly a Bolshevik and probably a thief as well. And when, some few months past, Ambassador Claudel made a speech in Washington paying the sort of compliments which an ambassador is supposed to pay, he was denounced in various French newspapers as little better than a traitor for having dared to say that America possessed certain excellences. Yet every ambassador to France (the American included) regularly makes speeches full of the most fulsome platitudes about the unrivaled virtues and charms of his second fatherland, and these speeches are taken as a matter of course. Every man has two countries. But for Claudel to reply in kind—that is treason. French editors who have never crossed the ocean quite regularly write leaders explaining the true inwardness of our manifold defects, but their own attitude was well expressed by La Fouchardière (clever essayist of *L'Oeuvre*) who devoted a column to a reply to a book by Upton Sinclair in the course of which a character made some remarks unfavorable to France. Many of these things, said La Fouchardière in effect, are true; but we do not permit foreigners to criticize France.

Doubtless various explanations and some excuses may be made for the arrogance of this attitude. The very frequency with which the superiority of all things French is insisted upon may be in part due to a feeling of insecurity; to a fear lest that artistic and intellectual leadership which was once a reality should become a shadow. Certainly the same newspapers that profess indifference to the unfavorable judgments of others reprint with an almost pathetic eagerness every compliment paid by a foreigner; and when, for example, Lunacharsky, the ex-commissar of education in Soviet Russia, recently told reporters that "after all Paris is still the capital of the spirit" this not very original utterance was blazoned forth in type of scarehead size. Such remarks are usually hardly more than the mechanical compliments which one pays to an aging belle because one knows that she expects them and it may be that France, like the same aging belle, receives them with all the greater eagerness for the very reason that in the bottom of her heart she fears that they may no longer be justified. But that is hardly a matter of concern to the American who, as the representative of a new, imperfect, but very important culture, needs a point of view which shall be critical without being, as it too often is, subservient to an opinion which is far from detached. He may well be humble before the past of Europe. It is much less certain that he need be so before her present.

The denunciatory articles occasioned by the alleged misdeeds of the fashion buyers have already been mentioned. In one of them the writer proclaimed that America had not the artistic gifts necessary to create fashions. We French, he continued, can make clothes for the same reason that we could build cathedrals. But such a remark implies its own answer. The cathedrals were not built yesterday and if, in the course of a few centuries, French genius has declined from the builders of Chartres to the designers of Paquin and Worth, what is likely to be left of it a few years hence?

IV

As for us, our greatest defect is often said to be our faith in the universal desirability of speed, of system, and of mechanization. We seek to introduce them into realms where they do not belong and we are accused of insisting that even culture should hum. But however true the charge and however absurd the results may be, it is hardly to be concluded that where machinery itself is concerned, there is any positive virtue in inefficiency. An art school run like a factory is scarcely more ridiculous than a factory run like an art school, and temperament is out of place in an elevator or a telephone system. The American who flees from too much mechanization at home may be understood if for the moment he discovers, as he sometimes does, a restful charm in the chronic failure of European machines to run; but his delight with this novelty hardly justifies one in concluding that the future lies with those races which cannot be persuaded to take the trouble to make the complicated machinery of modern life function as it should. Whatever the temperamental preferences of some of us are, God is going to be on the side of the nation with the best machines, and Art (wretch that she is) will continue in the future, as she has always in the past, to seek out the lands where wealth and power and ease are to be found in most abundance. Poverty and humility may be excellent things for the soul of the individual artist, but he is so nearly always poor and humble in the midst of a prosperous society that history hardly furnishes an example of a nation which was conspicuous for its achievement in the arts and sciences without being at about the same time conspicuous for wealth and power.

Europe learned to use the machine as a middle-aged man learns to drive a car—dubiously and without ceasing to feel that it is alien to his nature. America took to it with the enthusiasm of youth and manipulates its levers as though they were the muscles of its own body. And thanks to that fact, she has an advantage for which nothing can compensate.

A year or two ago a much-touted French novel told the story of an industrial family in France. At the end one of its members returns from a sojourn in America with tales of the methods he had observed and he concludes with the statement: "We have much to learn from one another. We can master in ten years what they have to teach us but it will take generations for them to acquire what we have to teach them."

Undoubtedly the author who put these words into the mouth of his character thought that he was being generous, but one wonders if the truth might not better be stated almost, though not quite, the other way around. What Europe has to teach may take a long time to assimilate but at least it is something teachable. What Europe has to learn from us is not learnable at all. The young man of twenty will come in time to know all that the man of fifty ever knew. But the man of fifty cannot learn the enthusiasm, the courage, and the eagerness which his pupil may gradually lose but which he can certainly never communicate.   —*Harper's Magazine*

. . . . V

Other Lives

. . .　　. . .　　. . .

One of the greatest of men who made one of the greatest of mistakes

When a big man makes a mistake it is frequently a big one, sometimes big enough to be really worthy of his genius. And that is a good thing to remember when the weight of some authority presses too hard against our common sense. An especially appropriate time to remember it was the three hundredth anniversary of the death of René Descartes, one of the greatest of men who made one of the greatest of mistakes.

That anniversary was recalled by a good many tributes to his genius. But precious little was said about the evil he did, of the evil that lived after him and survives even today in a curious form of which he would have been the last to approve. Descartes, though he thought so brilliantly, and with effects so permanent that it is hard to imagine modern science or modern technology without him, was also the man who convinced half the intellectual world that animals are machines without consciousness or will and incapable of feeling anything, even pain. Hence Descartes is also the real father of the mechanistic theories of man current today. He put man in a class by himself but the science which he fostered rejected ultimately the sharp distinction and behaviorists today make man something very much like that machine which Descartes declared every animal except man to be.

Descartes was born in 1596 with what looked like every good gift except robust health. His parents were substantial citizens; they gave him the best education of his time, and they left him an income sufficient to live where he liked, to think what he liked, and to do what he liked. He was famous before he was thirty, and before he died "cartesianism" was almost synonymous with the new spirit of scientific inquiry. He was philosopher, astronomer, physicist, physiologist and perhaps above all, a creative mathematician whose revolutionary methods made Newton possible.

In early manhood Descartes was already an intimate of the leading mathematicians of Europe and, according to his own statement, he was only twenty-three years old when, on a particular day and in a particular place, the substance of his famous "Discourse on Method" occurred to him and he was "filled with enthusiasm" for "the marvelous science" whose foundations he had discovered.

The "Discourse" includes, besides the discussion of scientific method, both a sort of intellectual autobiography and a metaphysical discussion of the meaning and origin of knowledge. He was anxious to determine the minimum assumptions which could be considered as safely self-evident, and the awareness that one *is* and can think, was the minimum. This conviction was expressed in one of the most famous of all philosophical pronouncements, "Cogito ergo sum" (I think, therefore I am), which became as fundamental to rationalist systems as "In the beginning was the Word" was fundamental to Platonistic theology.

Except for the "Cogito ergo sum," everything was to be investigated by logic and by experiment; absolutely nothing taken either on faith or on authority. It was, in other words, the method which science has ever since professed to follow and his formulation was demonstrably far more influential in establishing the method than Francis Bacon's "Advancement of Learning" or "Novum Organum."

And if the "Discourse" gave science a method, Descartes' "Geometry" gave it an indispensable tool—namely a new system of mathematics that could deal with the mechanics of the world machine as neither the algebra of the Orientals nor the Euclidian geometry of the Greeks could. According to the story (and it makes a good deal more sense than the story of Newton and the apple) Descartes was lying in bed staring at the corner of his room where the three walls came together when it suddenly occurred to him that points in space could be located definitely by reference to three imaginary intersecting planes and that either a series of points making a curve or a moving point could be described by an algebraic equation.

Without Descartes' invention only a very small part of modern technology would be possible. Analytic, or as it is still often called, Cartesian geometry is the foundation of the calculus and the calculus is the indispensable tool of the physicist, the electrician and the engineer.

How then could he have gone so disastrously, so preposterously wrong in his thinking about the nature of living things? How could he have set up so cruel and so absolute a distinction between man and everything else that shares existence with him?

Perhaps the answer is that he could do so because his intellectual character included two tendencies which make a singularly dangerous combination—absolute skepticism concerning whatever comes from authority, tradition, or mere common sense, along with an absolute trust in the conclusions of pure reason. By the latter he was led to the astonishing conclusion that all the animals except man are mere machines; or, as he put it, that they "act naturally and by springs, like a watch."

Man, he argued, is like an animal except that something, the soul, has been added. Only God can bridge the gulf between matter and consciousness, and God bridges it only in man. Awareness is a function of the soul and since a soul is the possession of man alone, only man can reason and only man can suffer. The instinctive behavior of the animal is not analogous to human habits but to merely physical laws. A dog is not glad when he wags his tail, or in pain when he screams. He seems to us to be experiencing joy or agony only because the soul which we possess would experience those emotions if the mechanism of our bodies led us to react physically as a dog reacts at the sight of an old friend or the rending of a limb. As Nicolas de Malebranche, one of his disciples, put it in 1678, the animals "eat without pleasure, they cry without pain, they grow without knowing it; they desire nothing, they fear nothing, they know nothing."

A little later the poet Jean de la Fontaine—whose common sense was a better guide than Descartes' pure reason—described how some of the latter's disciples amused themselves with the animal-machines and the realistic way in which they seemed to suffer but of course did not:

They administered beatings to dogs with perfect indifference and made fun of those who pitied the creatures as if they felt pain. They said that the animals were clocks; that the cries they admitted when struck, were only the noise of a little spring which had been touched, but that the whole body was without feeling. They nailed poor animals on boards by their four paws to vivisect them and see the circulation of the blood which was a great subject of conversation.

The folly of the foolish is more than likely to begin and end with the circle of the few who are in some way dependent upon them; but the folly of the wise can have consequences beyond measure. Descartes, a wise and good man, very nearly shut the gates of mercy—if not on mankind, then at least on every living creature that was not man. For a generation, thinking men were divided between those who accepted and those who did not accept the Cartesian theory of the animal constitution. Because of his authority—or more terrible yet, because of the greatness of mind which had won him that authority— sensible men turned their backs upon their good sense, and in the laboratories of virtuosi bone and flesh were cut and torn, sometimes for no purpose other than to marvel at how convincingly a mere machine could simulate suffering.

Perhaps never before in the history of the world had cruelty been so ingeniously taught or fellow creatures so effectively deprived of their last defense—the pity which "runneth soon in gentle heart," and which may, indeed, at last appear even in hearts not gentle. The Man of the earlier Renaissance could be both refinedly cruel and coarsely brutal. We may shudder to think of what went on in the bear rings that stood almost side by side with Shakespeare's theaters. But the spectators knew that the bear was suffering and sooner or later some among them would protest and rebel. How can cruelty be protested against, however, if cruelty can be proved by pure reason neither to exist nor to be possible?

The license that it gave to cruelty was not the only or perhaps even the most important of the effects of Cartesianism. Growing interest in and familiarity with the world of plants and animals might tend to provoke the sense that all life is one and that we share it with other creatures no less wonderful than we. Descartes would persuade us, on the contrary, that these others are far less "fellow creatures" than the Western world had ever before believed them to be. The assumption that man alone has a soul may be ancient enough, but no such consequences of that assumption had usually been drawn. The Old Testament itself warns that a man may be judged by the treatment he accords to his beasts. A Christian writer could say, as Descartes could not, that God's power was displayed no less in the creation of a worm than in the creation of a man. In the older view, immortality might be impossible for the soulless, and so might reason be. Both might be exclusive possessions of men and angels. But it remained for Descartes to deprive the beasts of sentience itself. No other view had ever made man quite so lonely in the universe. Only he, among all created things, was not a machine. Nothing else could rejoice or suffer with him. The earth which he inhabited was, in effect, as alien and as dead as the moon itself.

Fortunately, not all philosophers and scientists accepted the Cartesian doctrine. In England the "Cambridge Platonists," Cudworth and More, set themselves against it. So, too, did Robert Boyle, of the Royal Society, and the microscopist Hooke. Had it not been rejected before too long a time by the common sense of mankind, the eighteenth century could not have become, as it did, preeminently a period during which, in countless ways, men felt themselves drawn more and more toward the contemplation of the whole spectacle of nature. But it was a near thing.

Today the influence of Descartes' monstrous notion lives on in a form he would never have anticipated. That "soul" which he made the only distinction between man and machine was something whose existence he believed to be objectively demonstrable. But it is precisely the thing which subsequent science has found it most difficult to demonstrate, at least in any fashion satisfactory to materialists. If the only thing that distinguishes man from the mechanical animal is something that cannot be shown to exist, then why, they may ask, is not man also a mere mechanical animal? Why may not his conviction that he is thinking and willing be only an illusion which the animals may or may not share with him? Why cannot he be explained wholly in terms of stimulus and response? Why may he also not "act naturally and by springs, like a watch?" And it is something very much like that of which behaviorists would convince us.

Truly the evil men do lives after them—sometimes in ways they never dreamed of. Descartes, who thought God inevitable, furthered the mechanists, who are convinced that even man, as distinguished from the machine, is not.

—*New York Herald Tribune*
AUGUST 27, 1950

. . .   .

A damnable pleasure

It would not be quite true to say that "some of my best friends are hunters." Nevertheless, I do number among my respected acquaintances some who not only kill for the sake of killing but count it among their keenest pleasures.

To me it is inconceivable that anyone should think an animal more interesting dead than alive. I can also easily prove to my own satisfaction that killing "for sport" is the perfect type of that pure evil for which metaphysicians have sometimes sought.

Most wicked deeds are done because the doer proposes some good to himself. The liar lies to gain some end; the swindler and the thief want things which, if honestly got, might be good in themselves. Even the murderer may be removing an impediment to normal desires or gaining possession of something which his victim keeps from him. None of these usually does evil for evil's sake. They are selfish or unscrupulous, but their deeds are not gratuitously evil. The killer for sport has no such comprehensible motive. He prefers death to life, darkness to light. He gets nothing except the satisfaction of saying, "Something that wanted to live is dead. There is that much less vitality, consciousness, and, perhaps, joy in the universe. I am the Spirit that Denies." When a man wantonly destroys one of the works of man we call him Vandal. When he wantonly destroys one of the works of God we call him Sportsman.

Now, the typical Sportsman will not accept this parallel. He has his rules, his traditions, his protocols. Apparently he feels toward random slaughterers much as I feel towards even those who observe the rituals. The Sportsman is shocked by a man who will shoot a sitting bird; I am shocked by anyone who will, purely for "sport," shoot a bird at all. To no creature, man or beast, who is full of the desire to live is it any great comfort to know that killing him was done according to the rules. There is a rather well-known short story (I have ungratefully forgotten the author) about a sportsman who came to the conclusion that man-hunting was the most challenging of all sports and used to give unsuspecting visitors to his island hideout a fair run for their money. Was this sport?

I am not a vegetarian and I am well aware that there are those to whom that fact makes me as shocking as the "true sportsman" is shocking to me, and the mere slaughterer shocking to the Sportsman. I can only ask that we recognize not too scornfully the possibility of these differences of feeling. My position is a rather extreme one, though obviously not the most extreme possible; but I do not think it can fairly be called fanatical because, I freely admit, the Sportsman is not necessarily the monster my own logic seems to make him. Yet, though hunting for food and the destruction of certain animals is probably necessary to civilization, to me it still seems that any activity that includes killing as a pleasurable end in itself is damnable. Even the hunter-for-food may be as wicked and misguided as vegetarians say, but at least he does not kill for the sake of killing. To kill for killing's sake is a terrifying phenomenon—like doing evil, not in the hope of gain, but for evil's own sake—as strong a proof of that "reality of evil" with which present-day theologians are again concerned as we could have.

Examples of three different but typical ways of refusing to acknowledge that any defense of such killing is called for may be plucked out of recent popular periodicals.

In the spring of 1955 a magazine called *Sports Illustrated* distributed a questionnaire intended to determine the public attitude toward hunting. An answer received from a woman in Tampa, Florida, was as follows: "I am not the sloppy, sentimental type that thinks it's terrible to shoot birds or animals. What else are they good for?" And *The New Yorker,* which reprinted her reply, answered the question with an irony likely to be lost on the asker: "Bulls can be baited by fierce dogs, and horses sometimes pay money."

About a year before, *The New Yorker* had also, though without comment and merely in the course of report of the personality of the new British Permanent Delegate to the United Nations, quoted Sir Pierson Dixon as remarking genially, apropos of some articles on sport which he had written for English periodicals: "I like this shooting thing, stalking some relatively large animal or, even more enjoyable, shooting birds. It's like the pleasure of hitting a ball."

A little later *Time* magazine ran an article about how duck hunters near Utah's Bear River Migratory Bird Refuge [*sic*] "could hardly shoot fast enough" to bring down the ducks they found there, and it adorned the article with a quotation from Ernest Hemingway's "Fathers and Sons": "When you have shot one bird flying you have shot all birds flying, they are all different and they fly different ways but the sensation is the same and the last one is as good as the first."

Of these three attitudes the first may seem the simplest and the most elementary, but perhaps it is not. The blank assumption that the universe has no conceivable use or meaning except in relation to man may be instinctive; nevertheless, the lady from Tampa is speaking not merely from naïveté. She is also speaking for all those minds still tinctured by the thought of the medieval philosophers, who consciously undertook to explain in detail the *raison d'être* of the curious world of nature by asking for what human use God had created each species of plant or animal. If any given creature seems good for nothing except "sport," then it must be for sport that it was created.

Hemingway's utterance, on the other hand, is the most sophisticated of the three and the only one that seems to make the pure pleasure of killing a consciously recognized factor. The mental processes of the Permanent Delegate are neither so corrupt as those of Mr. Hemingway, nor so intellectually complicated as those of the lady from Tampa. He is not, like the first, looking for madder music and stronger wine, nor, like the second, attempting to answer the philosophical question of what animals and birds "are for." Because of the dreadful uncomprehending innocence sometimes said to be found most frequently in the English gentleman, it has simply never occurred to him that the creatures whom he pursues are alive at all—as his phrase "like the pleasure of hitting a ball" clearly reveals. Birds are simply livelier, less predictable clay pigeons. And it is in exactly the same light that those of his class have sometimes regarded the lesser breeds without the law, or even the nearly inanimate members of all the social classes below them.

For the attitude farthest removed from this, Albert Schweitzer is the best-known contemporary spokesman. But one can hardly have "reverence for life" without some vivid sense that life exists even in "the lower animals"; and it is this vivid sense that is lacking in the vast majority of sportsmen and equally in, say, the abandoners of pets and, not infrequently, one kind of biological scientist. Often not one of them is so much as tinged with the sadism which Hemingway's opinions and activities seem to suggest. It is not that they do not care what the abandoned pet or the experimental animal suffers, but that they do not really believe he suffers to any considerable degree. In the case of the hunter, it is often not so much that he wants to kill as that he has no vivid sense that he is killing. For him, as for Sir Pierson, it is more or less like "hitting a ball."

Hemingway would, of course, say that there was more to it than that. He feels more of a man out there with his gun, bringing down the birds. It's healthy out of doors, good for muscle tone, and there's the challenge of a contest, etc. These are exactly the common arguments which, until a few years ago, were advanced to defend war as a legitimate activity. None of the real goods is actually dependent upon the killing of another living creature. How anyone can profess to find animal life interesting and yet take delight in reducing the wonder of any animal to a bloody mass of fur or feathers is beyond my comprehension. You can go into the woods to share them with your fellow creatures just as well as to slaughter them. Photography is more difficult and challenging than gunnery. The air is sweeter without the odor of spilled blood. And in my opinion anyone who does not recognize this must fall into one of two classes—the one composed of the innocently and the other of the guiltily evil.

Thoreau once remarked that many a man went fishing all his life without realizing that it was not fish he was after. That is the type of the innocently evil who have simply never dissociated the pleasurable incidentals of hunting from the killing which comes at the end of it. But I rather suspect that these are a minority, and that the majority belong to the other class—the class of those to whom the final savagery is of the essence. They are much like those drinkers who talk about either the fine bouquet of a wine or the conviviality of the cocktail, but for whom the "kick" of alcohol is the real *sine qua non*. And I don't like blood lust even when tricked out in the philosophy of a Hemingway.

When Thoreau allowed himself to be persuaded to send a turtle as a specimen to the zoologists at Harvard, he felt that he had "a murderer's experience in a degree" and that however his specimen might serve science he himself and his relation to nature would be the worse for what he had done. "I pray," he wrote, "that I may walk more innocently and serenely through nature. No reasoning whatsoever reconciles me to this act."

In general, however, professional students of living things are only somewhat more likely than the average man to feel strongly any "reverence for life." One of the most distinguished American students of birds told me that he saw no incompatibility whatever between his interest in birds and his love of "sport." Many, perhaps most, professional students find no reason too trivial to "collect" a bird or animal, though their habitual use of this weasel word may suggest a defensive attitude. And I have often wondered that sportsmen who find themselves subject to many restrictions have not protested as unfair the "collector's license," rather freely granted and sometimes permitting the holder to shoot almost anything, almost anywhere and at any time.

Obviously the problem raised by all this is not solvable in any clear-cut way. The degree of "reverence for life" which man or any other animal can exhibit is limited by the facts of a world he never made. When it was said that the lion and the lamb shall lie down together, the hope that they may someday do so carries with it the obvious implication that they cannot do so now. Even Albert Schweitzer's rule that no life shall be destroyed except in the service of some higher life will be differently interpreted, almost from individual to individual.

Just how great must be the good that will accrue to the higher animal? Interpreted as strictly as possible, his law would permit killing only in the face of the most desperate and immediate necessity. Interpreted loosely enough, it might justify the slaughter of the 20,000 birds of paradise, the 40,000 humming-birds, and the 30,000 birds of other species said to have been killed to supply the London feather market alone, in the single year 1914. After all, even fashionable ladies are presumably "higher" than birds and they presumably took keen delight in the adornments which the birds were sacrificed to provide.

Some pragmatic solution of the rights of man versus the rights of other living creatures does nevertheless have to be made. Undoubtedly it changes from time to time, and it is well that the existing solution should be re-examined periodically. Because the 1914 solution was re-examined, comparatively few birds are now killed for their feathers and it is not demonstrable that the female population is any the worst for the fact.

In India, members of the Jain sect sometimes live on liquid food sipped through a veil in order to avoid the possibility that they might inadvertently swallow a gnat. There are always "anti-sentimentalists" who protest against any cultivation of scruples on the ground that they can logically lead only to some such preposterous scrupulosity. But there are extremes at both ends. Those who have scruples are no more likely to end as Jains than those who reject all scruples are likely to end as Adolf Hitlers. The only possible absolutes are reverence for all life and contempt for all life, and of these the first is certainly no more to be feared than the second. If there is any such thing as a wise compromise it is not likely to be reached by the refusal to think.

In the old days, in this country, lines were not infrequently drawn by those students who had interested themselves in old-fashioned natural history and were brought thereby into intimate association with animals and plants. Its aims and its methods demanded an awareness of the living thing as a living thing; and at least until the rise of behaviorism, the suffering and the joy of the lesser creatures was a part of the naturalist's subject matter. But the laboratory scientist of our modern, supercharged day is not of necessity drawn into any emotional relationship with animals or plants, and the experiments which of necessity he must perform are likely to make him more, rather than less, callous than the ordinary man.

At best, compassion, reverence for life, and a sense of the community of living things is not an essential part of his business, as they are of the more vaguely defined discipline of the naturalist. And for that reason it is a great pity that the most humane and liberal of the natural sciences should play so small a role in the liberal arts curriculum. While still under the influence of an older tradition, field botany and field zoology were quite commonly taught in American colleges, even in the remoter parts of the United States. Today, few liberal arts undergraduates know anything of such subjects and often would find no courses open to them if they did.

The most important things taught by these disciplines were not the shapes of leaves or the calls of birds, but a philosophy, a certain attitude towards life. It is very hard to argue such a fundamental premise. The Sportsman, who kills living animals merely to re-create himself, obviously thinks that the right attitude is for man to use the life of the earth as he sees fit. This is not for me an acceptable premise. I do not believe that man has a divine right to the unlimited despotism of an oriental potentate; that he is justified when he says *"l'univers, c'est moi"*; or that, like the Calvinist God, he may legitimately damn all inferior creatures merely for his own glory. I believe instead that all created things have their rights and that the right to live is one of them—unless there are compelling reasons why it should not be.   —*Saturday Review*

AUGUST 17, 1957

. . .   .

Green thumb, green heart

The editors of this magazine [*Leisure*] have invited me to have a go at a column. For reasons which I shall explain in just a moment, I am even more flattered than one might expect. But before we go any further, you had better know what you are in for. I shall offer no practical advice for the very good reason that you probably know better than I "how to do it." To be perfectly frank, I am only an amateur botanist and an indifferent gardener whose somewhat chloritic thumb is not as green as it should be.

What, then, is my qualification for daring to chat with more learned and more skillful people? Only that I am what, for lack of a better term, I must call a passionate and devoted "plant lover" who has often wondered why that description isn't more often used.

After all, people are called "animal lovers" without implying that they are either zoologists or successful breeders of cats, dogs or cattle. The scientist or the breeder may be also a lover of animals. Not infrequently, but by no means always, he is. And the same is true of the botanist and the gardener. Perhaps disinterested love is a necessary virtue in the best of either, although there are botanists who only take plants to pieces in order to label them, and gardeners who grow flowers only to win prizes. I never expect to win a prize or to have a species named after me, but I have looked at many different plants with the eye of loving wonder and I have read rather widely in the writings of those who shared my feelings.

I shall not attempt to define "plant lover" very closely or list all the signs by which you may recognize one, but I should point out that members of the species do have several common traits. To begin with, they accept the living plant as one of the most convincing of proofs that beauty is its own excuse for being, and they have a passionate interest in the whys and wherefores of the infinite variety of the plant world. They are interested not only in *their* garden but also in anybody's and nobody's—by which last I mean those which Nature plants and tends by herself.

A plant is what they see first, whether it is in someone's living room or on a city street. When driving through the country, even on business, some people watch for gas stations and some read the Burma Shave signs, but the plant lover keeps a lookout for what is growing by the roadside. As for me, I am walleyed from watching the center line and the scenery at the same time, and I have got many an indignant scowl from passengers when I applied a quick brake in order to examine something which seemed to demand inspection.

Such behavior is not all there is to it, because the behavior is only the outward expression of emotional and intellectual attitudes. One dry kind of scientist, botanical or otherwise, is trying merely to learn *about* the aspect of nature he has chosen to study. But the lover of plants or animals believes he can also learn something *from* them. They, like him, are alive; they are part of the same great mystery and they bring him close to it. He may want to learn all that he can *about* them. But he is inevitably also a bit of a mystic. At least he knows what Goethe and Wordsworth were talking about when the first called the green world "the living garment of God" and the second caught from "the meanest flower that grows" a hint of "thoughts too deep for tears."

How does it happen that some of us—and that includes many great botanists and horticulturists from Linnaeus on down—are lovers of plants while others, even among ardent gardeners, seem to regard flowers as essentially inanimate and merely somewhat more attractive than wax replicas?

Some years ago Mr. Ross Parmenter, a music commentator on the staff of *The New York Times,* published a charming little book that deserves to be better known than it is, called *The Plant on My Window.* In it, he describes how, when he moved into a new apartment, he came across a little pot of struggling philodendron left on a radiator by the previous tenant. He had never really noticed any plant in his life before. Suddenly he was aware of this one as one might be aware of an abandoned cat or dog. He gave it water, put it in the light, and was amazed at the everyday miracle of its response in greenness and growth. He had undergone an unmistakably mystic experience and almost before he realized what had happened he was aware of the whole world of plants. Soon he was not only visiting the Bronx Botanical Garden but reading deeply in its library. He was both learning about plants and learning from them.

Such late conversions are probably unusual. Most plant lovers can remember their special interest and susceptibility from childhood and often can connect it with a specific incident or moment. Some will say this incident must have followed a childhood "conditioning." Perhaps. But perhaps it was simply the first remembered instance when something native to their personality awoke to life. One of my own earliest memories is of performing, at the behest of some elementary teacher, the experiment of sprouting a bean in sawdust between two pieces of glass. I saw the protrusion of the root and the first tentative unfolding of the embryo leaflets as a miracle more impressive than any I had ever heard of involving water and wine. This was life out of death and whether or not my experience was the result of conditioning, it had a great influence on my life. I have spent much of my leisure time (and not a little of what I suppose I should call my working time) looking at plants, growing plants, and wondering about plants.

The great Linnaeus found perhaps his deepest satisfaction in realizing that it had been his privilege to see a greater number

of God's many creations than any man before him had ever
seen. I am far from being able to make any such boast. Except
for a few glimpses of the Thailand jungle, I know the really
deep tropics only from books. But I have kept my eyes open
for plants over most of the United States, including Alaska,
parts of Mexico, the Greek Islands, and the Mediterranean
coast as far east as the coast of Turkey. And I remember few
things more vividly than the giant cacti of the Sonoran desert,
the flame trees of Thailand and the blazing purple fields of
great willow weed in southern Alaska.   —*Leisure* Magazine
                                               A U G U S T , 1960

* * *   * * *   * * *

The delights of unnatural history

"Do not all charms fly at the touch of cold philosophy?" Keats
answered his own rhetorical question by saying that they did—
taking the rainbow out of the sky and clipping the angels' wings.

For this opinion he has been scolded, off and on, ever since.
Truth is stranger than fiction, and the wonders of science, as he
has been sternly reminded, are more wonderful than any others.
The rainbow is still there—not, to be sure, as evidence of God's
promise to Noah—but as an even more interesting demonstration of the laws of dispersion. The universe is wider than our
notions of it ever were and a treatise on biology, we have often
been reminded, is more amazing than any medieval bestiary.

Perhaps. Yet the two most celebrated animals that ever lived,
never lived—the phoenix and the unicorn. There must be some
reason other than perversity for this fact. To this day the simple
—and that includes many poets—prefer them (along with such
slightly less famous creatures as the kind pelican and the toad

who bears a precious jewel in his head) to the lungfish or the platypus.

The average man, though no poet, is more likely to believe that an elephant never forgets or that the hoopsnake rolls merrily along with his tail in his mouth than he is to know (or care) whether or not the 'possum is a marsupial. When the Emperor Franz Josef happened to see an eagle that one of his huntsmen had shot, he is said to have inquired wonderingly what had become of its other head. The Amazon may not be the only river named after women, but it is the only one which comes to my mind and it was so called because these warlike ladies were moved to South America when the original African homeland had become sufficiently well known to make it pretty evident that they were not to be found there. The imagination just couldn't bear to give them up, and if the Himalayas are ever thoroughly explored, the Abominable Snowman is sure to turn up somewhere else.

Though I have read a good deal about real animals and how they behave, though I have even written something about them in my amateurish way, I am at least as much fascinated by what is sometimes called unnatural history, as I am by the natural. Nothing could be more amazing than Von Frisch on the most recently discovered wonders of the bee, but for sheer delight I would rather take to bed with me that credulous Roman, Pliny the Elder; the better- (but not too well-) informed Edward Topsel in whom the actual and the picturesque era are charmingly blended; or, best of all, the medieval bestiary so admiredly and sympathetically translated by the late T. H. White.

Truth may be stranger than fiction but it is strange in a different way. That, I think, is the key to the mystery. As a naturalist I am always shocked at the thought of extinction. Like Theodore Roosevelt, "when I hear of the destruction of a species I feel as if all the works of some great writer had perished." But who misses the passenger pigeon or the dodo as he would miss the phoenix and the unicorn if they disappeared from the imagination? God made the first two; man made the second. And for that reason he has an especial affection for them. Since fiction is what we make up, it is inevitably what we would like to be true. Too much of what we find out, even when it isn't (as it all too often is) disconcerting, strikes no responsive chord in our nature. Unlike fancy, it is not the world we would have made had we had the making of it.

When a medieval monk explains to me that the peacock shrieks so hideously because he is vain, but has such ugly feet that he cries in rage every time he happens to see them, I feel that this is precisely what ought to be true. It is a pseudo-fact I shall remember long after I have forgot the latest experiment to demonstrate that 'possums "play dead," not because they hope to deceive me, but because fear has so overstimulated their adrenal glands as to paralyze the muscles.

How, until I have forgot that fact or alleged fact, can I ever again accuse anyone of playing 'possum? Like too many other scientific facts it just isn't humanly usable. A 'possum playing dead would certainly be more interesting if he knew what he was doing. So would a bird practicing the broken-wing trick—so much more interesting indeed that I am going to believe that it does know, until the mechanists get even better negative evidence than they have now. After all, none of them have ever been 'possums or birds.

Myth and unnatural history overlap. Each, no doubt, feeds the other. But they are not the same thing. Even those myths which were part of a living religion were not believed in the same way that pseudo-scientific facts were believed because, as that believer Samuel Johnson himself pointed out, the credence we give to "the truths of religion" is always different from that accorded to "the facts of ordinary life"—which latter is what unnatural history was supposed to be.

On the other hand, unnatural history, though distinguishable from myth, is also in part the product of similar tendencies and the needs of the human mind. Ignorance, misconception and credulity contribute to it. But it is not merely any or all of these things. It is also a creation of the human imagination and therefore, like the myth, a wish fulfillment which reveals something about human nature, however misleading its picture of external nature may be. Men believed in unicorns and believed that they had seen them not so much because they were inaccurate observers, as because such a beast would be a highly desirable addition to our fauna. Since he did not exist, it behooved man to invent him, and invent him he did. Indeed, he did much more than that. He invented a theory to justify the invention, not only of the unicorn, but also of any other possible beast which nature had, as we now know, unfortunately forgot to create.

This nature, as we all learned in school, was formerly believed to "abhor a vacuum" and we were probably told that Galileo took a great step into the modern world when he announced, after experimenting with a suction pump for water (and presumably with a touch of irony), that "nature does not abhor a vacuum below thirty-four feet"—which happens to be the height of a column of water which atmospheric pressure is sufficient to sustain. But perhaps there are some, even among readers of the *Scholar*, who do not know (and I apologize in advance to those who do) that the premise "nature abhors a vacuum" once covered much more than the physical. It meant that the universe is a *plenum*. The perfection of God implies that everything possible is also actual; and since a unicorn *could* exist it certainly *must* exist—somewhere, if not in any conveniently observable place. To say that it didn't was a blasphemous denial of the perfection of God and the consequent perfection of the universe He had created.

Here, for example, is what was said on that subject in a thesis proving the existence of the unicorn and published in 1661 by a certain George Caspard Kirchmayer who apparently stole it from a contemporary though he himself was a professor at Hamlet's alma mater in Wittenburg and a member of both the English and the Viennese Royal Academies:

> Who cares any longer to be of such simplicity as not to hesitate to oppose his own view to many proofs both divine and human, for the existence of the unicorn. . . . If, says the acute Scaliger, anything were missing, a vacuum would be created in the forms of animal life. This would be a far greater fault in nature than a vacuum in space without substance.

This same Professor Kirchmayer was, however, equally convinced that the phoenix was a mere fable and convinced for a similarly sound reason. All accounts of this bird agree that there is never more than one phoenix alive at a time. God would certainly not permit any creature to get away with so plain a defiance of his universally applicable injunction: Increase and multiply.

But where did all the delightful nonsense which the medieval mind was to elaborate so exuberantly come from? It must be very old since there are in the Old Testament various oblique references to some of the most familiar tales (like the refusal of the raven to feed its young until they show black) which seem to imply general familiarity with them. Yet there is not much of it in the surviving Greek literature of the Golden Age because that age, though obsessed by myth, was already developing too strong a sense of fact to write first-rate unnatural history.

Even Herodotus was cagey about the phoenix. "They have also another sacred bird . . . called the phoenix, which I myself have never seen except in pictures." (That would have been enough to convince any bestiary writer.) Aristotle, the master of those who know, knew quite a bit that isn't so, but he was a scientist who would never have permitted himself to believe anything just because it would be agreeable to do so; and when he goes astray for any cause other than the simple inadequacy of his data (a phenomenon not unknown in the most modern of sciences), it is not because he indulged his fancy but because he had rather too much confidence in pure reason—like the German in the familiar anecdote who evolved the elephant out of his inner consciousness.

For thousands of years date growers had been tying flowers of the male tree to the branches of the female in order to fertilize them but Aristotle could demonstrate by logic absolute that plants must be without sex and he proved it so convincingly that the scientific demonstrations of the eighteenth century had a good deal of difficulty in making headway against his authority. He could also explain why snakes have no legs: No animal with a backbone ever has more than four (which is true enough) and a snake is so long that four wouldn't do him any good (which is a bit farfetched).

It was the Romans, and especially Pliny, who passed on to the medieval masters in this field most of the hints which they elaborated. Because no age since has accepted a cosmology so completely homocentric, the medieval masters took it for granted that anything that would illustrate God's detailed provisions for the convenience or the instruction of man must necessarily be true. And since the universe was a metaphor, the metaphorical interpretation of any fact or imagined fact must be the most significant one.

The future Cardinal Newman had, for a time, great difficulty in accepting the claim of the Roman Church to infallible authority in matters of faith and morals. But the difficulty vanished when it occurred to him that such an authority would be very helpful to man, that God always provided what man needed, and that therefore he must have provided this convenience. This is precisely the line of reasoning which the monkish compiler of unnatural history followed out, even when dealing with the most specific details. Your modern who wants to find instructive morals in nature is often inconvenienced by the necessity of getting his facts reasonably straight; but the monk had no hesitation in finding the moral first, and he took it for granted that nature would necessarily illustrate it somewhere. He did not find it difficult to believe that the widowed turtledove never consented to a second marriage because that would set a good example to the human female and, if he had heard that the newborn lion cub lay dead for three days until his father breathed upon him, that was so pat an allegory of the resurrection that one need inquire no further.

On the other hand even Pliny, when recounting a wonder, often cites specific instances of the testimony of a supposed eyewitness. In his account of the elephant, for instance, he tells us that Mutianus (who was three times Consul and therefore presumably a responsible fellow) "states that he himself was witness to the fact that when some elephants were being landed at Puteoli and were compelled to leave the ship, being terrified at the length of the platform which extended from the vessel to the shore, they walked backwards in order to deceive themselves by forming a false estimate of the distance."

But just because the medieval writer had such complete faith in the *a priori* and almost as much in "the authorities" (*i.e.* anyone who had ever told a tall story before the writer's own time) he rarely felt it worthwhile to limit himself to what we should regard as acceptable testimony. That the medieval zoologist should have been ignorant does not surprise us much. Considering the circumstances under which he lived, it is, as a matter of fact, astonishing how much genuine information is mixed up with the extravagant nonsense in the better bestiaries.

The compiler was a long way from either Africa or India and from an elephant. It is extremely unlikely that he had ever seen one or even known anybody who had. Yet he tells us, for example, that their period of gestation is two years—which is almost precisely accurate. Then he goes on to repeat the oft-repeated tale that elephants cannot lie down because they have no joints in their legs and are compelled to lean against trees when they wish to sleep.

What does surprise us is the medieval zoologist's calm confidence that this is the best of all possible worlds; that God's ways are not mysterious but plainly evident to anyone who will observe them; and that there is nothing in nature which does not either supply a need or at least present a useful moral. Being a monk, as he usually was, he had renounced the wicked world of men but he had no doubt that there was nothing wrong with the universe except man's wickedness. One could not possibly get further than this from existentialism or radical alienation. To the monk the physical world was an allegory of the moral and the spiritual. To him, it seemed therefore perfectly obvious that the soundest scientific method was simply to ask of every observed phenomenon, "What purpose does it serve?" or "What lesson does it teach?" If the only answer he could come up with was one that must have seemed rather farfetched even to him, he accepted it for the same reason that the modern physicist accepts the paradoxes of his science: "What other explanation is possible?"

To us it seems that no "scientific method" could be more completely unscientific than the usual medieval one. "Teleological" has become the dirtiest word in the vocabulary of the modern interpreter of natural phenomenon. But the medieval scientist was not merely silly. Given his premise that the universe embodies a purpose and that this purpose is human welfare, his methods followed as naturally as the method of our science follows from the premise that man is merely an accident in a universe which knows nothing of his peculiar desires, needs and standards of value which he has somehow or other most improbably acquired.

One assumption leads naturally to another. We think "the doctrine of signatures" extraordinarily silly, but if you take it for granted that God created the various members of the plant kingdom to serve human purposes, then what is more likely than that he would give a key to the various uses so that, for instance, the liver-shaped leaves of the liverwort inform us that it is good for diseases of the liver; and the habit of certain saxifrages to grow in the disintegrating fissures of rock indicates that it will similarly disintegrate kidney and gall-bladder stones?

The only cause for astonishment is how long such beliefs lingered into the age of science. A mid-seventeenth century herbalist writes of the herb commonly known as horse tongue: "The little leaf-like tongue, growing upon the greater, is no light argument that this plant is effectual for sores in the mouth and throat." Though John Ray, the first great English biologist and a true scientist in our understanding of the term, rejected the doctrine of signatures as unsupported by convincing evidence, he was still sufficiently inclined to teleology to write:

One observation I shall add relating to the virtues of plants, in which I think there is something of truth, that is, that there are, by the wise disposition of Providence, such species of plants produced in every country as are most proper and convenient for the meat and medicine of the men and animals that breathe and inhabit there. Insomuch that Solenander writes, that from the frequency of the plants that spring up naturally in any region he could easily gather what endemical diseases the inhabitants thereof were subject to: So in Denmark, Friesland, and Holland, where the scurvy usually reigns, the proper remedy thereof, scurvygrass, doth plentifully grow.

The more we have learned, or think we have learned, about the universe, the less tenable such assumptions have come to seem. In fact, the intellectual history of Western man is often summed up as consisting of the various stages of his disillusion with the assumption that the world was made for him; that he is the most important thing in it; that it has a humanly understandable meaning, and purpose; that "all evil is good not understood." Copernicus and Darwin are conventionally, and no doubt correctly, regarded as the key figures because they mark such clear and such radical steps toward a new concept of man's place in the universe. They are angels with flaming swords who stand guard at the gates of the fool's paradise from which we have been expelled.

If any reader has begun to suspect that I suffer from so much nostalgia for this Paradise Lost that I plan to defy the guardians of the gate and reenter it, I hasten to assure them that I neither believe that possible nor wish that it were. I have more faith in the doctor with his syringe full of antibiotics than in any herbalist, however skilled he may be in reading plant signatures. Preparing recently for a trip around the world that would include some unusually unhealthy regions, I had myself inoculated against nine different maladies instead of planning to cull along the road those symbols which, if I believed Ray and his authority, the learned Solenander, would surely be growing where any of the nine diseases were especially prevalent. But I do have one more comment to make.

In quite properly rejecting the assumption that a theory must be true if it is comforting or consoling we have acquired, it seems to me, a tendency to lean over backwards in the opposite direction. The more any sociological or physiological or psychological theory offends our dignity, or seems to deprive us of the power either to control our destiny or even to understand our own aims and motives, the more likely it seems to us to embody the truth. If Darwin tells us that we are the product of blind chance, Marx-Leninism that our ideals and ideas are mere ineffectual "ideologies"; Freud, that we don't know what is going on in our own minds, and sociology that we are what our own society makes us rather than what we choose to be, the very fact that all these theories are rather dispiriting makes us inclined to accept them. Sometimes I find myself suspecting that if we really did understand the universe and our place in it, this universe might not be as completely alien as we have come to assume. After all, we too are a product of it.

—*American Scholar*
SPRING, 1964

• • • • • • • •

Another good word for unnatural history

The late Will Cuppy kept several *bêtes noires* in his mental zoo, and he frequently trotted them out in such delightful works of more-or-less-natural history as, *How to Become Extinct* and *How to Tell Your Friends from the Apes.* A favorite target was Aristotle, although why he chose him rather than that amiable, industrious and boundlessly uncritical gossip, Pliny the Elder, I was never able to understand.

After all, Aristotle did know a lot and he took his responsibilities seriously. He did not, to be sure, realize (as we do) that most biology is highly improbable and that it is, therefore, very dangerous to put any faith in *a priori* logic because the facts usually turn out to be what no sane man would ever be inclined to suppose. Nevertheless, and aside from this tendency to believe that an absent fact could be supplied by reason, Aristotle did very well indeed, even by the standards of this factual age. When he undertakes to explain why snakes don't have legs, his explanation may sound rather like one of Kipling's *Just So Stories,* but that is not his general tone.

Pliny, on the other hand, is something else again. Whenever he abandons summaries of other writers to enter upon speculations of his own, he gives a certain amiable imbecility full range, and becomes a delightfully foolish companion. For one thing, his complete abandonment to the most farfetched of teleological explanations is a not unwelcome relief from modern science, which so firmly represses any reassuring assumption that the universe is in any way adapted to our needs and wishes, or has ever had any idea whither it was headed. Those of us who have been rebuked (as I have) for teleology or anthropomorphism, just because of some such figure of speech as "the cactus is a tropical plant which learned how to live in the desert," and have been sternly told to say instead—"has become adapted to desert conditions"—are tempted actually to applaud when Pliny comes up with something like his comment on the cork oak: "When this tree is debarked, it does not die as other trees do because Nature, like a farsighted mother, dressed it in a double bark, knowing well that it would be frequently debarked." This is an example of cart-before-horse almost as entertaining as the observation said to have been made by a Mohammedan theologian in the Middle Ages, when he cited as one of the most striking examples of God's kindly concern for the welfare of His children, the fact that He never sent rain to the desert where it would be wasted, but only to the fertile valleys where it would do some good.

In both of these cases, the interpreter was at least interpreting an actual fact. Pliny, at his best, thinks up an absurdity in order to explain something that isn't true to begin with. For example, he tells us that snakes have such an aversion to the ash tree that they will go through fire rather than touch its leaves or branches and that it is, therefore, "a wonderful courtesy of Nature that the Ash has flowered before serpents come out of hibernation and does not cast its leaves until they have gone again."

As for me, I have never been quite sure that there is not something immanent in Nature which inspires it with a sort of purpose and I think it is possible to imagine that without recourse to any crude teleological interpretation of Nature's phenomena. Moreover, I do find something at least intriguing in the fact that the very sciences that reject such notions have been compelled to reveal correspondences between the needs of human beings and the conditions of our physical world that would have impressed believers in design far more than Pliny's ash tree or cork oak—although the correspondences I have in mind also are, no doubt, carts rather than horses.

It is a commonplace, for instance, that the higher manifestations of life as we know them seem to require a set of conditions so special that none of the other planets in our system comes anywhere near providing them and that, therefore, those who believe that these manifestations exist elsewhere in the universe are forced to fall back upon the probability that, among the billions of planets outside our own system, some may be very much like our earth.

And while I am willing to grant that life may have begun as the result of a "fortunate accident," which has never during our earth's megabillion years' history happened again, that accident would seem a lot easier to take for granted if we still believed, as our ancestors did, that the miracle was repeated thousands of times a day when insects, reptiles and other forms of life were created out of mud or "corruption."

Consider also the fact, not only that water is necessary, but that it must also exhibit a peculiar property. It must get heavier as it grows colder but, oddly enough, reverses this process at about 39° Fahrenheit and begins to get lighter again. Because it does behave in just this odd way, the bottom of the lake is warmer in winter than the top; ice begins to form at the surface rather than on the bottom; and by thus providing an insulator it limits the depth of ice. If water got heavier and heavier as it got colder and colder, the ice would start forming at the bottom and in all but the warmer regions lakes would freeze so solid that they would hardly melt by the end of summer. Hence most of our surface water would be locked up in ice. Not long ago I asked a distinguished geologist what would have happened if water had not had this peculiar property. He replied, "Well, we would probably all be dead; or more probably still, none of the higher forms of life would ever have evolved."

Now all this is more or less commonplace, and I do not cite it in any effort to revive teleology or to suggest that it represents more than another of the many happy accidents that explain our universe. But I do like to consider things curiously and the other day a curious fact, which I do not remember to have seen commented upon before, happened to occur to me. It led to some reflections which I am going to call "Seeds and Civilization."

The seed is, of course, a rather recent invention, as recent goes in the time scale of the earth. Plants reproduced without seed for a much longer time than has passed since seeds were invented, and flowering plants did not become dominant until a mere sixty or seventy million years ago. Yet, as I shall attempt to demonstrate, if seeds had not been invented in what might be called the nick of time, civilization could never have developed, and we might still be hunters and food-gatherers instead of masters of a technology which, unfortunately, may be about to turn the tables.

Anthropologists still use the old terms Paleolithic and Neolithic to distinguish between the men who came before and those who came after a sudden leap forward. But they now know that it was not polished stone weapons that made the difference. Men were able to make better implements because they had invented agriculture. Thus the seed of our civilization was literally a seed. And before man could discover how to use the seed, Nature had first to invent it. And it took Nature herself millions of years to invent step-by-step this wonderful device. The plant kingdom could get along very well without them, but human civilization would be impossible.

Green plants, something like the scum that grows on ponds, may be a billion years old, but neither they nor many later vegetative types produced seeds. They reproduced themselves in a variety of complicated ways of which the most advanced was the formation of spores like those upon which the ferns still depend. This almost microscopic spore has to lie on the moist earth until a single tiny cell divides repeatedly to form a flat thallus; the thallus develops male and female organs; the ovules produced in the female organ are fertilized by a kind of sperm; and from the fertilized ovum what we recognize as a fern develops.

It is possible, of course, deliberately to raise a fern from a spore, but it is vastly more difficult than raising a plant from seed. Moreover, the processes are so difficult to observe that even as late as the eighteenth century they were not understood. A seed, on the other hand, is a wonderfully convenient device. It is a kind of egg that differs from the ordinary animal egg in one important particular. It is an egg that starts to hatch, then arrests the process and enters upon a dormant period in which it may remain alive but unchanging for many years, or even— in at least one known case—for centuries. The advantages of this arrangement for man, as well as for the plant, are obvious. And the most obvious of all is the fact that a seed, unlike an egg, can be kept until a convenient or suitable time has come for it to make itself into a plant again.

The fresh egg of a chicken contains nothing that suggests what it will produce. And it won't keep. Only if it is warmed for a time, while still fresh, does even the outline sketch of the primitive fowl begin to develop. But the seed, before it had ripened, had already formed a miniature plant or embryo, which anyone who has ever broken open a bean or a peanut has seen nestled down between the two halves of the seed proper which contain a food supply. Upon this food supply, the germinating plant will depend while the roots and leaves of the embryo plant are developing to the point where they can draw nourishment from the soil and the air. In the embryo itself are enzymes so powerful when aroused into action that peanut butter would not keep fresh if the embryo had not been removed from the nut before it was crushed.

I am not going to arouse the ire of science by suggesting that when Nature invented the seed she did so with the intention of making civilization possible. We may grant that it was only another happy accident. But Nature did invent the convenient seed and took, as I said before, a very long time to perfect it. Essentially, and enormously simplified, what happened, was this: Spores, like those of the fern, became pollen and the plant "got into the habit" of going through an abbreviated form of the thallus stage of the fern on the parent plant itself, and it thus created a seed with an embryo. Our confidence in the astonishing fact that if you plant a pea you get a pea and if you plant a petunia you get a petunia is sublime. Any fool knows that—now. But our primitive ancestors did not know and they were so far from being fools that, as so many anthropologists maintain, the Cro-Magnon caveman had as much native intelligence as we do. Yet he and his forebears had been on the earth many hundreds of thousands of years before it was discovered— quite recently, indeed—that one can plant the seed of a plant in the ground and get another plant just like it.

Anthropologists say, also, that before man knew how to grow things he was compelled to be an aimless wanderer following game animals and wild crops wherever they could be found. Once he had grasped the secret meaning of the seed, he could have a dependable food supply that didn't have to be searched for. He could settle down, have a home, form a community, become a sort of domesticated animal instead of a wild one, and then rapidly develop, one after another, the characteristics of civilization. For several hundred thousand years his advance had been at less than a snail's pace and his numbers so few that he was an unimportant, barely surviving species. Within only a few thousand years after agriculture had begun, he was to become lord of the earth with a written word, religion, philosophy, literature, and a hundred material possessions to contribute to security and comfort. When those of us who like to consider things curiously buy (perhaps in a dime store) a package labeled peas or petunias, we are not likely to realize that we hold a miracle in our hand—something that took Nature hundreds of millions of years to invent and man several hundred thousand to find out his use for. We could still be civilized men without steam or electricity or telephones or automobiles—many men before us were highly civilized without them—but we could not be much more than very clever animals with little use for our intelligence if nature had not invented the seed; and if some genius, forgotten thousands of years ago, had not been seized by one of the most prodigious notions ever to visit the human brain.   —*American Scholar*

SUMMER, 1965

. . . .

What are flowers for?

"Nature," said Sir Thomas Browne, "is the Art of God." And of all Nature's works the most delicately perfect, as well as the most universally admired, is the flower.

There are those who are indifferent to the sea or oppressed by the mountains, who find forests gloomy and animals repulsive. There are even those who say that they hate the country. But no one ever hated flowers, and no other beauty— not even woman—has been more often celebrated.

There is nothing to which poets have referred more frequently, and the poetry of everyday speech pays its own tribute in a score of familiar phrases: the flower of youth; the flower of chivalry; the flower of civilization. Nothing else, either natural or manmade, seems to embody so completely or to symbolize so adequately that perfect beauty which, if the expression be permissible, flowers in the flower.

Grass and leaves are grateful to the eye. No other color is so restful as green. But how monotonous the earth would be if this green were not shattered again and again by the joyous exclamation of the flower! It seems to add just that touch of something more than the merely utilitarian which human beings need if they are to find life fully satisfactory. Flowers seem like a luxury that Nature has grown prosperous enough to afford.

The stern scientist will, of course, dismiss this last statement as an absurd fantasy. Flowers, he will insist, are strictly utilitarian—except, of course, in the case of those which man himself has perverted in cultivation. Flowers are the plants' organs of generation and their purpose is not to be beautiful, but to produce seeds with a maximum of efficiency. Yet, even the stern scientist will admit that Nature invented many remarkable devices before she hit upon anything at once so useful and so pleasing to the human eye.

It was—so he will tell us—a mere hundred million or so years ago that the very first flower opened its petals to the sun. And though that was a long time ago as we measure time, though ninety-nine million of those years were to pass before the first member of our own species was there to see a flower and to begin, no one knows how soon, his long love affair with it, still it was not long ago in the history of living things. Primitive green plants had already been thriving in the water for perhaps a billion years or even more. They had come out upon dry land many millions of years later, and the great forests that laid down the coal beds flourished at a time which antedates the first flowers by a longer stretch than that which separates the first flowers from us. Then, quite suddenly as such things go (so suddenly indeed that evolutionists are still puzzled by the phenomenon) the earth burst into bloom. Moreover, some of the earliest blossoms of which a record has been preserved in stone were already quite spectacular, and the late dinosaurs may have looked with dull eyes on the dogwood and the magnolia that their sluggish brains were no doubt incapable of admiring.

Having granted that much and instructed us thus far, the scientist will go on to say that the poets have, as usual, preferred their own silly fantasies to the truth and preferred them so persistently that it was not until about the time of the American Revolution, when mankind was already half a million years old at the very least, that he cared enough about facts to discover that the flower, like everything else in nature, is merely part of the struggle for survival. Thomas Gray could just possibly be forgiven for babbling about the flower that "wastes its fragrance on the desert air," because most of his contemporaries did not know that this fragrance was not wasted if it enticed the insects it was secreted to attract. But Wordsworth was only deceiving himself when he found in the meanest flower that blows "a thought too deep for tears," and as for Tennyson, who lived in one of the great ages of science, he ought to have been ashamed of himself to write anything so foolish as his apostrophe to the "Flower in the Crannied Wall":

> . . . if I could understand
> What you are, root and all, and all and all,
> I should know what God and man is.

The flower, the scientist will go on, was not invented (or rather did not mechanically invent itself) to please us. It flaunted its petals and spread its perfumes because the pollen wasted when distributed at random by the winds could be conserved if an insect could be tricked into carrying it directly from flower to flower. What we call a flower's beauty is merely, so he would conclude, a by-product and a human invention. The perfume isn't there to please us; it pleases us because it is there and we have been conditioned to it. A few flowers pollinated by flesh-eating flies have the odor of rotten meat. If that were usual, rather than unusual, we would by now love the stink.

In some of these contentions the scientist is right, or at least partly right, if you grant him his premise that man is a mere accident in nature, a freak to whose desires and needs Nature is serenely indifferent. But there are other ways of looking at the matter. Nature did create man and did create his unique qualities, among which is the ability to believe that beauty, even if useful, is also its own excuse for being. That conviction is, therefore, as natural as anything else—as natural, for instance, as the struggle for survival. Man is quite properly proud of the fact that he sometimes succeeds in transforming the sex impulse into something beautiful, and he finds some of what the anatomists call "secondary sex characteristics" very appealing in themselves. But the plants were millions of years ahead of him, and if flowers are merely the organs of reproduction, they are the most attractive of such in all animate nature.

In fact, it was in this light that the eighteenth century tended to see its new realization that plants also could "love." Aristotle, the master of those who knew, had proved by logic absolute and to his own satisfaction that the vegetable kingdom was sexless; in spite of the fact that the people of the Near East had known since Babylonian times that their female date palms would bear no fruit unless they were married to the male blossoms from another tree. But even Linnaeus, the prince of botanists, saw this as a reason for, not an argument against, the poetic interpretation of the flowers he so much loved. And he described them in quaintly rapturous terms: "The petals of the flower contribute nothing to generation but serve only as bridal beds, gloriously arranged by the great Creator, who has adorned with such noble bed curtains and perfumed them with so many sweet perfumes that the bridegroom may celebrate his nuptials with all the greater solemnity." The grandfather of Charles Darwin wrote an enormously popular poem called "The Loves of the Flowers" in which he included such lines as these (which, incidentally, seemed very embarrassing to his famous descendant):

> With honey'd lips the enamoured woodbines meet,
> Clasped with fond arms, and mix their kisses sweet.

If that is extravagant, it is hardly more so than the sternly scientific view which sees nothing but mechanics in the evolution of the flower.

Is it wholly fantastic to admit the possibility that Nature herself strove toward what we call beauty? Face to face with any one of the elaborate flowers which man's cultivation has had nothing to do with, it does not seem fantastic to me. We put survival first. But when we have a margin of safety left over, we expend it in the search for the beautiful. Who can say that Nature does not do the same?

To that botanist who said that "the purpose of a flower is to produce seeds" John Ruskin replied in high indignation that it was the other way around. The purpose of the seed is to produce a flower. To be able to see the way in which Ruskin was as right as the botanist is itself one of the flowers of human sensibility and perhaps man's greatest creative act. If Nature once interested herself in nothing but survival (and who knows that she did not care for anything else?) she at least created in time a creature who cared for many other things. There may still be something to learn from one of the first English naturalists who defended his science by insisting on man's duty to admire what he called The Works of God because "no creature in this sublunary world is capable of doing so, save man." Even if Nature was blind until man made his appearance, it is surely his duty not to blind himself in the interest of what he calls "sober fact." It will be a great pity if science in its search for one kind of knowledge should forget to exercise a peculiarly human capacity. Gardeners who believe the purpose of seed is to produce the flower should keep that capacity alive.

—First published in *House and Garden*
MARCH, 1964

. . .   .

Dam Grand Canyon?

"In Grand Canyon Arizona has a natural wonder which, so far as I know is in kind absolutely unparalleled throughout the rest of the world. . . . Leave it as it is. You cannot improve upon it. The ages have been at work on it, and man can only mar it. What you can do is to keep it for your children, your children's children, and for all those who come after you as one of the great sights which every American, if he can travel at all, should see."

Grand Canyon's Magna Carta should be those words, which Theodore Roosevelt pronounced when he first visited the region in 1903.

For more than sixty years his wisdom has been tacitly recognized. True, certain roads have been built and certain other facilities provided, without which it would not have been possible to accommodate the millions who have come for the legitimate purpose of admiring Grand Canyon's beauty and learning the lessons it teaches.

But, so far, nothing has ever been done for any purpose other than making accessible the Canyon's grandeur and its messages. There has been no talk of even that specious doctrine "multiple use" which, however seductive it may seem, blindly refuses to recognize the fact that some uses are incompatible with others.

Grand Canyon, so everyone seems to have agreed, is so stupendous and so nearly unique a natural wonder that it should not be "used" for anything except the purposes it has served since Theodore Roosevelt so clearly saw and defined them.

In none of the other most-visited national parks have the problems involved in providing for millions of visitors—without destroying the natural character of the region—been so well solved. All the restaurants, overnight lodges, shops and so forth have been concentrated in one spot instead of being spread, as they are in some parks, throughout the accessible areas. In accord with the wise policy of unique use rather than multiple use, even the one mining concession granted before Grand Canyon became a national park has been bought out and will cease to operate after a certain number of years.

Because this policy has been consistently followed, Grand Canyon National Park is a demonstration model of how a national park should be managed, just as Yellowstone is an awful warning of what happens when tourist facilities take over the whole area.

The Grand Canyon is, after all, one of the most visited spots on the face of the earth. Yet solitude—and almost completely untouched nature—can be found by those who desire it. Those who are merely checking another three-star sight off the list gather around the hotels and the terrace. They form there the crowd that many of us come to such places as the Canyon to escape. But it is very easy to evade them and have the whole landscape to one's self.

Roads along the rim stop only a few miles west of the tourist center. A few primitive roads, not thrust upon the visitor's attention, and just rough enough to discourage those who fear to leave the asphalt, lead to other points on the rim where one may sit in absolute solitude. There is no sign that man has ever been there before. An experience of that kind is one not easily come by and is uniquely valuable.

I am not happy in opposing the position taken by my friend Representative Morris Udall. Like his brother, the Secretary of the Interior, he has been, and still is, one of the best friends the move to preserve natural beauty has ever had. Nevertheless, he has, in this instance, taken what I am bound to consider the wrong side in the present controversy concerning the proposal to build one, and probably two, dams on the Colorado River, neither of which could possibly contribute to natural beauty. Ardent dam advocates, when pushed into a corner, can say no more than that the dams wouldn't after all, do the Canyon serious damage.

The dam proposal, and the arguments which have been used to support it, are already familiar. (See "Ruin for the Grand Canyon?" by Richard C. Bradley, *Audubon,* January-February, 1966.) I shall recapitulate them only briefly before stating what seems to me to be the strongest and the least emphasized argument against it.

The plan is to build two power dams, one in Marble Canyon just upstream from the main gorge and the other in Lower Granite Gorge; the latter would be the highest dam in the Western Hemisphere. This proposal is made as part of the Central Arizona Project, intended to supply Colorado River water to Arizona farmers. But when pressed, its proponents admit that the main purpose of the dams is not to further this project directly, but to generate power which, so it is claimed, could be sold for enough money to defray the expense of the water project and thus make a "package" more acceptable to Congress.

To the objection that either of these dams would destroy the natural scenic, geologic and biological character of the area—one of whose chief values is undisturbed nature—it was at first stated that the dams would do nothing of the kind. When it was pointed out that the dams would destroy the whole river ecology and create a reservoir one hundred miles long, flooding the entire length of Grand Canyon National Monument and some thirteen miles of the national park itself, the reply came that the changes should be regarded as improvements because they would increase the "recreational" facilities.

As one propaganda publication exultantly proclaimed, "A blue lake at Bridge Canyon Dam would make this spectacular canyon easy of access for those who love to boat, fish, and swim." And whatever may be said of such activities—for which there are many opportunities elsewhere—it can hardly be said that they do not turn Grand Canyon into something quite different from that natural wonder which, as Theodore Roosevelt said, *man can only mar*.

These facts seem to me to constitute a conclusive argument. But it is even more important to point out that the proponents of the dams make a general assumption which could lead to the violation not only of Grand Canyon, but of the whole national park and monument system and the wilderness system. The most fundamental question they implicitly raise is simply this: Is the preservation of natural beauty a major or merely a minor objective? Does utility, economy even, always take precedence over every other consideration?

The arguments to which dam proponents always return as fundamental and unanswerable are these: Farmers need the water and this is the cheapest way of providing it. Alternate proposals, notably that of an atomic generating plant, are dismissed as more costly. The dams would make the whole project self-liquidating, the alternative proposals would not.

I will not go into the question of whether a further development of agriculture in the desert is actually in the interests of the country at large as distinguished from the interests of a group of Arizona farmers. But assuming, as I do not, that these water needs are real for the nation as a whole, the dangerous part of the argument is the assumption that the *cheapest* way to supply that need is obviously the one that must be adopted; adopted even though it involves what is treated as a very minor disadvantage—namely, the modification of, the tampering with, what is widely regarded as the most thoroughly unique of all the American natural beauties and wonders.

Are we really so poor that economy must always be the *first* consideration, cost what it may in terms other than the material? If that principle is accepted, then there is no limit to where it may lead.

Of how many existing parks can it be said that they could be used to meet some real or fancied need more *cheaply* than it could be met in any other way?

A recent editorial in a Phoenix newspaper ridiculed the "outsiders" who presume to teach Arizonans the value of Grand Canyon, and went on to assure readers that the state would not permit any damage to what is its most spectacular scenic feature and one of which it is very proud.

As a matter of actual fact, such confidence would be seriously misplaced. Arizona's attitude toward its unique characteristics has been, if anything, more careless than that of most states. Arizona tends to define the progress to which it is devoted, exclusively in terms of population growth and wealth, and it boasts of natural beauty only in the advertisements that are directed at the tourists who are expected to spend money there.

Arizona has been conspicuous in its preference for billboards over scenery. In fact, I cannot think of a single instance in which the tendency has not been to assume that beauty, comfort or even health are mere frills which only impractical sentimentalists put first.

In Tucson, where I live, the problem of smog grows. But a recent editorial in one of the two local newspapers dismissed it with the remark that to control gases discharged from smelters would be (like the alternate proposals to the Grand Canyon dams) "too expensive," while the exhausts from automobiles would necessarily become heavier as the city continues its growth.

I am not suggesting that Arizona is very different from many other areas in this respect. But the real question is simply, What is *too expensive* when health and natural beauty are at stake? Our government does not demand that schools be built in the cheapest possible way, or that a health program must be self-liquidating. We can afford untold billions to get to the moon. Is that so much more important than clean air and the grandeur of this earth that we must dismiss as *too expensive,* their effective preservation?

Does anyone seriously believe that a technology that can solve the innumerable problems of space exploration could not quickly find a practical method of controlling automobile exhaust—if one-twentieth of the funds available for the space program were alloted to a crash program for solving the smog problem?

Does anyone seriously believe that a nation that can afford the space program must consider nothing except cheapness when it comes to supplying the supposed needs of agriculture? Is the moon that much more important than our own earth and its disappearing beauty?

Do not forget that, whatever the proponents of the dams say, the minimum possible effect upon the Grand Canyon region will be to make artificial what is now one of the few remaining examples of what nature herself can do.

Is there nothing that man will keep his hands off of? Is he determined that he will "conquer" nature completely and leave not even a few examples of what she can do without his help or hindrance?

It is again the words of Theodore Roosevelt which say so succinctly what we should not allow anyone to forget: "Leave it as it is. You cannot improve on it. The ages have been at work on it, and man can only mar it."

A dozen years ago English naturalist James Fisher toured the West with Roger Tory Peterson. In the last chapter of *Wild America*, the book they wrote together, Fisher summed up his impressions:

> [Americans] show us too little of their earthly paradise and publicize too little their determination to share it with wild nature. . . . Never have I seen such wonders or met landlords so worthy of their land. They have had, and still have, the power to ravage it, and instead have made it a garden.

Both of these statements were true then and, all things considered, they still are true. But national parks and the extent to which they should continue inviolate have recently become increasingly "controversial"—which means that while more people are actively alarmed for their safety, those who advocate encroachment of one sort or another are also more active.

The proposal to alter the character of Grand Canyon is one of the most serious threats, not only because of the extraordinary character of the Canyon itself, but because the arguments used to justify the dams might, if accepted, open the way to similar invasions elsewhere.

If the question is not whether some "use" of the park is necessary to supply a real or supposed need, but simply whether such an invasion is the *cheapest* way to satisfy it, then it is hard to see how any natural area, even a city park, can be considered safe.

Surely we can afford to say that Grand Canyon, at least, is not the place to save money. What is all our boasted affluence worth if we cannot afford to recognize the value of that beauty which is its own excuse for being?   —*Audubon* Magazine
SEPTEMBER-OCTOBER, 1966

. . .   .

. . . But not good-bye

The first appearance of this column ["If You Don't Mind My Saying So." *American Scholar*] was in the Spring of 1955. If my mathematics are correct, that makes just fifty installments including the present—certainly many more than I thought at the time I would, could or indeed would be permitted to make. Many readers must have dropped out and I wonder if any who read the first are with me today.

In that first installment I suggested that Mr. Bennett's famous nudge to his piano-playing daughter, "You have entertained us quite enough for one evening," would be a convenient formula for the editors when the time came for me to bow out. The morning mail has not yet arrived, but so far, I have received not even a hint and I do not plan to quit just yet. It has, nevertheless, occurred to me that the series might be terminated by an event originating beyond the control of either the editor or me. At my age one cannot expect, and I certainly do not desire, a warning long in advance that the bright day is done and that one more of us is for the dark. This may serve as an excuse for a discourse a little more explicitly personal than usual, in which I shall make some general remarks about my attitudes towards various things, including my own life and times. Should I disappear suddenly without leaving a testament the editors might dispose of me by saying simply: "See the issue for the summer of 1967."

I have been tormented by many anxieties but most of them were needless. I have suffered no great tragedies, conspicuous failures or public disgraces. On the contrary, I have had and got much more of what I wanted than most people have or get.

Never having been insatiably ambitious or even normally aggressive, I am not wholly dissatisfied with my unspectacular achievements. I wanted to be a writer and I wanted even more to have an interesting life—in the sense that I myself would be usually interested in it. Both of these hopes have been fulfilled at least to the extent I ever seriously hoped they would be.

Some years ago one of my acquaintances dropped in upon an aging professor of entomology at the University of Arizona. The old gentleman, who was at the moment pinning bugs in a museum case, looked up and exclaimed: "You know I can never get over my astonishment that I get *paid* for doing this." In a way I share his feeling. For the most part I have been engaged in pursuits which only a small minority of our population would be willing to pay me for following, and yet society (perhaps just because it was too busy and too prosperous to pay attention to what was happening) has somehow maintained me in modest comfort while I made very little effort to please it.

From a purely selfish standpoint I have, therefore, no reason to complain about the world I live in. And yet, despite my feeling that my own existence has been for me a success, the world of my day has moved pretty steadily in directions which I find distressing.

Most men of my age feel, I suppose, that the world is going down the wrong road. I certainly do. It isn't that I am politically or economically a reactionary. On the contrary, I go along with most of the liberal and welfare legislation. But in another respect I find the world I live in increasingly alien. Those aspects of the physical world that make me happiest are certainly disappearing as a result of industrialization, exploding population, and urban sprawl. To my mind, New York has become almost a horror; Arizona, vastly less attractive than it was fifteen years ago. The latter's willingness—its eagerness even —to cloud once-pure air with smog, to expand two cities in a most helter-skelter way, to be greedy for money at the expense of most other contributions to the good life, are all typical of the country as a whole, and public figures who once seemed to set themselves against all this yield to political necessity and come out in favor of it. To me it seems that the majority of my fellow citizens are crassly and cynically materialistic while most of the intellectual minority which one might expect to oppose them are nihilists interested chiefly in destruction and violence, in non-art, non-music and non-painting. Philosophy is bent on destroying itself as it becomes Logical Positivism on the one hand or Verbal Analysis on the other. The persons who appear to be most likely to shape the future are the scientists and technologists who, as in a recent issue of *The Scholar*, tend to agree that all the culture of the past is irrelevant and that the world should, and soon will be, a science-fiction writer's dream. Thus the physical, intellectual, esthetic and moral world in which I want to live seems to be disappearing.

The death wish is perhaps among the more dubious creations of psychoanalysis. Though some people do seem to seek self-destruction, the notion that it is an element in all men is harder to demonstrate. But a case could certainly be made out for the contention that modern man as a race has the death wish. Otherwise he would not be marching so resolutely toward literal extinction. But what impresses me most is not this wish for literal death but the desire for another sort of death which manifests itself so consistently in his thoughts about himself. Can anyone deny that for at least a hundred years we have been prejudiced in favor of every theory, including economic determinism, mechanistic behaviorism and relativism, which reduces the stature of man until he ceases to be man at all in any sense former humanism would recognize.

I am not unaware that I enjoy many conveniences and comforts which were unknown only a generation or two ago. I realize also that, if it were not for recent advances in hygiene and medicine, I would probably be dead by now. And yet, though I consider this last fact a boon as far as I am concerned, I am not sure that it is such for mankind as a whole. The population increase is responsible for a number of the other developments I deplored in the preceding paragraphs, and a curious characteristic of our society is the antithetical attitudes of the two major sorts of intellectuals. Scientists and technicians tend to be optimistic and to predict a glorious future. The most esteemed and perhaps the most talented writers portray the present as ghastly and absurd and can have little hope for the future since the source of their despair is not economical, political or technological but what they regard as the radical meaninglessness of the universe and, therefore, of human life.

Some will, no doubt, insist that this difference in mood means merely that science and technology represent the maturity that intellectuals of the other sort are unwilling or unable to understand or to face. But though I do not share the view of the universe held by so many contemporary intellectuals, I find it hard to believe that technology will be applied successfully to the solution of what seems to me the most serious threat to the better (or even a reasonably good) life for the future. I am ready to believe that smog, pollution, the horrors of war and so forth *could* be controlled by technology, just as the population explosion could be controlled by the means already at hand. But I see little indication that any of these things will be done since mankind as a whole—so bold in its attack upon the problems of achieving more speed, more power, and more wealth—

is very timid in its attack upon any of the other problems—partly, no doubt, because any such attack seems unfavorable to the increase of speed, of power, of wealth, or sometimes of all three. People demand high-speed automobiles no matter how dangerous, and economists tell us that our prosperity will collapse if we do not maintain sales by giving people what they want. Thoreau said, "One world at a time," but we would spend billions on an attempt to go to the moon while being very careful not to pay the price of pollution control—especially any price that includes outraging those most responsible for pollution. We have a crash program for getting to the moon, but there are always people of influence to urge slow-moving caution when it comes to regulating any of the forces that are destroying the healthfulness as well as the beauty of our country.

Tennysonian optimism—and yet we hope that somehow good will be the final goal of ill—is very old-fashioned indeed in terms of what Tennyson was hoping for. But it is precisely what technologists say in their different way when faced with the threats they have created. Sometimes they even go so far as to be sure that "somehow good" will be the final goal of atomic fission, though so far it seems the greatest disaster of modern times. And it takes a faith at least as strong and as gratuitous as Tennyson's to believe that.

Security depends not so much upon how much you have as upon how much you can do without. And that is true for society as well as for the individual. Every technological advance is also a hostage to fortune. And the more we teach adjustments, group activity, getting along with the group and so forth, the less any individual is prepared for the time, so likely to come in any man's life, when he cannot or will not call upon group support. Ultimate security for him depends upon the ability to stand alone or even just to *be* alone. Belonging is fine. But to belong to anything except oneself is again to give a hostage to fortune.

Many of those who do profess a faith in the somehow good would be willing to grant that the benefits of what they call progress are often not entirely unmixed; that we take one step backward for two steps forward as when, for example, automobiles pollute the air and good roads destroy the charm of the countryside. In other words, the Emersonian law of compensation works in reverse. For every gain there is a loss, and to me one of the most depressing aspects of this truth is the fact that a moral step forward seems so often to be accompanied by another step backward.

Most of us are shocked and almost incredulous when we read how common it was throughout most of history for armies to pillage and massacre whole populations as, for example, the Crusaders are said to have done when they captured Jerusalem. Quite a long time ago we stopped regarding things like that as normal procedure. We don't put the inhabitants to the sword any more. Or rather we don't when we can see them face to face. But of course military necessity often compels us to do the same sort of job quite as effectively from a few thousand feet up, though the man who drops the bomb can't see his victims the way a Crusader saw the woman or child through whose body he thrust his sword. This seems to me a wonderful example of committing one of the oldest sins in the newest kind of way, and I do not see how the most enthusiastic proponents of the theory that technological advance is an unmixed blessing can deny that only technology has permitted us to put a city to the sword without quite realizing what we are doing.

Not only technology but much of the so-called science of man seems to be leading us toward less and less interest and less and less awareness of that inner life of which only the imaginative writer now seems to recognize the importance or even the existence. If the extremists are right and consciousness is a mere epiphenomenon, then we may gradually lose it and become, in fact, that man wound up like a watch which Thomas Henry Huxley said he was willing to become. Something like that may just possibly be what happened to the insects when they became so efficient that they no longer needed to think, even at the level of the lower organisms, and instead became efficient machines with perhaps no consciousness at all. Could the obsession of the avant garde with violence and unreason be a desperate effort to retain a hold upon something violent enough to prevent the lack of awareness?

The fact that I have led a reasonably satisfactory private life in a world which I find increasingly unsatisfactory raises in an unexpected way the whole problem of free will or in more concrete terms the question of whether or not mankind is, as he tends increasingly to believe, controlled by forces outside himself. My own paradox—a satisfactory life in an increasingly unsatisfactory world—suggests to me a kind of answer.

I think that man is free to make those choices which can be made without reference to the way in which society is evolving, but that neither he nor, perhaps, collective humanity will resist the tendency of society to be molded by processes it cannot control. When Emerson said that things are in the saddle and ride mankind, he did not mean that we must let them do so; but that is exactly what the Marxists do mean when they talk about society as the product of evolving technology, and I think there is a good deal of truth in the contention. A Thoreau can go to Walden Pond and (as he said) refuse to live in the bustling nineteenth century. But neither he nor millions of others could have prevented the nineteenth century from bustling. The paradox is something like that of the unpredictable atom and the predictable behavior of any large aggregate of atoms. We can predict with a considerable degree of accuracy how many people will go to the seashore on a day when the temperature reaches

a certain point—even how many will jump off a bridge. And
though neither you nor I am compelled to do either, the statistics show that the group considered as a whole—like the group
of atoms in a physical object—must obey the laws it does not
formulate. That is why I believe that though man's individual
potentialities are much greater than commonly assumed today,
he will probably not realize most of them, at least in any near
future.

I think that I understand quite well what Natalie Barney
wrote to Marguerite Yourcenar in a letter a fragment of which
was recently published. It translates something like this:

I tell myself that you are lucky to have lived during an epoch
when the idea of pleasure was still a civilizing idea (which today it
no longer is). I am especially pleased that you have escaped the
grip of the intellectuals of this half century; that you have not been
psychoanalyzed and that you are not an existentialist nor occupied
with motiveless acts; that you have on the contrary continued to
accept the evidence of your understanding, your senses, and your
common sense.   —*American Scholar*

SUMMER, 1967

A Note About the Author

Joseph Wood Krutch was born in Knoxville, Tennessee, in 1893. He received his B.A. degree from the University of Tennessee and his M.A. and Ph.D. from Columbia University. His honorary degrees include an LL.D. from Columbia, received in 1955, and a Ph.L. from Northwestern University in 1957. From 1943-52 Mr. Krutch was Brander Matthews Professor of Dramatic Literature at Columbia University. In 1954 he received the National Book Award for Non-fiction for *The Measure of Man*; *The Desert Year*, published in 1952, won him the John Burroughs Medal. Other books by Mr. Krutch include: *Henry David Thoreau*; *The Twelve Seasons*; *More Lives Than One* and *If You Don't Mind My Saying So*.